DON'T BITE YOUR TONGUE

DON'T BITE YOUR TONGUE

HOW TO FOSTER REWARDING RELATIONSHIPS WITH YOUR ADULT CHILDREN

Ruth Nemzoff, Ed.d.

Preface By
Rosalind Chait Barnett, Ph.D.

DON'T BITE YOUR TONGUE
Copyright © Dr. Ruth Nemzoff, 2008.

All rights reserved.

First published in 2008 by
PALGRAVE MACMILLAN™
175 Fifth Avenue, New York, N.Y. 10010 and
Houndmills, Basingstoke, Hampshire, England RG21 6XS
Companies and representatives throughout the world.

PALGRAVE MACMILLAN is the global academic imprint of the Palgrave
Macmillan division of St. Martin's Press, LLC and of Palgrave Macmillan Ltd.
Macmillan® is a registered trademark in the United States, United Kingdom
and other countries. Palgrave is a registered trademark in the European
Union and other countries.

ISBN-13: 978–0–230–60518–4
ISBN-10: 0–230–60518–4

Library of Congress Cataloging-in-Publication Data

Nemzoff, Ruth E.
    Don't bite your tongue : how to foster rewading relationships with
your adult children / Ruth Nemzoff ; preface by Rosalind Chait Barnett.
        p. cm.
    Includes bibliographical references (p.) and index.
    ISBN 0–230–60518–4
    1. Parent and adult child. 2. Adult children—Family relationships.
    3. Intergenerational relations. I. Title.

HQ755.86.N45 2008
646.7′8—dc22   2007050069

A catalogue record of the book is available from the British Library.

Design by Newgen Imaging Systems, Ltd., Chennai, India.

First edition: August 2008

10 9 8 7 6 5 4 3 2 1

Printed in the United States of America.

*To my parents, Samuel A. and Sophie Nemzoff, and
my stepmother, Frieda Baxt Hohenemser Nemzoff, all of
whom taught me how to parent.*

*To my husband, Harris Berman,
with whom I continue to share a wonderful life.
He's been my partner in raising four fabulous adults.*

CONTENTS

DISCLAIMER

All characters and stories in this book are composites. If the characters and vignettes seem familiar to you though you have never met me, or even if you have had long talks with me, be assured, they are not you. They are familiar because the situations are so common that the stories were repeated to me in one version or another by many people. I hope, however, you will gain insight into yourself by looking at these composite characters, since we are all brilliant in advising others. Enjoy the book.

ACKNOWLEDGMENTS

I want to thank my editor, Luba Ostashevsky. By thanks, I mean that Luba was the force behind this book. She sought me out, she advocated for this book, and she had faith in me even though I had never written a book. She also read drafts and gave precise, insightful, and easy to follow comments. She is a brilliant teacher, great fun, and was the force and cheerleader behind me. My Barnard College roommate, Elinor Yudin Sachse, has been proofreading my papers for over fifty years. She undertook the huge task of editing all the chapters, wrote chapter nine with me, and gathered people for discussions. Her combination of precision, creativity, and loyal friendship is unmatched. Filmmaker and author, and also my Barnard floormate, Bonnie Sherr Klein provided constant encouragement. She and my Barnard "little sister" Carol Cardozo spent hours reading the manuscript and sharing their ideas. Another Barnard friend, Ellen Offner, a former editor and now principal of Offner Associates, Healthcare Consultants, edited yet more and kept my spirits up through the long years before publication. Rosalind Chait Barnett wrote the preface to this book and helped me write much of the book's contents. Additionally, I must thank my husband, Harris Berman. He has always been respectful of my perspective, but has enriched each of us in the family with his own. He meticulously read each chapter and corrected all sorts of errors. Melanie Grossman advised me on some of the earliest drafts and on the final copy. Her friendship, humor, and invaluable wisdom are part of this book. Sara Dickman, Holly Gunner, Wendy Belgard Hanawalt, Zahra Hendi, Jamie Josehpson, Anna Lanskoy,

Sophie Lee, Elsa Tranter, and Nancy Yanofsky added to my thinking as did my walking soul sisters, Chana Meyer, Lynda Fink, Myra Musicant, Harriet Robbins, Carol Singer, and Susan Murray. Bev Diamond and Phyllis and Barry Berman all read some chapters.

I am indebted to Shula Reinharz, founder of The Brandeis Women's Studies Research Center (WSRC) for creating an artistic and intellectual environment in which I could learn and emerge as a writer. I also want to thank all my colleagues at the WSRC, especially those in the Mothering Group and the Gender, Sexuality and Science Group, who have read drafts of this work and encouraged my professional growth. All of these people believed I could write this book before I did. In addition, Sheila Clawson helped me design workshops for parents.

The Brandeis Women's Studies Research Center has funded all my student-scholar partners: Naomi Chung, Alexandra Gelles, Danielle Friedman, Janine Evans, Saul Lipchik, Elizabeth Pederson, and Julia Tejbloom, shared their insights, researched, and edited. Janine Evans worked with me for over two years, researching and writing by my side. She also compiled the appendices. Brooke Rosenbauer has tracked down the footnotes, edited, and kept me organized. Both Brooke and Janine have added ideas to the book and have been true partners in helping me finish this manuscript. I have been privileged to work with and get to know such talented students. For technical assistance I turned, often in utter frustration, to my son-in-law, Farzad Mostashari, who has shown incredible patience. Maria Krings and her team at the Bentley College help desk were endlessly tolerant of my computer ignorance.

I am grateful to Andrea O'Reilly, for founding the Association for Research on Mothering (ARM), which demonstrates that parenting at all stages is a subject worthy of study.

This book could not have been written without all their help. But it also couldn't have been written without the insights from those who attended my speeches and workshops and all the men and women, some of whom were parents and some of whom were adult children, who shared their stories with me. I am also grateful to those who, throughout my years of active first stage parenting, offered support and counsel and provided the foundation for my learnings.

The names of those who helped me raise my children are listed in order of appearance in my life. I want to thank them all. My mother, Sophie Nemzoff, showed me that one can speak up, argue, and still love; my father, Samuel A. Nemzoff, encouraged me by saying, "I have made mistakes in my own life and you must make your own," thus relieving me of the responsibility of being perfect and of seeing him as all-knowing. My aunts, uncles, and cousins showed interest in my life. My sister, Judy, and brother-in-law, Alan Josephson, swapped weeks of babysitting and were at my side as we cared for our parents in their final years. Judy and I were a great team. We allowed each other to make decisions, while still providing counsel without recriminations—a good model for parenting adult children. My father-in-law and mother-in-law, Fred and Mitzi Berman, extended themselves to me with all sorts of services and affection. My stepmother, Frieda, provided friendship, wisdom, and babysitting, yet always honored the place of my deceased mother.

All my friends from elementary and high school and summer camp have given me good times and affection. In particular, Betsy Tarlin recruited discussants for me. My sisters from Barnard College have reassured me in difficult times and cheered me in happier ones. My friends from my stay in India and I learned together that there are many ways to create a family of fine human beings. In my New Hampshire years, partners and friends shared babysitting responsibilities, founded nursery schools, and promoted changes for women, men, and families. These actions helped me sort out the ambiguities of maintaining traditions and creating new ways for the future. Several parents of each of my four children's friends adopted me as their friend. All of these men and women have shared their understandings and affection and made the highs and lows of parenting richer. The spouses of my walking buddies have also helped me process life's happenings. Thanks too to all others who have gone though life's hurdles with me and helped me by driving car pools, accompanying field trips, and showing an interest in my children and me.

I am grateful to all my friends' children and children's friends who, now that we are all adults, have extended their friendships to me. My children's in-laws continue to teach me new ways of seeing and enjoying our mutual children. My wonderful in-law children, Farzad Mostashari and Mandy Lee Berman, continually amaze me in what they do for me and in nurturing my biological children. They have taught me new ways of communicating, from exuberance to silent observation to enjoying the joys of a chocolate cake. They have also given me delightful grandchildren. Finally, I want to acknowledge my four children, Kim, Seth, Rebecca, and Sarabeth Berman, who not only have been great critics of both me and the book, but also have brought me to the outer reaches of my limits and my abilities. They criticize with love and applaud me with enthusiasm. My grandchildren, Samson, Ana-Sophia, Ellie, Zoe, Aidan, and Zachary, also helped despite their young ages, or because of it. They have forced me to think about my values, given me great love, and have always asked, "Why?"

I have indeed been fortunate to have wise counsel, wonderful family and friends, and much love. I list all these people because I am indebted to them, and also to demonstrate the numbers required to help me raise my children, while still allowing me to do the work I have been privileged to do.

PREFACE

As a clinical psychologist and researcher, I am delighted that the important topic of the relationships between parents and their adult children is getting the attention it most urgently needs. Remarkably, forty years ago the term "adult child" was an oxymoron; you were either a child, meaning that you were still dependent on your parents, or you were an adult, meaning that you had left the parental nest and were building your own independent life. The boundaries between "child" and "adult" were clearly understood. Certainly for middle-class parents, a child ceased being a child when he graduated from high school or college. Parents could then comfortably turn their attention to their own future plans, confident that their parenting days were over.

Now that scenario seems quaint and terribly outdated. What has changed? In general, parents' expectations that their children would follow the same normative trajectory that they followed are not being met. For example, many adult children in their thirties and older are still dependent financially—and in some cases residentially—on their parents. Today, relatively few children follow the "traditional" path of graduating from school, leaving the parental nest, getting a job that pays a living wage, marrying immediately after schooling, and soon starting their own family. With the growth of the knowledge economy, many children are remaining in school longer to get the training that will make them professionally competitive. Graduate education is enormously expensive, meaning that grown children, and often their parents, are incurring financial debt that will take years to repay. Moreover, while still in professional training, many adult children are having their own children. All too frequently, the multiple strains on these young couples prove too stressful for their unions. In the aftermath of a divorce, many adult children return to their parents' home, often with their own children in tow.

Changes in life trajectories have also occurred for children who do not go on to college or for those who stop their education with a bachelor's degree. As we all know, entry-level jobs pay dismal wages, offer few or no benefits, and provide little long-term job security. In addition, housing and health-care costs have skyrocketed, leaving adult children with few options other than turning to their parents for a place to live or to subsidize their rent so that they can live "independently." Whatever the particular details, many older parents are now confronting emotional and financial challenges that they are ill-equipped to meet.

Today's parents of adult children are living longer and healthier than their own parents. Thanks in part to medical advances and to increased financial security, baby boomers can expect to live meaningful lives past their ninth decade. With this longer perspective, many look forward to doing things they have put off for years. When adult children re-enter their parents' lives as financial dependents, they may be shocked and ill-prepared when their parents do not automatically comply with their requests. Indeed, parents may be confused and resentful when they are thrown back into the role of provider. Parents are well-advised to realize that their adult children may still be seeing them as they were decades earlier and not as they are today. And their grown children need to learn that the assumptions they are making about their parents' lives may no longer be valid.

Along with the obvious advantages longevity confers, there are new problems. The American family is growing vertically and shrinking horizontally. We are having fewer children but are more likely to stay around to see them marry, have children, and even grandchildren. Among other things, these changing demographics call for a new vocabulary. It seems odd to describe the relationship a ninety-year-old mother has with her sixty-five-year-old daughter as a "mother-daughter" relationship. That term has for so long conjured up the image of a young mother with a small girl in tow—a term that, although biologically accurate, sounds strange. Yet we have not created any other term to describe these long-lived older parent-adult child relationships.

In the past, adult children's relationships with their parents centered around care-giving—emotional, physical, and financial. Children were their parents' bulwark against loneliness, frailty, and poverty in old age. For a long time, children's education and income exceeded their parents' and the flow of resources was from adult child to parent. Children were expected to provide for their parents as their parents had provided for them. Because of financial challenges, that paradigm has almost completely reversed. Now grown children in their twenties, thirties, and beyond often look to their parents for support of every kind. Adjusting to this new reality poses significant problems for parents and for adult children.

In my clinical practice, I often work with individuals who are grappling with questions about how to relate to their grown children. Should they continue to support their adult children who can't seem to get their lives on track? What will happen to those children when they are no longer around to bail them out? And, what will happen to the parents themselves when they need help? On whom will they be able to rely on when their time of vulnerability arrives? These questions are particularly difficult when a parent has only one or two children. In today's smaller families, each parent-child relationship is especially charged. But having multiple children can also cause strain, especially when they are in different places with respect to meeting their own dependency needs.

Further complicating these relationships is the fact that they are often conducted over long distances. In the past, families tended to be far less mobile. Many people lived out their lives close to their parents and their children followed suit. When there was so much interaction, there was ample time to iron out misunderstandings. And proximity often fostered shared interests and experiences.

This is not so today when infrequent contact is the norm. One woman I work with in my practice has two children; the mother lives in Boston, her daughter lives in California, and her son lives in Texas. Another client, also a Boston resident, has a daughter who lives in Costa Rica and a son who lives on the West Coast.

Such situations are not unusual. These long-distance relationships raise the ante. If you only get a few opportunities a year to visit with your adult children, there is little chance to build connections, to get to know the ins and outs of their lives, and to let them know what you are all about. Most importantly, there is limited opportunity to let small hurts heal. A missed birthday card, an unreturned call, an insensitive remark can easily escalate into a major rift or be left to fester when there is so little opportunity to work things out.

I first became intrigued about these relationships in the 1980s, when I realized how little research was available to help me address these issues in my clinical practice. Unfortunately, much of what we know about parent-adult child relationships comes from the popular culture. Thanks to a sensationalistic media, we are all only too familiar with situations in which parent-adult child relationships have gone sour. Today the big stories are about the troubles between celebrities such as Britney Spears and her mother or Lindsay Lohan and her father, and the rift between fathers and children in political families. Yet countless regular families like yours and mine are struggling to make our relationships work away from the camera.

The fact is that rich or poor, with or without formal education, this life stage affects us all. Yet there is precious little research to provide guidance. Why is this so? Geropsychology, the study of the mental health of older adults, was not formally recognized as a specialty within psychology until the early 1980s. No wonder so little systematic study had been done on parent-adult child relationships. Moreover, most of the research has been done from the perspective of the adult child, not the older parents!

How did it happen that as a society we have been so slow in recognizing the centrality of these relationships to the well-being of parents and their grown children? A quick overview of how clinical psychologists have come to understand the factors that influence individual well-being may shed some light on this question.

Until roughly 1950, clinical psychologists concentrated largely on critical developmental events in their patients' early years. What were their early relationships like with their mothers?

Their fathers? Their siblings? Much less attention was paid to developmental events that took place after the early years. Even when career development was the focus, the classic studies of Donald Super[1] failed to consider events occurring after people turned eighteen years of age. Then in the late 1960s, psychologist Bernice Neugarten[2] described the period of life we now comfortably call "middle age," focusing on the individual between the ages of thirty-five and fifty-four. She brought to light the impact of age on the course of family development. For example, how long children stay in the educational system and the age at which they marry and have children shape the nature of the relationships they develop with their parents. Fifty-year-old grandparents will have different relationships with their adult children and grandchildren than will seventy-year-old grandparents.

Other researchers and theorists followed suit. Much was written, for example, about menopause and its effects on women's well-being and self-perception. This focus also generated interest in the question of how middle-aged people bring meaning to their lives. What is it that gives them pleasure? What are their sources of distress? Even with this change, the focus on the individual patient remained the same. One especially relevant finding from this line of research is that older parents' self-esteem is based to a large extent on their children's success.

Over time, however, the focus of much clinical work moved from an exclusive concern with the individual per se to a recognition of the important role of the family network. The view that a person's mental health is shaped by the family was introduced by Kurt Lewin, often referred to as the founder of modern social psychology. Lewin sought to not only describe group life, but to investigate the conditions and forces that bring about change or impede change in groups. And he insisted that group life be viewed in its totality, not on an individual basis. One of his most important insights was of the interchange between people and their social context. If you adjust elements in the social dynamic, particular types of psychological experience predictably ensue. In turn, a person's psychological state influences the social field.

From this perspective, it was a short step to the emergence of couple's and family therapy. These approaches, which have considerable following today, view the family as a dynamic, interactive system in which what happens to one party affects the others. In other words, a change in one part of the system will result in a change in another part of the system. For example, parent-adult child relationships are multidirectional: What your adult child does affects you, your spouse, your other children, and so forth. Similarly, what you do affects your whole family system.

Such interconnectedness is a characteristic of all interpersonal systems: workplace groups, social groups, and religious communities, to name a few. However, family systems are the ones that are apt to have the greatest impact on our well-being. As we all know, parents often view themselves as critical influences on how their children develop, so the way the children "turn out" can constitute powerful statements about their own success or failings as a parent.

Confronted by a dearth of empirical data, I undertook a series of studies to help understand the dynamics of these relationships. Although most of these studies were focused on the relationship from the point of view of the adult child, much can be gleaned about the parents as well. In one study of married employed adult daughters and their parents, even the daughters who described their relationships with their parents as positive and who reported that they had frequent contact with their parents, grossly misperceived their parents' needs. For example, they saw them as in poorer or far better physical and financial shape than the parents saw themselves. Perhaps the parents did not discuss their lives because they did not think their busy daughters would be interested, or they may have held back, fearing that they would be a burden. Conversely, adult daughters, respecting what they perceived as their parents' reticence, may have been reluctant to pry. One likely outcome of such inadequate communication is that daughters' efforts to be helpful will be misdirected. Another is that parents are likely to miss out on opportunities to find common ground with their daughters and build open and meaningful relationships. Parents who do not want or do not need help may be offended by interference; adult daughters may feel underappreciated. When so much miscommunication can occur with frequent contact, just imagine the possibilities for problems when families live at a distance, see each other infrequently, and probably meet in situations not conducive to open communication.

In our other studies we found that, on average, daughters between twenty-two and fifty-five have positive relationships with both of their parents. Moreover, the quality of their relationships with their parents had a beneficial effect on their own psychological well-being. Daughters who had positive relationships with their parents also reported low levels of distress and high levels of well-being. Similar results were reported in a study we did of sons aged twenty-five to forty. Overall, adult sons reported positive relationships with each of their parents. And, having a positive relationship with their mother or father was associated with their own reports of low psychological distress and high well-being. To the extent that older parents derive benefits when they see their grown children doing well, their children's well-being will be a boon to their parents.

These findings challenge two widely held beliefs in our culture: grown daughters have closer relationships to their parents than do grown sons, and mother-adult daughter relationships are closer than father-adult daughter relationships. Undoubtedly, these beliefs affect the behaviors of older parents and their grown children. For example, mothers may "naturally" turn more often for help and companionship to their daughters than to their sons. One result is that adult sons may have fewer opportunities to do things with and for their parents and as a result, are unable to build closer and more meaningful relationships with them. As members of this society we all share these beliefs, to some degree, albeit unconsciously. We need to become more aware of these kinds of limiting beliefs and do our best to challenge them. We have to do better if we want healthy intergenerational relationships as we age.

New research results suggest that the mental health of mothers is linked to their relationships with their adult children. These results come from an unusual study of older mother-adult child relationships from the perspective of the parent. Mothers who were initially interviewed in 1951, when their child was between five and six years of age, were re-interviewed in 1996, when the mothers were, on average, over seventy years of age and their children were in their early fifties.[3] Among other topics, the interviewers asked about the mothers' relationships with their adult children, especially the "study" child from the original project. The researchers found that the older mothers' sense of self in 1996 was related to how close they currently feel to their adult children, with their ability to exchange ideas with them, and with how well they get along with each other. Moreover, mothers with a positive sense of self reported high psychological well-being and few symptoms of depression. These results show that their relationships with their older children matter. When these relationships are close and sharing, mothers describe themselves as confident, satisfied with themselves as persons and as mothers, and compare themselves favorably with their peers. When these relationships are troubled and distant, mothers' self-reports are far less favorable. Much more research needs to be done to flesh out the aspects of these relationships that are particularly helpful and harmful to both older parents and their adult children.

Most of us had to figure out how to renegotiate our relationships with our grown children without the benefit of a practical, down-to-earth guide. We discovered, often painfully, where the road blocks were and how to avoid them. We also learned how to create and sustain positive experiences. Now, thanks to *Don't Bite Your Tongue*, we have the practical and much-needed guidebook we all wish we had had. Ruth Nemzoff brings to this book her expertise in family dynamics, and her experiences as a mother of four grown children and a group leader who has talked with hundreds of parents just like us. She provides us with glimpses into the real-life situations of many parents who, like us, are struggling with these critical issues. What have they learned? How have they managed? What situations made matters worse for them? What situations or interventions have helped them?

In addition to learning from the many parents with whom she has worked, Ruth helps us learn from ourselves. She asks provocative questions that make us think hard about who we are and what we want from our relationships with our adult children. Ruth's guidance is not in the form of simple rules to follow. Rather, she provides us with tools for self-examination and self-discovery. Rather than focusing on who's "right" and who's "wrong," Ruth avoids the "blame game" in favor of a much more constructive approach that focuses on practical steps that you can take today (and tomorrow) to strengthen your bonds with your adult children.

Rosalind Chait Barnett, Ph.D.
Senior Scientist
Director, Community, Families, and Work Program
Women's Studies Research Center
Brandeis University
Waltham, MA

INTRODUCTION

Get Comfortable with Ambiguity

*D*on't Bite Your Tongue: How to Foster Rewarding Relationships with Your Adult Children* is a tale of two perspectives: that of the parents and that of the grown children. When these perspectives clash, fireworks can erupt. This book suggests ways to reduce the "fire" and increase the "works," for the parents and adult children alike. It is written from the parents' point of view, but encourages parents to talk with their children to get their perspectives, and suggests ways to do so. It also puts these changing relationships in context. Use this book to begin conversations with your children.

Don't Bite Your Tongue focuses on that continually lengthening period of life when both parents and their children are relatively healthy adults. Of course, what we mean by "healthy" takes on new dimensions when many of us live our whole lives with chronic diseases or disabilities.[1] Because we live longer, we are likely to spend many more years relating to our children as adults than we did as children. Our relationships will continue through many life stages and transformations. The task of what I call second-stage parenting is to constantly modify the balance between intimacy and independence. Finding the "right" combination of nurturing and autonomy for each child and parent over life's course is not easy and changes frequently occur, often in unpredictable ways. This book is intended as a guide as you invent your own ways of parenting during this second stage.

Ambiguity, uncertainty, lack of definition, past habits, and social customs join to put both parents and children in a quandary.

What is adulthood? When does it begin? How do we yield control to someone for whom one once had full responsibility?

As my four children entered adulthood I often found myself perplexed over how to approach them. Do I tell them what I think they should do? I knew I needed different approaches and behaviors now that my children were launched into the world. I figured if I was puzzled, others were, too. I began reading and interviewing others and then sharing my findings at lectures and workshops. Those attending my workshops typically have questions like these:

- How can I express my concerns without sounding controlling, judgmental, or punitive?
- How can my children and I remain friends, maybe even confidants or mentors to each other?
- How do we create a relationship in which we are mutually independent and also sufficiently dependent so that we can count on each other in times of need?
- How can I share my truths and sorrows without burdening my child?
- How can I say what I want to say in a way that will be heard as a suggestion, a perspective, and not as a command, an order, a threat, or a guilt trip?
- How can I still worry about my child's safety without crippling him or her?
- How can I deal with the disappointment when my child fails to follow the life trajectory I expected? For example, what if my child will not have children? Or will not look for a job? Or is marrying someone I think is inappropriate? Or is raising the kids in a way I find troubling?
- How do I leave behind my fantasy that my child and I would be very closely connected forever, and instead embrace our new relationship for its strengths?
- How do I react when my child makes a decision with which I am not happy?

There is no one way to answer any of these questions. The solutions have to evolve over time and through dialogue with our adult children. Just as we are learning to be parents of adults, our children are learning how to be adults in their relationship with their parents. We are all learning and inventing together. No one-size-fits-all pattern will show the way because families and relationships are as diverse as snowflakes.

In the first decade of the twentieth century, average life expectancy was less than fifty years. By 1950, women lived into their seventies. Men, however, didn't catch up to that standard until the 1970s. Since that time, life expectancy has grown steadily so that, as of 2006, women can expect to live an average of eighty years, and men are close behind at about seventy-five.[2] If we are on the upside of average we can expect to live well into our nineties, or even to 100. We are likely to see our grandchildren attain adulthood. We could share with our children their experience of first becoming a grandparent. This second stage of parenting, being a relatively healthy parent to a grown child, can be far longer than the first, raising our children; it covers most of our lifespan and may involve creating adult relationships with two or three and sometimes even four generations.

Defining "adulthood" becomes more difficult as the old markers of childhood's end—such as school graduations and marriage—become temporary posts along a meandering highway. This road goes back and forth between work and education, marriage and single life. Both parents and children have new timelines, and just as the children drift from one phase to another, so do parents. In the United States, 7.3 million people over the age of sixty-six are taking adult education courses.[3] Men over the age of sixty-five constituted 3 percent of the labor force in 2005, compared to the 1.9 percent in 1980; women over the age of sixty-five accounted for 2.3 percent in 2005, a jump from the 1.2 percent in 1980. It is predicted that men over sixty-five years old will make up 4.8 percent and women 3.9 percent of the labor force in 2014.[4] Just as the children move between single and married status, so do the parents. In 1990, 22 percent of the population over eighteen had never been married, 8.3 percent had been divorced, and 7.6 percent had been widowed. By 2005, these numbers had changed to 24 percent never married, 10.2 percent divorced, and 6.4 widowed.[5] With everything in flux, old models of parent—adult child relationships are out-of-date.

No matter how much domestic models and cultural norms change, one thing stays the same, and that is the importance of family. Because families are meaningful, the individuals in them need to "get along," and to find ways to communicate. Thus, the conventional wisdom that parents should "let go" and "bite your tongues" is not helpful in forging bonds as we, our children, and our circumstances change. Chapter one, "Don't Let Go, Don't Bite Your Tongue," points out the flaws in this old advice. It reimagines the process of second-stage parenting as a time to get to know our children as adults, and to allow them to get to know us.

Within each of us there is both an adult and a child, and we move back and forth from our most adult selves to some of our most obnoxious childhood behaviors. This complicates all of our relationships. While we all try to behave maturely, or like to think we do, there are times when we act like two-year-olds having a tantrum. Road rage and checkout-counter rudeness represent daily manifestations of adults acting in their child mode. When our adult children anger or confuse us, it's tempting to revert back to this childish state and perhaps fall into habits of accusation, guilt, or silence. It's vital to understand our own emotions and the reasons for them. Chapter two, "Know Yourself," probes the ways in which our own upbringing and lifelong habits can influence our relationships with our children.

Chapter two encourages parents to reevaluate their own upbringings in light of this new stage of life. Parents who envision living next door to their children and babysitting for their grand-children may find that life brings different situations—perhaps their children live miles away or have no children of their own. When parents' expectations are unmet, they may be disappointed or feel like failures. Children likewise may face disappointment; they may expect their parents to be always available to them and are thus unhappy when their parents have jobs or plans that keep them otherwise occupied. Whatever the particular hopes and dreams of the individual, the reality is often different, in part because what constitutes a family is changing. Chapter three, "Say Goodbye to Fantasy and Hello to Reality," considers how to recognize and explore our fantasies and how to reconcile ourselves to reality.

Not only psychologists but also social custom recognizes the importance of the parent-child bond. Parents are congratulated for their children's achievements even though the kids may have moved out of their homes decades before. Children of politicians and movie stars appear in the newspaper for escapades that would not warrant a line of type for the children of the not so rich and not so famous.

There is a declining value on respecting elders, as the older generation is no longer viewed as the greatest source of wisdom or even the repository of the best information. Parents born before the advent of the birth-control pill may have far less sexual experience than their children. Most children are far more technologically savvy than their parents. Also, language that was used to honor adults and mark a shift from childhood to adulthood has all but disappeared. Once, most children called adults by title— "Mr.," "Mrs.," "Aunt," or "Uncle"—as an honorific, until they reached maturity. Now many toddlers call adults by their first names.

Complicating any discussion even further, we have no vocabulary to describe the maturing parent-child relationship. The same words, "parent" and "child," are used to describe the participants in the parents—dependent children relationship as are used for the one between parents and grown-up offspring. Language further erodes family solidarity as the custom of spouses calling their in-laws "Mom" and "Dad" fades. Many parent and in-law children address each other with first names, a pattern that can emphasize friendship rather than obligation or respect. Even clothing, the traditional marker of age and class differences, no longer differentiates. Grandmothers wear jeans and elementary-school children wear high heels. All this blurs our understanding of our relationships. We don't know when childhood ends and adulthood begins. We are uncertain about the strength of bonds and about the honor we owe one another.

It is no wonder we are all perplexed about when childhood ends, when adulthood begins, and when it is appropriate to have information and when it is not. The legal system promotes ambiguity. At eighteen one can sign up for military service, but one must be twenty-one to drink alcohol. The definition of "dependent" differs from one public agency to the next. The Internal Revenue Service (IRS) parameters are not the same as those of the courts. The state and federal governments differ on their definition of the age of majority. For example, under the Massachusetts Health Care Reform Act beginning on January 1, 2007, parents can include their children on their health care plans, and pay for them until age twenty-six. But according to the Federal Health Insurance Portability and Accountability Act (HIPAA), parents have no access to their child's medical record after age eighteen. The 1974 Family Rights and Privacy Act (FERPA)[6] forbids colleges and universities from giving a student's grades to parents, yet these educational institutions require parental financial data when awarding scholarships. Privacy laws also mean that colleges cannot report to parents, except in an "emergency" (undefined), that their eighteen-year or older child is having problems. Chapter four, "Emerging Adulthood," delves into the ambiguous stage of adulthood and its implications.

As the relationship we share with our children changes, so too does the world change around us. What was once taboo is now commonplace; what was once expected is now ignored or actively disdained. Careers, living situations, and relationships have all taken on new forms. Our children, a full generation younger than we are, take these changes as a matter of course, while we sometimes struggle to keep up. Our children will often live with various roommates and lovers well into their twenties, thirties, and even forties, and might consider it none of our business what their relationship status is. Cohabitation, homosexuality, shifting career paths and interests, and what we may consider to be bizarre hobbies and fashions are all matters in which our attitudes may differ from our children's. Chapter five, "Refilling the Nest," Chapter six, "Relationships," and Chapter seven, "Weddings," all deal with the changed world around us.

This is not the first time that the basic dynamics of family relationships have changed. History shows that the family has adapted to major economic and social changes throughout time. In fact, the traditional family as we think of it emerged only in the late nineteenth century as a result of the Industrial Revolution. Although we, along with politicians and fundamentalist religious leaders, idealize the nuclear family, it has only existed for a relatively short time.[7] And this model now applies less frequently. For example, dads can no longer rely on moms to maintain communication with grown kids; neither may be living with or near the mom. Young parents can no longer expect grandparents to provide childcare, especially in light of the projections that by 2014, the number of people sixty-five and over participating in the labor force will skyrocket from 5.3 million to 8.7 million.[8] Chapter eight, "Grandparenting," details the changing roles of grandparents. It looks at the relationships among the three generations, as well as ways to negotiate problem areas, such as when to intervene with our children's parenting, how to become a part of their busy lives, and how to stay involved over long distances.

Parent-child associations are a mixture of choice and obligation.[9] On one hand, parents want their children to be independent. On the other hand, parents need to stay connected. They have devoted time, energy, money, and their deepest love to their children. There is no law in this country requiring children to provide even minimal care for parents in old age, when their Social Security and insurance benefits may not be adequate. Many studies suggest that older adults in America expect assistance from the younger generation.[10] Thus, if parents want their children to care for them, they need to have a real relationship with them. These relationships don't guarantee care, but children are much more likely to find time and motivation to share the burden if they feel some intimacy with their parents. Adult children also want and need to know their parents. Maintaining the close connection with a parent fosters a sense of security and love for them. Parents can also be the bulwark against life's uncertainties, a home to go to when finances weaken or marriages crumble, or a place to find comfort should disease strike. With few relevant laws in place and so many outmoded conventions to consider, some of the most important and difficult decisions in life depend entirely on the quality of the relationship between parents and children. Chapter nine, "Money," explores the nature of one of the most complex and uncomfortable aspects. Deciding how money should be dispensed within a family—from petty cash to medical help to inheritance—is rarely easy, but is nearly always too important to be kept under wraps. This chapter helps traverse this difficult terrain.

The parent-child relationship is not merely a friendship, entered into freely, which can be acquired and discarded at will; it persists over time and despite great distance.[11] Even when parents and children have little contact, the relationship remains a significant one. Reams have been written about the strength of the parent-child bond.[12] Psychologists and psychiatrists make their livings helping both parents and children figure out how past family interactions influence their current behavior and moods. Knowingly and unknowingly, both parents and children have expectations for these relationships based on past experiences and on societal myths. These expectations shape the conversations between parents and their offspring. Collective family experiences and history lead each member of the family to slip into familiar roles, often to adverse effect. Chapter ten, "Eternal Triangles," investigates the tensions that arise between parents, children, and the various other members of their families and lives—spouses, in-laws, or friends—and offers ways to navigate these multiple loyalties.

Add to all this bewilderment the fact that habits are slow to change. Caring for daily needs and assuring safety were the staples of the parental job with dependent children. Some parents were more authoritarian than others. All parents used rewards and punishments to teach their children the skills required to take care of their own needs. Some used bribery, others withheld privileges. These techniques may have been effective when the children were young and dependent, but create barriers with grown children. Parents and children find it difficult to shift their former modes of interacting in tandem with shifts in life circumstances. It takes time and practice. Just as you don't necessarily hit the ball the first time you play tennis, you don't always say or do the right thing when talking intergenerationally. Communication with our children is paramount, especially when we are frustrated, concerned, or overwhelmed. Chapter eleven, "Communication Tips," discusses the importance of communication, and suggests different ways of going about establishing healthy, open relationships with our adult children.

Perhaps the most important matter in this book is that of personal growth and fulfillment. Our relationships with our children are of the greatest importance to us, for practical reasons as well as emotional ones. A good part of our lives has been devoted to raising our children, and now that they are grown we want to enjoy the fruits of our labors. Yet as essential as these relationships are, they are not the totality of our lives. We have half a lifetime and more of experience behind us, and some of us have more time on our hands to enjoy what we have and pursue what we have always wanted. Others must find ways to share what they have learned as they coped over a lifetime with disease, poverty, or great responsibility. Chapter twelve, "Conclusion," explores the importance of making a life for ourselves apart from our children and the importance of our children knowing about our interests. From sharing well-practiced skills to learning new ones, from taking up hobbies to taking up a career in politics, there are a million and one ways to improve ourselves and the world around us.

My intent with this book is to explore many of the sensitivities in interactions between parents and adult children. It examines competing loyalties. It proposes positive ways to stay involved. It does *not* give you solutions for every type of incident, but provides suggestions to ease the transition from parenting a younger child to maintaining a relationship with your adult child. You, your child, the people surrounding you, and society are in constant flux. New situations require new responses.

My suggestions are based on the belief that each of us has the power to change our behaviors,[13] that we can learn from observing, talking with others, and reflecting on our own words and actions, and that we, as parents, have learned a lot since we brought our babies home. We can employ the skills we've used as friends, workers, and even some skills we learned as parents of young children, and apply those to communicating with our adult offspring.

If parents were lucky when their children were younger, they had friends with whom to share their uncertainties; but sharing their concerns about grown children is more complicated. Parents may not wish to invade their children's privacy by discussing their worries, or may be reluctant to divulge what they see as their own parenting failures. We all need a new roadmap, one that matches each individual's life circumstances. One reality we all share is that the assumption that parenting is over when a child becomes an adult simply isn't true.

This book gives some steps to start you on your journey; some of you will opt for the highways, others for the byways. I hope the ideas in this book will assist you on your way. You can read alone or with a group. Others may prefer to respond to these questions with their children or with a group of friends. For those who prefer to explore by themselves, I have provided questions to help guide your thinking. The goal of these questions is to help you gain insight into yourself, your children, and society. Enjoy the self-reflection!

Questions for you to consider alone, with a friend, with your child, or in a group:

- When do you feel uncertain about when to intervene with your adult child?
- What do you wish you could "make" your child do?
- How do you feel when you intervene? What circumstances make you feel good? What makes you feel bad?
- Whom do you go to for advice?
- When do you consider your kids adults?
- What in this chapter resonates for you? Why?

1

DON'T LET GO, DON'T BITE YOUR TONGUE

In some ways parenting an adult child is like parenting a first child. We have never done either before and have to learn a lot over many years. We learn to be flexible as our infants' needs differ from those of our toddlers. Infants need feeding and hugging; toddlers need to exercise their newfound skills of walking, running, and jumping. We stop holding them all the time and let them run. You could say we let go, but actually we modify our behaviors to accommodate their new skills. They lead, we follow. They feel our support and are encouraged to take the next step. And so it goes.

When they are old enough to walk to the school bus, we accompany them and teach them the route. We practice with them. Then, our hearts in our mouths, we let them walk on their own. Gradually we extend the routes they are allowed to travel on their own. First the smaller, less-traveled streets, and then the wider, busier ones. You could say we let go, but, in fact, we use incremental learning to teach skills and then let the child apply them. They lead, we follow. They watch our reactions, feel encouraged, and take the next step. And so it goes.

During the teenage years, we bolster them, try to reinforce their strengths, and encourage them to build new skills and overcome weaknesses. We no longer do everything for them. They make their own friends and choose their own activities. You could say we let go. More accurately, they show us where they want to go and we try to give them a guiding hand, sometimes even on paths we wouldn't choose ourselves. Both parties in these interactions have to be sensitive to each other's moves, sometimes for better and sometimes for worse. When done well, both parent and child contribute equally to the interactive choreography of their relationship. But, as we have learned from years of parenting, things don't always go well. There are plenty of tears. We could not then and cannot now control the behavior of our children. Only our own behavior, the situations we create, and our expectations, can change. Of course, the successes, failures, and rough spots in any relationship depend on both parties. The recognition that children, too, contribute to building a relationship relieves parents of total responsibility for the outcomes. But it does not prevent parents from exploring their own contributions to the emotional ups and downs of any interaction.

Our most important task as new parents is to help our children develop the competencies they need to cope with what life will bring. It is not our job to have all the right answers. Our generation is not the source of all wisdom. Each of us has complex emotional reactions to social, economic, and even spiritual happenings. We, too, are changing and we, too, need new competencies. Sharing reactions as equals can lead to intimacy; believing that our own vision is correct will not. Listening is key because it is part of any good communication. We cannot "make" our children share; some are just *not* the sharing sort. We can offer thoughts, ideas, set examples, rather than advocate one position or another. Drawing on accumulated experiences, we can craft relationships with our adult children that will meet their current needs as well as ours. Instead of letting go, we can call upon all the skills we have used in the past. Just as experience with your second (or third or fourth) child is, perhaps surprisingly, quite different from that with the earlier ones, so it is with parenting them as adults. No one set of instructions fits. Parenting is more akin to looking in the fridge and conjuring up a meal from what's in it, than following a recipe. Parents work with what they have; the child's temperament and skills inform our behavior. And as in the past, we need to modify our behaviors to accommodate the changes in our children, in ourselves, and in the circumstances.

Don't Let Go

Parents have been hearing the advice to "let go" since they first dropped little Johnny off at day care. The goal in popular wisdom is to raise a child who is independent, who doesn't need parents anymore. Teachers, camp directors, and scout leaders all repeat these words to parents, and in one sense this is true. But we all need people who care about us, and we all need cheerleaders, people who are interested in our daily lives and our accomplishments and our sorrows. Exhorting parents to let go is only half the story.

The latest version of this advice is the admonishments to parents not to hover after sending their children to college. Like previous versions of the overbearing mother, these parents are demonized as they attempt to find the right degree of separation and connection as their children emerge into adulthood. Caryl Rivers, author of *Selling Anxiety: How the News Media Scare Women*, hypothesizes that the controlling, obsessive, and overindulgent and overprotective "helicopter parent" is yet another media-fueled invention.[1] A June 2007 *Newsday* article exhorts parents to leave their children at the college door and let them develop on their own.[2] Note that it is the experts who define what "too much" is, not the parents and children involved in the relationship. Only now are colleges stepping forward to guide parents and to examine their own institutional role change from the protector of students, *in locus parentis*, that they held until the 1960s.[3]

While we do need to let our children write their own papers and make decisions about personal and professional behavior, we also need to focus on finding new ways for us to be involved in each other's lives—ways in which we teach and learn from each other. The task is not to let go, but to figure out how to be available yet not controlling of each other's lives. We need to let our children know we are interested in their lives, and hopefully they will be interested in ours. Together parents and emerging adults need to craft a way of finding a balance between losing touch and smothering each other. It is a journey into unknown territory and will remain so for the rest of our lives.

Georgia, age forty-six, a community activist who stayed at home when her kids were young, found the experience different with each of her two children. She explained what occurred the first weeks after her oldest child left home: "I waited for my daughter to call, thinking that I was giving her a chance to grow up and to be on her own. Besides, I did not want to be intrusive the way I found my own parents." After several weeks at the university, her daughter called rather upset, "You never call me! Everyone else's parents call them all the time."

Georgia realized:

> I was acting on my own intuitions and my past experience without consulting my child, who had her own opinions, needs, and feelings. I apologized and explained my reasoning. We agreed on a plan where I would call weekly and she would call whenever she felt the need or desire to chat. As these years have gone on, we constantly modify this plan and check in with one another about how we feel about our communications. When my daughter's babies were young she would shoot off an e-mail when she had a free moment, and now she calls more frequently. I thought I understood the rules of communication with adult children until my son left for school. He was different because he called regularly, but was annoyed when I called him. He did not like the interruptions. I don't know why my son's needs were different from my daughter's. But to this day, I find what is satisfying communication with one child is not with the other and I need to constantly ask and listen.

Letting go is not a solution. It is better to craft new ways of connecting, ways that recognize our mutual needs, including our own feelings about being interrupted or being disconnected.

We need to develop ways of relating to our grown-up children at each stage of their maturation. If we are not thoughtful and careful, we can unwittingly and gradually phase our children out of our lives—first with sleepovers, eventually leaving them at college, and finally by creating completely separate lives. The result can be disconnected families. Rather than letting go we need to develop ways to stay appropriately connected, finding ways of communicating over time and distance without actually living our children's lives. *The Research and Action Report* (Spring/Summer 2007) of the Wellesley Centers for Women featured a piece called "The Human Brain: Hardwired for Connections." Amy Banks and Judith Jordan from the Jean Baker Miller Training Institute discuss how, neurologically, social connection directly affects brain development.[4] Jordan said, "We now know that we need [human] connection to grow, and that isolation actually damages our neurobiology." Banks added, "If we can start thinking neurochemically about the way people's brains and bodies work, then we can learn how to interact across differences and find mutuality in relationships."

Here is what Nadine, a fifty-seven-year-old lab technician, has to say about the letting go advice.

LET GO! Are you kidding? You want me to let go of my child? That's worse than telling me to rip up the diploma I worked so hard to earn. It's worse than telling me to walk away from the house into which I put so much love, money, and time. Those efforts are nothing compared to what I put into my kid—I lost sleep, worked myself to exhaustion, and you want me to let go? I don't want to let go. I am tired of professionals and friends telling me to let go and disconnect. I know my children have their own lives, but so what? Does that mean that we can't have a relationship? I don't need to know every gory detail of their lives, but I would like to know some of the big picture.

Not being involved in events, values, hopes, dreams, and not sharing the joys and sorrows of life, makes Nadine think she does not want to let go. She reacts against the all-or-nothing term itself— Let Go. She wants some window into her children's lives; some intimacy and acknowledgment of past shared experiences. She, like so many parents, has no desire to live her children's lives, but does not wish to be cut off, either.

Maureen, a former housewife, exemplifies the attitudes of another group of parents. "I hate to admit it, but I don't have much in my own life. I would love to be involved in my children's lives—babysitting, going to school plays, joining them on trips—but I live thousands of miles away and they have so little vacation time, they don't want to waste it on me. I wish I knew how to keep some ties despite the distance and time constraints."

Other parents are busy with careers and friends. Many are enjoying a taste of freedom, absent for twenty or more child-rearing years. They do not want their children to be their main focus, although they enjoy some interaction. Ideally, they want each person to be one piece of the mosaic that is life, to have a connection and a continuing thread. As Ron and Betty, a couple in their fifties with satisfying careers and lots of friends, put it, "We're excited about our daughter's wedding and it is a big marker, but it just doesn't feel like the culmination of our lives. We both have jobs, we have friends, and we have so many other interests. It seems like heresy to say this, but the wedding is just one of many big events in our lives."

In some dyads, it is the child who complains about the lack of intimacy. Kevin, a thirty-seven-year-old laid-off engineer, said it well. "I'm at a real low point now. It would sure be helpful to me if my Dad would tell me that he had a wrinkle or two in his career. But he is of the old school. He doesn't tell me anything about himself. He has to maintain himself as an authority figure. My Dad is a role, not a person, so I don't tell him much about my feelings now."

Whatever the wishes for a continuing relationship, the notion of letting go is too simplistic to serve the needs of either parent or adult child. Letting-go advice doesn't work because it ignores the intricate and complex ties between parent and child. What happens to one generation affects the other. When your son loses a job, he may ask to borrow money, or vice versa. When your daughter decides not to have a child, your dreams of having biological grandchildren fly out the window.[5] When your parents die, you become an orphan. Letting go does not recognize traditional family bonds nor does it acknowledge that in some countries and some states, required portions of a parent's estate go to the next generation. Although the legal system does not require families to take care of each other, centuries of tradition and great social pressure direct family members to care of one another. For all of its simplistic appeal, just letting go is not a workable prescription for building healthy relationships with our grown children if life-long relationships for both generations are the goal.

Don't Bite Your Tongue

Ten years ago, when our first child, a daughter, became engaged, my husband and I were recipients of another type of folk wisdom. One after another of our friends would give us congratulations, and with it, "Let me give you the same advice I was given. Keep your mouth shut and your pocketbook open!" A knowing laugh always followed. With the engagement of our second child, a son, the advice expanded, "All the mother-of the-groom needs to do is be quiet and wear beige." I was stunned at the consistency of the warnings. Why did this momentous change in our lives and the lives of our children elicit a warning to keep quiet? I had learned over the years that the way to avoid misunderstandings and develop a friendship was to talk. I was curious why no one was suggesting that this new stage of life required creativity in finding new ways of engaging with our children. We too, after all, were about to embark on an entirely new phase of our lives, symbolized by the fact that we would no longer be the next of kin on our children's legal papers.

My dissatisfaction with friends' advice led me to the bookstore. Books by Dr. Spock, T. Berry Brazelton, Selma Fraiberg, and Chaim Ginott had guided me when the kids were young. I figured I could look for wisdom on the bookshelves. There I found little advice for the parent of an adult. I was shocked that a relationship so significant in my life and the lives of my friends received so little attention. It was as if this were an invisible relationship.

In contrast, on planes, trains, and buses and pretty much any place, strangers would talk to me about their adult children, declaring over and over again, "I bite my tongue, I don't say a word." I found other parents were as confused as I. Some felt that, "Parenting is over when they leave home," but most felt that parenting, at least in the sense of a special concern about one's children, continued forever. The discussion sessions I've held over the past few years have been "standing room only," proving that everyone wanted to hear about and talk about dealing with their adult children.

The relief and excitement these people felt as they talked about their relationship concerns with their children reminded me of the 1960s, when women began talking honestly to one another about their thoughts and feelings. Relief stemmed from the recognition that many of the problems, which they thought they had created, were widely shared and were actually societal and political. Parents of adult children often express that same relief when they learn that others are struggling with the ambiguities of the new status in their families.

Their adult children also expressed confusion about this relationship. For many, the choices seem to regress to childhood, or to stay aloof. They have no more clues how to be an adult vis-à-vis their parents than their parents know how to relate to the adults their children have become. Talking about problems allows us to begin solving them. It felt liberating to break the silence, to declare that children are still important to parents and that the relationship with them is constantly changing.

As I talked with more and more people at lectures and workshops, I found that there were many reasons that parents silence themselves. Some like Florence, an administrative secretary at a university, said, "I don't say a word because I might make a mistake. How do I know what's normal now?" Developmental psychologists tend to skip over the intervening years between late adolescence and aging. Parents have long been conditioned for insecurity by parental-advice books that stress the notion that our words can damage our progeny.[6] Advertisers reinforce insecurity by exhorting parents to buy the "right" toys to avoid the risk of putting their children at an intellectual disadvantage, thus inculcating in us a timidity which lasts even after our children are grown.[7]

Parents who say nothing out of fear of making a mistake may find some reassurance in the fact that they probably have already made many mistakes and their children have survived. Others react to their insecurities by silencing themselves for fear their adult children will follow their advice and it could be wrong. Alex, a mid-level executive, said, "I'm proud of myself. I didn't say a thing because my kids think they have to follow every suggestion I make." These parents are so worried that their words would injure *their* children that they squelch their own ideas. They keep silent to allow their adult children to express themselves. The parents have lost their own voices and need to reclaim them, as words are an important element in building more equal and adult relationships with our kids. When we try to silence ourselves our feelings slip out in our body language. It is practically impossible to hide strongly felt opinions. What is unsaid often puts more pressure on loved ones than what is spoken, since the receiver of the silence makes his own interpretation and has little chance to correct misunderstanding. Asking questions or offering opinions that encourage interaction rather than making pronouncements or remaining silent can be supportive of a child's independence. Sometimes, however, if we wait until our anger has passed, until a moment when we can see the other's perspective, we can select words that are more loving and calm rather than angry or insulting. We do this in our work lives, after all; we do not confront every situation at the moment it occurs but wait until we have calmed down.

Others, like Gabrielle, a school teacher, reported, "I never say a thing no matter how upset I am with my adult children. I don't want to be viewed as an overbearing mother." Much as we hate to admit it, images from popular culture and stereotypes influence our behaviors.[8] Mothers in particular worry about being overbearing. Their fear may be a remnant of the time-honored prejudice against women speaking their minds. Or, their fears could be well-founded. They may in fact be coming across as controlling or pedantic. An overbearing nature may not be due to what is said, but how it is said. Perhaps the impression is correct, and only more fundamental change can modulate the behavior.

Many parents have such tenuous relationships with their children and in-law children that they keep quiet for fear that they will not be allowed to see their grandchildren. Current ambiguous laws about grandparent rights, particularly in cases of divorce, add to that insecurity. Those who are concerned about this disconnection must seek legal advice. Where divorce is not the issue, find an intermediary to help grandparents and parents come to a workable solution.[9]

Other parents keep their mouths shut because past experience has taught them that their words lead to flare-ups. Claudia, a community volunteer who did not follow this advice, got into trouble with her forty-year-old professional daughter, Audrey. Claudia felt comfortable commenting on whatever was happening in Audrey's life, and did so liberally. Finally, when the daughter could take it no more, she screamed, "Why do you always voice your opinion? I don't want to hear it anymore." Without anger and with love the mother responded, "I see a situation, I verbalize." Both mother and daughter now understood that an opinion was not an order. Claudia would repeat her line whenever tension was getting high between them. This became a code that reminded Audrey that Claudia was expressing her love, not criticizing, and this reinforced their bond.

When talking about their relationships with their adult children, most parents express two messages. The first is, "I'm proud of myself, I didn't say a thing," followed by an expression of their discomfort, "I was dying to ask him." Or, "It kills me that I can't tell her. I just stew inside!" The pride in not speaking exists side by side with the desire to speak and the discomfort of not speaking. Rather than get into conflict with their grown-up children, some think it is better to say nothing at all. But is it better? Relationships are complex; controversy and conflict are part of their texture. The speaker at a lecture I once attended summed it up perfectly: "Intimacy and irritation go hand in hand."[10] Those who we know best annoy us the most. Interestingly, most parents neglect to remember that they have already survived numerous conflicts with their children and have somehow managed to maintain communication. When we were legally responsible for our children, professionals from schools, the justice system, or religious institutions sometimes intervened to help or force us to communicate. Now our communications and responsibilities toward each other are voluntary and self-initiated. Not talking about what we care about is a sure way to create barriers. Timing, however, is always important, and sometimes just waiting allows our children or the problem itself to resolve.

Forget trying to bite your tongue at all costs. Instead, use the skills you employ in other situations to communicate. Figure out your reasons for muting your words and find ways to mitigate the problems. We all know there are reasons in any interaction why one might choose not to speak. However, making the decision to wait to speak is far different from being silenced. Think about all the other people with whom you interact. Who are the ones you feel close to? Who are the ones you want to be with? I'll bet that the ones with whom you feel most comfortable are the ones you can share your thoughts and feelings with, and the ones with whom you have a good time. Why should it be different with your children? If we examine our relationships with people who are not our children, we find that before an intensely felt communication, we often think, ruminate, maybe even listen to them and others, and then decide how best to broach a subject. Rather than side-stepping difficult topics, we use the energy that restrained us to shape communication.

Another problem with silence is that it leaves the intended recipient of the communication with questions. Does your silence mean approval, disapproval, or just disinterest? Children "hear" or read into our silences because our body language, our actions, and our moods convey content-filled messages. Silence is not golden; it can lead to tension and misunderstanding. Much as parents like to remember the good old days when they could talk about "anything, any time" with their children, in actuality, they are quite practiced in choosing the right moment to speak. Few parents of toddlers would mention tomorrow's trip to the circus at bedtime if they ever hoped to get their children to sleep. Moreover, parents had to listen to their children if there was to be a meeting of the minds. I remember when my son was four, I wanted him to get up and get his cereal before he awakened me on Sunday mornings. I explained, "You are old enough now to get your cereal on Sunday morning." He protested, and I lovingly and patiently explained the step-by-step process: "Go over to the cabinet, open the door, take out the box, etc." He continued to protest, until finally he said, "But, Mommy, I don't know when Sunday is." We have always had to listen to our children if we had any hope of being understood.

Many parents have a more authoritarian style. What they say is the rule of the house. This may be a perfectly legitimate style for parenting young children, although my previous example illustrates some of its pitfalls. However, this style rarely works with adults in American society. The cultural emphasis on independence is too great. The authoritarian model may mean some in the next generation replicate that style, leading to a power struggle between parent and child; or, in order to distance themselves from their parents, children rebel.

We all also know many ways to communicate without words. A hug, a smile, or a frown often conveys more than words. Our children are well-practiced at reading our nonverbal signs. When feelings were hurt or friends had deserted, a trip to the playground or a special food might serve better than words. With all the energy you save biting your tongue, you can think of how you want to express yourself. It may be in words or it may be in deeds.

Answering the questions below will help you define when you want to speak and when you want to remain silent!

Questions:

- Do any of the vignettes in this chapter describe your relationship with your adult children?
- In what situations have you "let go" and it turned out well?
- In what situations have you "let go" and it turned out badly?
- In what situations do you silence yourself? In what situations does it feel good? In what situations does it feel frustrating or bad?
- Has your gown child ever "heard" your silence, that is, reacted to your nonverbal cues? When?

- What particular concerns do you have with or about your grown children that you are not discussing with them, separately or together?
- What difficult conversations have you had with a friend or a boss or a neighbor? What made the conversation work successfully? What led to ending the conversation?
- How do you regain equilibrium after you have had a disagreement?

2

KNOW YOURSELF

Those of us who weren't orphaned young were adult children of our own parents. Some of our parents were born around the turn of the previous century, long before women's suffrage, when the horse cart still delivered milk and when men and women had very clearly defined and distinct roles. Like all humans, our folks parented imperfectly. No doubt they did some things right and some things wrong. Since the older generations influence our current parenting, it is helpful for each of us to reflect on our own upbringing. Many parents fear either being like their own parents or not measuring up to them. Our own parental actions are controlled by the memory of what our parents did in raising us, and their parenting was likewise conditioned by their own upbringing. Our task is to forgive imperfections—our parents', our own, and ultimately our children's. The parent-child bond is a strong and enduring one. My own mother died thirty-nine years ago, yet her exhortations to write thank-you and condolence notes are with me to this day. When I have the urge to squeeze one of those luscious-looking chocolates in a box of fancy liquor-filled bonbons to find out what is inside, I hear her reprimanding me, proving that, for better or for worse, even death does not part us.

For many parents, children represent immortality. The parents will live on through their children and their children's children. So when the child "makes a mistake," the parent fears not only the immediate consequences of the mistake but the future impact on their own legacy. Many children feel this as a burden. Others revel in knowing they are passing on the traditions, wisdom, and hopes of their parents. Many of us do both, hating the constraints of carrying forth the past, and feeling good doing and being something that reminds us of our parents (like not squeezing the chocolate!) that would gain parental approval.

In religious and minority groups, the desire of parents to honor their own parents, their own traditions, and their group history may conflict with the desires of the children to be part of a more mainstream America. The "hyphenated" American (Mexican American, Chinese American, Cambodian American, Italian American, Irish American, Jewish American) is rapidly becoming a multihyphenated American as subsequent generations intermarry. Some groups—like American Jews—are concerned that their communities may disappear as they have out-marriage rates of 50 percent.[1]

For immigrant children the pressure to succeed is fueled not only by their parents but also by the great national myth that America, the land of opportunity, will give the next generation a better chance. That chance may involve better economic status, more education, or freedom from oppressive regimes. This story is so powerful that millions leave their own countries and take great risks to arrive in America; over one million legal immigrants came to the United States in 2005.[2] Presidential candidates vie to tell the most compelling rags to riches story. The American dream is that children will do better than their parents. Thus, any deviation from the family definition of "better" leads to disappointment.

Many parents and grandparents made huge sacrifices to make this American dream come true. We can see in the new immigrants some of the ways our parents cared for us, which many Americans take for granted. Several semesters ago, I asked my students, "How do you know your parents love you?" One Cambodian boy responded, "They feed me!" My American students were stunned: feeding and clothing middle-class American kids is so expected, none of them even thought to credit their parents for this. However, having done these things for your own children, you now know those are no small tasks! When I repeated this scenario to an American-born Chinese friend who has lived in the States since college, she said, "Yes, in China parents remind their children of their obligations by saying, 'I brought you up and fed you.' In the United States if you say that, you are accused of laying on a guilt trip." Forgiving your parents requires taking a new look at your own understanding of how you were raised. First, list all the things your folks did right. Start with the basics— they fed you, clothed you, saw that you got to school in the morning. When you make a list, try not to take anything for granted.

Then start with the things your own parents did that you might resent to this day and find the good in them. Sort out what good you got from "bad" parenting. For example, many of us were embarrassed by moms who loudly demanded the best seating or service anywhere and everywhere we went, or dads who humiliated us by yelling at the soccer coach for not putting us in the starting line-up. Alternately, many of us were disappointed in parents who did not speak up for us. In fact, both taught us in very different ways to speak for ourselves.

This is called reframing. You review the past and see it through new eyes, reframe it through the lens of experience and compassion. This takes work. It is a new way of remembering all the hurts, misdeeds, and real or perceived trauma some of us have survived. Instead of looking at the bad, focus on the good, however meager, that came from the unhappy events. Positive thinking can be habit-forming. Certainly focusing on the positive is a good skill to model for your children, and focusing on the good and ignoring the bad can be an effective way of relating to your child.

It may also help to consider your parents' reasons for performing whatever action you're focusing on. Sometimes impossible standards of perfection guided them. Others reacted out of their own unhappiness. Understanding the motivations of our own parents helps us develop compassion. Another way to increase our compassion is to stop, look, and listen to ourselves. Often we do some of the same things our parents did. Understanding that some of the actions we hated in our parents might have had good consequences or been well motivated is all part of modifying our own narratives. And, looking in the other direction, our children can help us as well. We can ask them what they see, and sometimes they will answer openly.

Sadly, some of us really did have inadequate parents. They just did not know how to take care of us, or advocate for us. But those of you reading this book who had those parents got something good enough out of their caring, however inadequate it was. Maybe you simply learned what *not* to do as a parent. Maybe you learned that you needed to take care of yourself. If your parents died when you were young, you may have learned the same lesson.

Joyce and Artie were both children from divorced families. Both had suffered financially and socially from the acrimony between their parents. Both were constantly playing the role of peacemaker. When they married, they committed to working things out between them. They would not put their children through the trials they had suffered. When their relationship did become strained, they sought help from their clergy. They gave each other space to make personal peace, and they focused on the positives in their marriage. Clearly Joyce and Artie turned the lessons of a painful childhood into something productive. They used the peacemaking skills they had learned to make peace in their own nuclear family.

Another method that is useful in understanding your own parents is to try retroactive empathy. Put yourself in your mom's or dad's place. What was it like to have two screaming kids and be locked in a house all day? Or what was it like to have no money and two babies to feed? What was it like to be trapped in a loveless marriage? What was it like to go to a job you hated? What was it like to be crushed by responsibility? This exercise will help you understand your parents' motives, maybe even help you understand their dreams and disappointments.

In short, when we look at ourselves as the object of parenting we can gain insight into our own feelings and actions. If you never express an opinion for fear of being critical, try to just express your thoughts without the critical component. You needn't remain silent. Hopefully this exploration helps us understand the effect our forebears have on us and on our progeny.

Just because you are similar to your parents, your children may not share your same characteristics. As Louis, a fifty-seven-year-old web designer, discovered, you can share traits but react quite differently. "My son Jake and I are both disorganized. I feel my disorganization is hidden if my house has a Victorian cluttered look. My chaos fits right in with the decor. Clutter makes my son feel even more disorganized and out of control. He is strictly a white-walls man. It took me a while to figure out we have different solutions, though we have the same trait."

Forget the Guilt

Another trap for parents is wasting energy on guilt. Guilt helps you to learn right from wrong as a child, but as an adult it serves little purpose. We cannot undo our past mistakes. We can learn from past mistakes, but endless berating serves no purpose. Instead try to use that energy to forgive yourself. It is easy to feel fearful and guilty. Which of us hasn't made mistakes? We know we are fallible, mistaken, and imperfect, even if we don't like to admit it. We know teachers, peers, pop culture, and world events help mold our children. We don't need experts to tell us we can't control all the outcomes. By this point, our adult kids have figured out that we aren't all-powerful. They know the environment changes them. They know that their friends, siblings, and spouses play roles in their lives. We, too, need to believe that forces beyond ourselves influence our children and we need to free ourselves from the heavy weight of responsibility for everything that has happened to our children. When your children were young, you were responsible for keeping your kids clean, well-fed, clothed, healthy, and well-behaved. You were expected to intervene if they were having a hard time or getting into trouble. As the years went on, they became more and more responsible for their own actions. Hard as it was to get kids to take responsibility, it's equally hard to allow children to be responsible for their own mistakes.

Most parents find it easy to allow their children to take credit for their accomplishments. When your child earns a degree, gets a promotion, wins a prize, finds a loving, supportive relationship, you enjoy it and give your child due credit. You don't stay up all night wondering what you did right. You delight in your child's accomplishments, credit good luck and your child's wondrousness.

The problem comes when things don't go well. When your adult child can't handle challenges on the job, you may wonder where you failed. What might you have done differently? When your twenty-eight-year-old son is still living at home and can't seem to figure out how to get his life on track, you are consumed with thoughts about what you did or did not do to create this situation.

Why is it that when difficulties arise, you take on the blame, even though you know you are not omnipotent? You wonder about your own failures. Regardless of what you have taught your child about the importance of personal responsibility, the truth is that you feel and behave as if you were the responsible party.

Like so many, you have absorbed our culture's pervasive parent-blaming message. Many have bought into the "caring trap"—if something goes wrong in your offspring's life, then you must have done something wrong. If only you had been more caring, more sensitive, less self-absorbed, things would be just fine. Their success is their own, but their failure is yours.

You must also learn how to embrace your own wins, not only your losses. Without being able to appreciate your own achievements, how can you appreciate those of your children? How excited can you be about your child's hard-won promotion to middle management, if you had always wanted to be CEO yourself and don't see how your child is ever going to make it to the top of the corporate ladder? Whatever you hoped for yourself that has not happened can hamper your relationship with your child.

The sense of parental failure when things go wrong is so strong and omnipresent, so much a part of our culture, that it seems like it would take a seismic event to unseat it.[3] Women in the 1940s, 1950s, and early 1960s were told their purpose in life was to raise children. Those women were judged by the success of their offspring and therefore they judged their offspring as a reflection of themselves. Thinking, "If only I had . . . things would have been different" perpetuates the illusion that we can control outcomes. We cannot go back. While it is important to reflect and reconcile our relationships with our own parents, times change, we change, and we cannot hang onto the past. We must create our own relationships with the new and different people who are our children.

Successful second-stage parents, by whom I mean parents comfortable with their role and their relationships, have learned how to engage with their children as adults. They use the same skills in dealing with their children's failures as they do with their successes. They may need reminders from time to time, but they understand their role in their children's lives—they are caring, emotionally open observers. They get to cheer or commiserate, but not to change. Sometimes they can smooth the path, give aid if asked, and provide a willing and interested ear. But they have relinquished the responsibility for their offspring's choices, successes, and failures.

These engaged observers are involved in the lives of their children. Before they jump into action or comment mode, they *reflect*. They ask themselves why they want to jump in. What fears or hopes of their own are working in the background? What mistakes do they wish they could change? Only then can they decide to share their thoughts about themselves and their child's situation. If they do share, it's helpful too to *ask* their children to comment on both the parental view of themselves and the parental view of the child's situation. Such honesty is not easy on either side. We might hear something painful, something we do not want to hear. However, without listening and responding, there can be no change; dissatisfaction, probably mutual, will prevail.

One advantage to sharing an event you remember as a failure, is that your child may see it as a fond cherished memory. And although we may not like it, our children force us to reevaluate our own life stories. Maybe you are an immigrant who made tremendous sacrifices to come to America. Or, you are a woman who gave up a promising career to take care of your children or you kept at a steady job to support your family and gave up dreams of fame and fortune. You expected your children's success as payment for all you lost out on or all you suffered. However, children are rarely grateful for what they have not experienced personally. Expecting our children to understand all we have endured is unrealistic. As the old Yiddish proverb says, "You can't feel your grandmother's toothache." Parents who reflect on themselves and the forces that influence their children realize, though often with great difficulty, what has happened has happened, and cannot be changed. They say goodbye to fantasies, even the fantasy that they will be rewarded for all their sacrifices, and accept reality.

Acknowledge Your Dreams for Yourself and for Your Child

Being honest with ourselves about our imaginings and shortcomings can help us understand our current behaviors. For example, think back to the first week you brought your baby home. I suspect you will find your feelings were a mixture of panic, fear, incompetence, pride, joy, and elation. Most parents felt a jumble of mixed thoughts during those first days. That jumble never goes away. The complexity of the parent-child relationship begins on day one and maybe even before.

All parents have dreams for their children. All too often those dreams are totally unrealistic, contradictory, and grandiose. You might have wanted your child to be tall and blond as well as short, petite, and dark. You might have wanted your child to be an Olympic athlete, a world-class violinist, and a Nobel Prize-winning scientist *and*, at the same time, be loving, relaxed, and giving. You might want them to be loyal to you forever and married with five children. What dreams did you have? Answering that question can help you assess your disappointments. It can also help you realize how much has turned out well. Just as we hope our children will not take for granted our efforts to take care of their daily needs, parents must acknowledge and appreciate the ordinary achievements of their children. The following vignette illustrates some of the complexities of the parent-child bond and some of the ways our histories play out in our relationships.

Beatrice, a fifty-two-year-old successful interior designer, was flattered when her son, Evan, a twenty-seven-year-old engineer who had moved to another city, asked her to help his wife Sarah and him move into their first house. Beatrice thought that not only would she have a chance to use her decorating skills, but she would also get to know her daughter-in-law better. Beatrice had cosigned their loan from the bank for a mortgage, and felt she had contributed to the purchase. She was pleased to think that her son was finally acknowledging her career. Her own mother had been a stay-at-home mom, so Beatrice especially resented the way her son seemed to think of her as "Mom," never showing any interest in her career, which had supported them both since her divorce when Evan was twelve. After the weekend, Beatrice met her best friend Mary in the supermarket. When Mary asked, "How'd it go?" Beatrice responded:

I was a bit tense about the trip. Evan, Sarah, and I get along fine, though there's still slight stiffness between Sarah and me, maybe because we've only met a few times. I felt good that I could help the kids. The house is tiny, but I could position the couch so that the living room looks okay. Where they were going to put it totally blocked the already too small room. I know they spent everything on the house and have none to buy new furniture, so I was also really proud of myself that I didn't comment on the big flowered fabric on the couch—so wrong for the room. Then the house is next to what they call "woods"; I'd call it a vacant lot. I'm so proud that I didn't say a thing about that either.

Later that day, Mary ran into Evan, whom she had known since he was born. He had driven his mother to her house to pick up some of his treasured belongings. Mary said, "I heard you've got a new place. Did you have a nice weekend with your Mom?" Evan replied:

Well, it was OK. We were just so excited about our new place. Compared to our apartment, it's a castle and we worked long and hard for the down payment. Mom's first comment was that the living room was too small. I was ready to kill her. Then she proceeded to play interior decorator. You know Mom; she thinks she is the artist of the century! Sarah was really miffed. Her mother would

never have come in and taken over like Mom did. This is
our first home and we want to make it OUR nest. Now it's
awkward. Do we leave the couch where Mom wants it or
put it where we want it? Sarah is so burned up, she never
wants to ask Mom an opinion ever again. I'm miffed that
Mom never even noticed the woods next door. This is the
real beauty of our place. Green trees; it makes our land
look really big. Mom never even mentioned the beauty.
She just rained on our parade!

Embedded in this incident between a parent and an adult child is
not only a tale of two perspectives, but also the seeds of tension.
Beatrice thought, rightly or wrongly, she had been invited to
come because of her decorating experience, not just to provide
physical labor. She took extra pride in that, unlike her own
mother, she had expertise to offer. Because she had never
respected the advice and help her own mother had given, it did
not occur to Beatrice that she might be useful without her
professional mantle. Moreover, she felt she had acted with real
sensitivity to the economic and social limitations of the couple's
situation. Where Evan felt his mother had intruded on his new
family's right to make decisions, Beatrice felt that she had some
claim to voicing her opinion because decorating was her field.
Beatrice was at once intimately connected, someone with a
financial stake in the home and also a guest—a complex and
ambiguous status. Clearing up expectations in advance might
have led to a smoother weekend, though it would not have
completely erased the complexity of the role.

Furthermore, Evan was caught in the triangle between his
mother and his wife. However well-respected Beatrice might be
in her field, Sarah felt her mother-in-law was intruding on her
place both literally and figuratively. All were caught between the
cultures of two families: Sarah's, whose parents never interfered,
and Evan's, whose mother always expressed her opinions. Like so
many of us, Beatrice hardly knew her daughter-in-law. Yet she
was a close relative by marriage. That Evan and Sarah lived far
away increased the difficulty in communicating. Beatrice was
caught in the uncertainty of how to treat Sarah, and Sarah was

similarly uncertain. It is hard to treat someone you barely know as kin. Evan was caught in the middle.

Mary was privy to the perspectives of both Beatrice and Evan. Like so many friends and disinterested third parties, she could see what Beatrice could not. We all need others to broaden our perspectives. Mary could sense that Beatrice was disappointed that Evan could not afford a new couch, a better house, and a better location, and that Beatrice did not realize how much that disappointment was evident in her tone. Beatrice recited to her friend the mantra of parents of adult children: "I am proud of myself that I did not say everything I wanted to say," her variant on, "I bit my tongue." She followed the folk wisdom of "not saying a word," but Evan sensed her disapproval nonetheless.

Maybe her problem was that she didn't realize that the economics of owning a house has changed dramatically over the years. When she had bought a house in the 1970s, the average person spent only a fourth of his or her income on housing. Now, 17 million families use more than 50 percent of their income to pay for housing.[4] Had Beatrice understood this, she might have not felt quite so responsible for Evan's lack of success. The economy had changed around her and she, like most of us, did not realize its implications.

Evan, on the other hand, may or may not have sent mixed signals to his mother in his invitation. He asked her to help. He may have wanted her physical labor, not her opinion. He did not make that clear, possibly because he did not know what he wanted. He wanted admiration for his achievement. To him, the house was a symbol of success and adulthood. He was, after all, paying the mortgage. While he is married and independent, he still claims privileges typically reserved for dependants. For example, he had left his personal belongings in his mother's home. Because Evan was her child, Beatrice was happy to be of help with moving and storage. She might not have been so forthcoming with her ideas with all her friends. Although she was happy to share her expertise, Evan instinctively viewed this expertise as criticism, since in the past her role as mother had been to temper his excesses. He felt that his mother focused on the flaws of the house rather than on celebrating his great purchase. He reacted to her the way he might have when he was young and she was trying to civilize him. Evan wanted the intimacy that allows one to impose on another, and was hurt when his mother treated him like another adult, that is, like a client. Beatrice willingly allowed her son to depend on her, but failed to fulfill his expectations of her as a cheerleader. And of course their differences in perspective were made concrete when Evan saw the lot next door as a beautiful wooded enhancement to his home, while his mother saw it as a vacant lot, an eyesore, and a liability.

Beatrice and Evan's difficulties arose over one seemingly trivial matter, the placement of a couch, and a bigger one, the reaction to a new home. The real issue was that neither knew their role. They kept shifting behaviors, from the familiar ones of their parent-child relationship, to the unpracticed ones of an adult-adult association.

Like Beatrice, our own aspirations for our children often inform our advice to them. In the following chapters we will explore many examples in which parents allow their dreams to be conflated with those of their children.

Enjoy the Advantages of Having Adult Children

Now that our kids have grown, we may have more time for ourselves. We can go back to hobbies long forgotten or never pursued. We can rekindle or develop new friendships. We can learn new tricks! For some, life may already be rich with work, family, friends, and hobbies. Others need to develop these. We give our children the gift of modeling how to create a full life. Parents may instinctively want to seek immortality in their children, but must instead find it in their own deeds. Medicine has added years to our lives. We cannot rely on the children to fill those years—it is up to each of us to use the gift of time. No matter how old you are, fifty or sixty or seventy or eighty or even ninety, you are not dead yet. Whatever dreams you have, it is time to attempt to fulfill them yourself. Our job now is to make things happen for ourselves. When we are interesting to ourselves we are interesting to others. We must create our own new adventures.

At the Democratic National Convention in August 2004, Nancy Pelosi, current Minority Leader of the U.S. House of Representatives, told this story, which typifies the attitudes of most children. Pelosi recounted, "I asked my five children who were off to college if I should run for the U.S. House of Representatives. They responded 'Ma, do it, get a life!'" This is great advice for us all. This can be the time for us to take risks, try new things, and continue to grow and to learn.

The questions below aim to help you sort out your own dreams, successes, and disappointments and the role they have played in your parenting. Thinking about them will help you in the next phase of your own life. This diagnostic journey may help you forgive your parents, yourself, and your children for things that have gone wrong. Hopefully it will help you appreciate all that has gone right and yield new confidence that you can grow, develop, and learn.

Questions:

- List all the things your parents did right—from clothing and feeding you as a child to helping you as an adult.
- Now list all the things that they did wrong—all the things you want to avoid.
- Take another look at these lists. Did anything good come out of the bad, and did anything bad come out of the good?
- List all your strengths as a parent.
- List the "mistakes" you feel you made as a parent. Does your child see them as mistakes?
- Are you shortchanging yourself because you did not do *everything* you had hoped to do?
- Do things that did not get done overshadow those that did?
- What are your current expectations, wishes, and fears for your children?
- How do you think your own past impacts them?

- How are your own hopes, desires, and disappointments expressed in your conversations with your grown children?
- In what ways have they been fulfilled, and in what ways unfulfilled?
- What dreams do you have left to fulfill, i.e., what do you want to do with the rest of your life?
- What new skills and interests do you want to use or need to develop?
- How can you create support systems?

If your children are willing, you can ask them to respond to the above questions. Reflect on and discuss their response with them. It can clear the air of past hurts and misunderstandings.

Again, try to be both the performer and the audience in your life. First try to see what you do, think, and say, considering what you have in mind when you do them, as well as how others may perceive your words or actions. Then think. Is this the way you want things to be? How can you change things? Being honest with yourself facilitates communication. With the freedom that comes when a parent's children are grown, and the freedom children feel when they are no longer under the supervision of their parents, both generations can live their own dreams.

3

SAY GOODBYE TO FANTASY AND HELLO TO REALITY

Before rock songs and heavy-metal anthems, there were ballads. One from the 1940s that still brings a lump to my throat is, "You Always Hurt the One You Love, the One You Shouldn't Hurt at All," by the Mills Brothers. If there were a national anthem of parents and adult children, this would be it! We have indeed loved each other with passion. Who but our one-, two-, and three-year-olds has ever wept when we left the room and then greeted us like royalty when we returned? And for whom but our children did we endure hours in the icy cold rain, or the sweaty gym, or the chlorine-filled air to see a one-minute moment of their athletic prowess? Yes, we have loved. And like the adult lovers in the song, we have hurt each other numerous times. We have disappointed each other because neither could live up to the ideal the other held. It is the complete irrationality of our love that gets us into trouble, the yearning for an unattainable dream. As parents, we give so much in time, energy, and lost opportunity to raise children that sometimes we feel entitled to overlook the impact our words and actions might have on them. Children feel betrayed by the parents they fantasized would love them eternally and unquestioningly. Our bonds give both of us the power to hurt. We know each other's sensitivities and fears. We have let down our guard with one another and stood literally and figuratively naked before one another. We can never have a neutral relationship. Our words have the power to give each other pleasure or pain, our gestures to say more than we realize or intend.

We have hurt our children by limiting their options because we were concerned for their safety, or by restraining them from doing everything they wanted because we did not approve of their choices, or because our experience told us that the outcomes would be dangerous. We have rejected their help when they offered it so lovingly. We have also hurt them inadvertently by being unavailable, by putting someone else's needs ahead of theirs—our work, a sick sibling, or an ailing grandparent. Because we were bigger and stronger and knew more, we had even more power to wound our children than to wound our friends, partners, or spouses.

Our children have hurt us, too. Their very honesty can be painful. When they were young, their imitative play provided a very real and sometimes unpleasant look into ourselves. We have all heard our own voices coming from our children's mouths. At some point our children began saying, "No." The disagreements began. And fantasies, on both sides, began to crumble. We both fell short, our disappointments all the greater due to the heights of the fantasies. In their early years our children lashed out with words or fists, and in high school most disobeyed as they struck out for independence. We may have had real concern for their safety; we may have found it highly unpleasant to live with moody, sometimes angry teens who slept until noon and promised to do anything we asked "later." As they emerged, sometimes years later, into adulthood, they had the audacity to make decisions different from the ones we would have made! Sometimes it feels like they have destroyed our dreams. We are hurt and angry. But we are embarrassed to share these feelings with our children. The result is tension.

This is not the first time we have been disappointed by fantasies. We have imagined perfect relationships with friends or lovers with never an argument and never a fight, only to be disillusioned. Like these other unrealistic imaginings, the one that we would walk blissfully into the sunset of our lives with our adult children at our side will never happen. We have had to modify the Hollywood happy ending with our friends and spouses. Those of us who managed to stay in each other's lives have done so by focusing on the positive, by coming to some sort of accommodation, and by not focusing on the wounds. We long ago laid to rest the illusion that any one friend or spouse would fulfill our needs in every way. Some of us changed the picture completely and left the friendship or the marriage.

However, we cannot unbirth our children. Unlike a marriage, the parent-child relationship is really and truly, "for better or for worse and until death do us part." And like all relationships it can have its tough times, its fights, and its regrettable words. If we expect a smooth ride with no aggravation, we are doomed to discontent. Many of us never thought about what we expect from our children, and thus feel a diffused malaise with the relationship. Some find they really do not want to spend much time with their children. Some imagine they will still be "hanging out" together every weekend and holiday. Many hold on to an illusion that doesn't suit either them or their children. We can live the rest of our lives longing for those dreams, or we can accept and enjoy the new reality, so long as it is not dangerous or unhealthy. The choice is ours. We can choose to blame our children for our losses or we can admit they have the right—the same right we claimed decades ago for ourselves—to make their own choices. We can choose to forget our fantasies, mourn our disappointments, and then embrace what life has brought us and them.

Kevin, a plumber, age forty-nine, always thought he wanted his boys by his side all the time. "When John and Shawn were young, it was the boys and me every Saturday. We went to the store, we played sports, we were together all the time. I thought it would remain like that forever. But now that the boys are married and have kids of their own and in-laws, I hardly ever see them, or so it seems. A part of me longs for those old days, the days when we were together, just the three of us, but then I realize if that were to be true they would never have developed, I wouldn't have grandchildren. I don't really know what I want now."

Kevin had grown up in a close ethnic community. His eleven cousins and all his aunts and uncles lived within a few blocks of each other. Every Sunday after church the whole clan gathered at his grandmother's house. His cousins and friends all married "the girl next door" and settled close by. Paradoxically, Kevin's goal to help his children gain good educations led to their leaving the community. His boys all earned scholarships to college, landed good jobs, and moved away. Kevin's dreams for his boys were realized, but the result came at an unexpected cost: his boys were gone. He had unknowingly expected to grow old, just as his parents had, with the whole family living close by and young kids running underfoot. His mind was so frozen in the past that he couldn't even begin to envision a different future.

Had he looked around his neighborhood, he might have noticed that other families around him were getting smaller and many of his friends were experiencing the same life change. Of course, he understood, and was proud of what his sons had achieved, but he couldn't help feeling spurned. Like so many others, Kevin felt jealous of his children's new intimate connections—jealous, angry, and discarded, but at the same time, proud and pleased at their accomplishments. He kept this morass of feelings to himself. Kevin feels unable to talk with his boys about how he would like to be included in their lives because he doesn't know what he wants. No one encourages him to explore his own needs. His friends reassure each other that the separation is natural: it is time to "let go." Besides, they reason, it would only cause problems to talk about what can't be changed. Unless Kevin lets his sons know his feelings, neither he nor they can begin to make things better.

If Kevin brought this up with his boys he might find that they pine for a more traditional family structure, too, and regret that their children are not close to the grandparents. Together they might come up with ideas of how to improve not only Kevin's situation but also his sons'. There are a vast variety of options to be explored between minimal contact and daily integration of lives. Perhaps his boys too would like to recreate the old intimacy, possibly in short spurts. Planning an outing might mitigate Kevin's longings; regular phone calls are another possibility. His sons and he might decide to include his grandchildren in their plans. Kevin might find he could help his sons out by doing activities in person or by computer with his grandchildren. Creativity is in order. Kevin might find he enjoys leaving the old neighborhood to travel to see his sons, or just to travel to see other places. In fact, he could develop new interests of his own.

These steps, asking for affection and working together, are monumental. They mark a change in their past interactions. In traditional homes, the children are expected to do the courting, the lobbying, and the deferential work. The parents have seniority. If Kevin shares his feelings with his sons and asks for help, he is no longer the all-knowing father, but shifting the parent-child relationship to a more egalitarian one in which all parties have knowledge, feelings, and opinions. If Kevin does these two things he has begun the process of developing a new way of communicating with his sons, one more suited to their new stage of life and better suited to handling the ambiguities of the parent-adult child relationship.

Corinne, age sixty-three, has a different problem. She knows what she wants, but cannot dismiss the scripts she grew up with and the fantasy she has held for so long. She has five children. Her life revolved around their lives. In her forties, when her last two kids were in high school, she went to college. She loved it and went on for a master's degree. She now has a doctorate in psychology and a thriving psychotherapy practice. "I always thought I would spend the rest of my life helping out my kids, babysitting, pitching in, but I became enthralled with my studies and now I have a great career. I love seeing the grandkids but I have done my time, I don't want to be stuck with kids anymore. I'm willing to help out in a crisis, but that is it! I think my kids are disappointed and I feel guilty about it."

Corinne was surprised that she grew to love having a career and really did not want to be with her grandchildren all the time. She felt guilty and selfish. She had been brought up to believe a woman's role was in the home, but new opportunities had opened up for her. She was proud of all she had achieved in her career. She had exceeded all her own expectations and wanted her family to revel in her accomplishments. After all, she had cheered them on for years. Some of her children did applaud her. Others disappointed her by not even asking her about her work or by quickly changing the subject when she talked about it. In order to save herself from the sadness of feeling cut off, she stopped talking about her work. "I feel like I have a secret life, that somehow I had broken a contract with my family. This makes me feel even guiltier." As we have seen, though, complete silence is rarely a solution.

Corrine's oldest son Paul is particularly aggrieved. He was the first of her children to start a family. He is the father of a five-month-old and a two-year-old. Both he and his wife work full time. They are overwhelmed by diapers, work, and too little sleep. Paul still wants to be his mother's top priority. He resents the fact that she is not completely available when he needs her. "I just assumed my Mom would help out with the kids. She taught us family is the most important thing. Now she cares more about her patients than about her kids and grandkids." Like Corinne, Paul can't let go of old scripts. He may be upset with his mother, or he may be upset with himself, feeling that he cannot provide well enough for his family so that his wife could be a stay-at-home mom. Paul might even be upset that his wife loves her job so much and is actually happy working outside the home. She also expects him to be an equal partner in childrearing, which Paul resents. He is early in his career and is madly trying to climb the corporate ladder. He resents his wife's insistence that he share the house work. He wants to support his family financially, but can't see how to do it *and* help with the kids and the house. His inability to understand his mother is mirrored in his inability to sympathize with his wife. Paul does not know that 64.8 percent of married couples with children under eighteen both participate in the workforce.[1] In 1970, 10.2 million married women with children participated in the labor force. By 2005, that number had almost doubled!

The economy has changed and so have the attitudes and goals of many women. Corrine is not alone in relishing her professional experience and success. While responsibilities for grandparents are increasing, their workforce participation is growing. Fifty-eight percent of grandparents who were responsible for their own grandchildren under eighteen years of age were also in the workforce in 2002.[2]

Despite her psychological training, Corinne cannot talk about her needs to her son because she feels so guilty about her selfishness. She feels inadequate: she cannot serve her patients and also be available on demand to her children, as part of her feels she should. Yet after a lifetime of putting others first, she feels it's now her turn: she wants and loves this time to develop herself and her own interests.

In addition, Corrine rationalizes that Paul is too busy to appreciate her situation. She's setting up an either/or world: either she handles her issues or Paul takes them on. She thinks she is protecting him, so she doesn't ask him to participate in a full and equal discussion of their individual roles in creating the tension that has developed between them. A frank conversation about unmet expectations might help them come to some compromise. It might also help Paul better understand his wife's demands for help with the household and children.

But Paul, like so many of us, wants it both ways—an ever-available parent and one who makes no demands. Paul is holding on to his definitions not only of his mother but of himself as *the* breadwinner and his wife as a stay-at-home mom. Therefore he cannot care for his kids in partnership with his wife; nor can he fully appreciate that his wife, like his mother, really wants to work.

Fantasy and reality are bumping uncomfortably into each other. Neither Corinne nor Paul has made peace with the changes life has brought. Neither has embraced the new phase in their lives. Corinne would have to override her own qualms to share her discomfort. She could invite Paul to talk about his issues with her and they could discuss how together they might work things out better. Letting go of the fantasy about his mother, he could ask her how she would like to be part of his children's lives. Though Corinne doesn't want to be a full-time grandmother, she can be a part-time one and a full-time worker; she might offer to set up times to babysit. As the two talk, Corrine can update Paul's outdated image of his mother. This might give him insight into his wife's attitudes toward her work and her requests for his greater participation at home. His outdated image of his mother is influencing his current thinking about his wife. Paul and his wife might also need to explore how she really feels about working outside their home, and to review their division of labor to accommodate both of their situations.

Davis and Candace are typical of many parents in that they face real differences between the dreams they had for their son and the reality of his current situation. Candace teaches third grade in a public school. Her husband, Davis, is a software engineer. They had hoped their thirty-five-year-old son, Dan, would be married by this time and settled in a career. He has done neither. They worry about him. They wonder if they did anything wrong to make Dan unable to commit to anything. They admit disappointment, and wonder if they should offer to help and how they might do so. They have given Dan a good education, and many enrichment activities. Yet Dan just can't seem to "find himself." Dan worked for an advertising firm, but he felt dirty "selling junk to the public." He then worked as a web designer, only to find that the company "just did not appreciate creative talent." He now partially supports himself with contracts designing restaurant murals. He pays his rent and food, but his folks supplement his income and pay for his health insurance so he can visit them and his friends and go out to an occasional movie. He works hard, his business is building, and he seems, at last, quite happy. However, contract work is unstable. Candace and Davis wonder whether they are enabling him to avoid commitment to a job—their view of how life should be—by supplementing his income. In his view, though, they are enabling him to develop his talent as an artist and entrepreneur, ultimately the founder of a successful niche company.

Money is not the only area in Dan's life in which Davis and Candace feel unsure of their place. Dan is a good, considerate son. They hate to leave him alone at holidays, but would like to have the freedom to travel during Candace's vacations. They had anticipated this as a carefree time in their lives. While they understand that Dan will survive if they are not around, they find the thought of his being lonely, without family at holidays, painful. Dan is not asking them to stay, but Davis and Candace can't help but feel they are abandoning him since he has no other family. In fact, Dan is part of a cohort of young adults who are not marrying until their late 30s; in 2005, 22.5 percent of men and 15.6 percent of women ages 34–39 were still not married.[3] Dan's parents resent that his slow life advancement is infringing on theirs. They have a son who cannot or will not support himself, so they feel that they cannot retire. They worry that if they spend too much money on themselves there will not be enough left for Dan. They understand that they are not obligated to take care of him, but it is hard for them to see him struggling. An outsider might say Davis and Candace need to let go to allow Dan to stand on his own two feet.

Career experimentation might, in fact, be part of a necessary process. The old markers of adulthood—early marriage and a lifelong job—are not in place. Candace and Davis avoid talking to Dan about both his social and economic life partly because, "We feel we put too much pressure on him. He knows what we expect of him and to rub it in is unfair and he is an adult. It is not as if he isn't trying to find his place in the world. His social life is private business. Maybe after he settles his own life, he will feel able to commit to a woman. Besides, if we bring up either work or social life, Dan either clams up or goes off in a huff, saying 'I know, I know.'"

It could be that Candace and Davis are embarrassed by their son's lack of success and Dan feels that. It is also possible that they sense that they are still responsible, yet have no control over their child, and this is paralyzing Candace and Davis. If they share their quandaries and assumptions with Dan, and ask him where he thinks he needs assistance, they could focus their help where he wants it, rather than wasting energy on fancied problems. If Dan did discuss his social life with his folks, they might find out that he has plenty of friends and a rich social life and rest easy that their worries about his loneliness are unfounded. He might allay their fears about his new business if he told them more about it. Or they might find that he too is concerned about his isolation. In any case, they would be better informed and feel more connected. At any rate, the situation must change or both generations will be frozen in a stage of life that has passed for both of them. Dan is still the dependent child with parents who put his needs before theirs. Dan can manage well enough by himself; he might need some financial assistance for health insurance, but that does not mean he needs assistance in all areas of life. It may be time to ask Dan for a plan toward self-sufficiency and decide together how long and at what level he will need to be subsidized. All this not talking about issues distances and upsets the family.

The paradox is that the complexity which drives us crazy is what makes human relationships so interesting. Assessing our roles in each other's lives goes on for a lifetime. Harry's mother was widowed ten years ago. Harry is a busy accountant with three high-school-age children and a wife. "My mother calls all the time and expects me to come over and change her light bulb or take her someplace. I am happy to help her out once in a while, but I can't jump every time she has a need. My wife and kids think I spend too much time with her already. I dread my calls to her. I always end up feeling guilty because I cannot meet her expectations." Harry's wife comes from a family where there is little expectation that the children will be so involved in their parents' lives. Just how much families expect to depend on or be involved with each other is a source of stress. The stress is complicated by the attitudes and expectations of other family members. Then the pressure escalates. Harry's mom expects her son to participate in her life, just as she took care of him when he was young and as she took care of her own parents. Because he is aware of everything his mother did for him and for her parents and in-laws, Harry feels guilty. He feels a duty to pay her back. But he has the same sense of obligation toward his own family. He is "sandwiched" between the generations. That sense of obligation can magnify tension, leaving no time to enjoy anything without guilt. Without conversations with both his wife and his mother, Harry cannot possibly meet all the demands placed on him. He fears that if and when he does have this discussion it will probably lead to hurt feelings. But he doesn't realize that avoiding that discussion also creates more unease.

And perhaps Harry needs to think about what he's doing to himself and why he is letting his own frustrations fester. It might be worth taking the risk to come to some compromise since whatever he is doing now is not pleasing anyone—not himself, his mother, nor his wife. The more each individual understands his or her expectations, the more they become explicit. Only then can negotiating new rules begin. Harry could invite his mother to help him out by attending some of his kids' school events when he is the busiest. Or, he might ask his daughters to call their grandmother, thus making her feel more a part of their lives. Instead of being a facilitator of family interactions, he is a gatekeeper. And the stress of keeping the obligations separate is making him feel inadequate.

Remember: a good relationship is not necessarily a smooth relationship. There will be ups and downs. We are aiming to grow connections—bonds that tie us, care and concern, not perfect bliss. Past experiences and current expectations are fertile soil for tension in the parent-adult child relationship. Equally confounding, each generation makes its decisions from a different perspective. Societal changes profoundly affect both parties in these intergenerational relationships.

If only you are willing to look at yourself, the relationships will benefit. After all, you only can change what you can control. And you can only control yourself. Hopefully, answering the following questions will help you better understand both yourself and your child. If your child is willing, it would be great to share this chapter. Whatever your relationship with your child, you need to know yourself and understand your own dreams and disappointments so that you can learn to deal with the reality of the present.

The questions below aim to help you sort out your own dreams, successes, and disappointments. Try to be both audience and performer in your life. First, try to see what you do, think, and say; consider what you have in mind when you do them, as well as how others might perceive your words or actions. Then ask, "Is this the way I want things to be? How can I change things?" This is hard work, but this book is intended to help you with your exploration.

If you know where you are or where you want to go, you can figure out how to get there.

Questions:

- What do you really want from the parent-adult child relationship for yourself?
- Do you imagine it as peaceful? Was your relationship ever conflict-free?
- What does the relationship with each of your children feel like now?
- Outline your expectations: Minimally, I would like . . . For example, I'd like him or her to call once a week. Maximally, I would like . . . At this point in the relationship it would be feasible to . . .
- What do you expect from your children? What do you think they expect from you? Have you asked them?
- What issues are you and your children dealing with right now that are troubling? What issues have you resolved? How did you resolve them?
- How do you think your child feels about your relationship? Have you discussed it together?
- What events in your life would you like to share with your children? How can you tell your life story so that your children will better understand you?
- How much do you think you should bend your life to fit your children's?
- Does your opinion vary by different situations?

4

EMERGING
ADULTHOOD

The post-schooling years are a tricky period for the parent-child relationship. Children step out, assert their independence, and choose cities and friends—all without supervision. There are no grades, no school rules, and no natural advancement from one year to the next. Everything is up for grabs. Parents see their authority diminishing, while children are making decisions that will have consequences for the rest of their lives. Parents feel left out or at the least uncertain. In some areas of their children's lives they are called upon for solace and support; in others they are not consulted. Kids switch between being very adult and rather childish. Parents fluctuate between wanting to protect their children as they have always done and believing they should let them spread their wings and make decisions for themselves. There is no consistency. Neither parent nor child knows what independence is and what dependence is. Both are trying to determine the role for parents in the lives of adult children. The next few years will be a quest to figure this out.

Again the 1974 Family Education Rights and Privacy Act (FERPA) fosters ambiguity as parents grapple with how much they should be involved in their children's lives after high school. High-profile incidents like the Virginia Tech massacre, where a mentally ill student opened fire and killed thirty-three students, call into question the wisdom of laws that prevent parents from learning of their children's problems. The college administration knew of the shooter's difficulties, but the parents were not fully informed. Sue Kayton, a parent of an MIT student who was found dead, has sued the university. When the student's friends reported her son missing, the administration refused her access to his room and his computer.[1] These incidents suggest the law may have gone too far in maintaining a barrier between parents and their emerging adult children.[2]

We cannot blame parents. Public and private secondary schools encourage parental involvement, but parents are suddenly shut out at the college door. Those who continue to remain closely involved with their children when they leave home are derisively called "helicopter parents," and are chided for their "hovering" involvement, whereas they should be encouraged to gradually convert their relationships to ones of mutual interdependence. Only by trial and error and lots of honesty with themselves and their child will parents find the right balance for their relationship. And, of course, once they have figured it out, the variables will change and they will have to work it all out again. Even if they have worked it out with one child, they will find the recipe doesn't work for the next. As with all relationships, this one is sensitive to all the ingredients. Both independence and dependence are fluid terms, open to interpretation, and susceptible to culture, personality, and life timing.

Many cultures in the United States and around the world expect their children to remain at home until marriage, while other families expect them to leave and build an independent life before starting their own families. Everyone is unsure of what to expect and what to demand. In some families, one can live in proximity to parents and be totally independent. In others the opposite is true. One study examined three generations of several families living in one town. It found that the number of interactions between parents and adult children was not as important as the quality of the relationships. More serious problems, such as anorexia, suicide, and depression, arose when the younger generation was expected to defer to the older generation. The younger women, who denied their own opinions and depended on the older generation to make decisions, were more likely to suffer from these problems.[3] While rules and regulations of family interaction can be comforting, they can also hinder communication, which ideally can allow for the freedom of expression of both generations.

Parents want to share their wisdom, to "save" their children from making the same mistakes they made, but their children see it as an infringement of their right to make their own decisions. Sometimes, it isn't *what* a parent says; it is simply the fact that a parent is saying anything at all. When parents offer advice, the child may misconstrue the parents' words as interference, distrust, or an attempt to control their lives. Remind your children they don't have to take your advice and that your advice is only one piece of data in many they will gather. Often a child just needs the chance to prove him- or herself capable of making independent decisions. Some children just want to find their own path. This can cause some parents to feel discounted and unappreciated.

Children's successes and failures can evoke mixed feelings and uncertainty in parents. If children enter higher-status jobs or earn more money than their parents, some are thrilled and take great pride that the support they gave their child led to this success. Others feel threatened. They see the balance of power shifting. Their child's success may touch off feelings of inadequacy. Other children are earning precious little income and need to be subsidized with money or shelter. Some parents believe it is worthwhile to continue to give their child a boost, while others feel it is not wise to coddle children any longer and that they must stand on their own two feet and pay their own way. They may be angry and upset that their children have not found a path to economic self-sufficiency.

Understanding your own feelings can help you pick your battles. Take a step back and decide if your grievances are based on your own insecurities and feelings of being pushed aside. If your children's decisions are not dangerous, or self-destructive, give your children the space they need. This can show your child that you believe he or she is competent and can create a more trusting, long-lasting bond that will carry you both into your child's adulthood.

A lot of anxiety arises around career choice. Sometimes the kid's knowledge may be more up-to-date than the parents'. All sorts of new careers have developed, many of which may be unfamiliar to the parents. Others have gone overseas. Both in the office and on the assembly line, some of the most lucrative jobs have become less lucrative and the most stable have become less stable. Examples abound. The Big Eight accounting firms have consolidated or been forced to spin off their consulting arms; they are now the Big Three. Working thirty years for a blue-chip auto company used to guarantee a good pension and health benefits, but now that company may go into bankruptcy and employees lose their benefits. Layoffs, downsizing, and right-sizing of employees with stellar work ethics and good credentials have transformed the notion of worker loyalty. Now hopping from firm to firm is frequently the path to success. Parental career advice may be out of date.

A college degree has become the new high-school diploma— an entry ticket, but not a job guarantee. For middle-class kids, graduate school and professional education often follow college. Educational institutions have changed their policies to accommodate these shifts. Professional schools now prefer students with some life experience to those straight out of college. Meanwhile, professional and educational paths have lengthened and educational costs have soared. When family assistance and support are needed to help children reach career goals, roles become unclear. Most parents and children agree that career is an individual choice. However, factors such as how much the parent is willing to subsidize and how much scholarship money the school gives all contribute to this decision. Money can control the verdict of where and maybe what profession a student can pursue. Parental control over money may seem to the adult child like control of him or her, and in some cases it may be.

Money as a Means of Control

In some families, children get along better with their parents when they begin earning their own salaries because for the first time they are financially separate. Money as a source of tension in the relationship is reduced. In others, parents may begrudge their children's right to make autonomous decisions and judge their children's choices by their own yardsticks. Not understanding changes in the environment, parents may also mistakenly interpret their children's behavior as rebellious and misread or read too much into their children's decisions. Not being honest with themselves and their children about their own motives can lead to ugly arguments.

Jan returned to her small town in Iowa after college. She lived with friends in an apartment and worked for two years in the human resources department of a mid-size local auto parts company. Opportunities for promotion were limited and she could find no other jobs nearby. Jan applied and was accepted at a prestigious business school many miles from her home in a big city. Its networks for post-degree job placement were legendary. She received some financial aid and some student loans and was adding to it the money she had saved over the past two years. She still needed some additional financing to foot the bill and even then would leave school with considerable debt. However, she was also accepted at her state university just a few miles from home. Her parents made it clear that they thought she should go to the state school and were willing to subsidize her tuition there. Jan considered the decision with her friends and finally asked her parents to use that same money to subsidize her at the big city university. Her parents said, "No, we will not give you the money to go away. You will be better off in the long run going to the state school, and leaving school without debt. Besides, we would think you would want to remain close to family and friends." What Jan instead heard was, "We want to control your life. We are afraid to let you go to the city and so we use the money as an excuse to keep you at home."

Her anger and disappointment were palpable. Jan said to them: "I am tired of hearing how ungrateful and irresponsible I am. Look, I am grateful that you sacrificed for me, but that doesn't mean that for the rest of my life I am ungrateful every time I make a decision that differs from yours. I am moving to the big city for educational and job opportunities, not to escape you. By moving and earning more and gaining new skills I will be in a better position to take care of you. I've been obsessing about which school to choose. I want to remain with my friends and family, but the opportunity is so much better if I relocated." Her parents were surprised at the outburst. How did a discussion about money devolve into a fight about her obligations to them? It seemed that anger from old arguments broke into the current discussion.

These arguments are rarely about a single issue. Had Jan's parents honestly shared their concerns, Jan might have been less emotional and more willing to converse. Because her parents did not express their worries, Jan, like most children, picked up on the emotional content of their message and rekindled old battles. Jan's parents were really worried about debt because they were children of the Depression. They did not want their money used to cultivate a debt and felt they had a right to decide how their money would be spent. They also did not want her to leave town because they feared Jan would become worldly in the big city, become too good for them, marry a city slicker, and never return. Had her parents honestly shared their concerns, Jan might have been able to mitigate some of them. Threats and power plays rarely lead to productive discussions, whereas openly sharing concerns may.

Jan owns part of the responsibility for the way this scene unfolded. Because Jan feared that her decision would be misunderstood as a deliberate attempt to break her parents' hearts, she never shared her thinking with her parents and discussed only the bare minimum. She did not give her parents a chance to understand her reasoning. However, parents can only influence their own end of the conversation. When the parents are honest, frequently the children respond in kind. Although exposing one's feelings can be risky, trying to continue to control your adult children also has a price. It can lead to cutting off conversation and connection.

There are many options to solve this impasse, but without a conversation both parents and children will be locked in a struggle for control. Most important, though, they miss an opportunity to discuss how they would like to stay in touch over the coming years as Jan moves further and further into adulthood. She or they could even suggest visits to explore the city jointly. This way they would grow in sophistication together and share some new experiences. They could begin to plan for a future different from the present.

Focusing on the money allows Jan and her parents to avoid the more sensitive discussion of differences in their values and their cultural contexts. A frank discussion will be quite uncomfortable for both parents and child, but probably no more so than the scene they are now having. Jan's parents are hurt because not only do they feel Jan wants to leave them, but they also think she is discounting all the values they have taught her. They have put the family in conflict with the individual. Jan does not see the two as mutually exclusive opposites, but rather as points along a continuum. She has chosen the point on the scale that is a comfortable mix of loyalty to family and loyalty to herself and her ambitions.[4]

Adults differ on the weight they put on the balance between individual wants and family desires. Jan is balancing her two important needs. Her decision is neither right nor wrong but represents a difference in individual values. In this case, her parents placed family closeness above individual achievement, and Jan did the opposite. Jan also weighed long-term gain in terms of career potential against the short-term loss of friends and family support far more than did her parents. Jan is not completely discounting her parent's values—in fact, she may see such investment in later, not instant, gratification, as a trait learned from her parents; she is just making an adjustment in priorities. In sum, many decisions are not right or wrong; they simply reflect the needs and values of each individual.

The Scenic Road to Adulthood: An Important Exploration

Blurring the lines between dependency and independence are not the only factors that lead to tensions regarding career decisions. The whole timeline of life has moved. The change in the timing of life stages leads parents and children to view the work world differently. This disparate sense of time can cause family conflict. The parents assume time and life are fleeting and the child wonders, "What's the hurry?" Working life has extended beyond age sixty-five and as the Social Security start dates creep upward, people are working longer.[5] Although we all know that an individual can never take continued good health for granted, statistics make it clear that our children's cohort can realistically assume that they will be healthy well into their eighties. Thus, as twenty-somethings, there is no rush to get started building a family, a career, and retirement benefits. They feel none of the pressure many of us felt in our twenties to reproduce fast. They may have an opportunity to choose one career at the outset and then change to another later, an option that was closed to us. They can, for instance, work in finance in their twenties and switch to a professional school in their thirties. They can go to graduate school in their thirties, forties, or even their seventies. Or they can see if their talents will get them to Broadway or their work into an art museum and then begin another career if their artistic dreams do not materialize.

Sometimes it is difficult to tell whether children are afraid to grow up or just experimenting with different interests to see which ones will give them the most satisfaction. They are marrying later, having children later, and using their twenties to explore many options. Adult children now have more time and more chances to experiment with several career choices before they settle on one. They may have one career for twenty years and then switch to another. It is not uncommon for an adult child to decide that the first career choice is not working. Parents, however, worry that their child is never going to choose a career and stick with it.

Since age ten, Alicia had wanted to be a doctor, like her mom, and had done outstandingly well in all her pre-med courses. However, she emerged from college uncertain if medicine was the right career choice for her. She went to her parents to share her doubts. "I am just not sure I want to make a seven-year commitment. I'm tired of school. I want to try other options. I want some adventures. I'm young and single now. I'd like to bop around the world a bit. I don't want to waste my youth. Medical school is expensive and I want to make sure it is the right choice for me.

Besides, I loved my volunteer work teaching, and I think I could be happy as a teacher."

Her mom reacted, "Your biological clock is ticking. If you are going to medical school, you can't afford the time to experiment with other options. By the time you finish residency you will be too old to have children. Besides, these days women need to be able to support themselves. Medical schools don't want indecisive people in their classes. There is nothing to be gained by going to Europe and teaching! Stop dilly dallying as if you were a child and get on with preparing for life."

Alicia decided she wanted to explore the world and found a job teaching in Europe. Her mom felt she was making a big mistake. But Alicia knew herself. She was burned out. She had worked hard in college. Between her work and study obligations and her volunteer activities, she was exhausted. She really wanted to enjoy life before the grind of medical school. She had loved her volunteer jobs teaching inner-city kids and thought that maybe teaching was her true passion. She creatively found work abroad as a teacher so that she could have the adventures she craved, test out whether or not she liked teaching, *and* support herself! Alicia was acting responsibly; she found a way to achieve all three of her goals. Why not applaud her? Her mom, Theresa, was so stuck in her image of medical school and its requirements of forty years ago that instead of praising Alicia's resourcefulness, she gave dire warnings.

Since the adult child had found her own resources, she did not need to follow her parents' advice, much to the consternation of her mom. She was going to Europe whether she had approval or not, but like many children, wanted some validation by her parents, if for nothing else just to keep peace in the family. Besides, she reasoned, "I am not committing murder; I am only going to Europe. I just don't get why you are so upset."

When her mom finally stopped fuming, she forced herself to think about her daughter's decision and her own reaction to it. She gathered some facts and found that today medical schools were now accepting older students and that many of Alicia's friends were working abroad. Theresa had been one of three women in her medical school class and by the time she was ready to start a family, she had difficulty conceiving. She realized the pain of that experience made her afraid for her daughter. She then acknowledged to herself, and only later to her daughter, that she was worried about her daughter traveling alone. When she was young, it was not "proper" for young women to do so.

These facts and self-reflection allowed her to reframe her thinking and become thrilled that her daughter had opportunities that had been closed to her. She realized that she would want to take advantage of the freedom open to women if she were in her daughter's shoes. In fact, she decided that she too wanted to travel and work abroad. The mother's reflection not only taught her something about the changes in society, but also helped her get in touch with her own longings. Theresa also realized that now that her daughter was gone she had the opportunity to act on her own dreams.

When Theresa reviewed the medical facts, she found that while it is true that at some point a woman's fertility diminishes, postponing maternity by one or two years does not have a big effect.[6] Her daughter could have adventures, a career, and children. Sure, her daughter would pay some prices, just as she had. Life would be hectic and hard, but it would also be enriching. Theresa also thought about all the teachers she knew who were living perfectly happy, though not affluent, lives and thought with great affection of some of the teachers who had influenced her. She gained new respect for her daughter, for teachers, and for the myriad of possibilities to create a rewarding life. She was therefore able to go back to her daughter humbly and say, "I thought about your plans for next year and I think you will learn a lot from living abroad. Your biological clock is not ticking so fast that a year or two will matter. I think you might actually be a more satisfied doctor if you should eventually choose that profession after having explored other options. You may find you want to teach and combine medicine with teaching or you may find that teaching is your calling. In any case, I know you will have a worthwhile year. I'd love to visit you and have some adventures of my own."

As she said this to her daughter, their relationship changed. It moved from one in which an all-knowing mother gave wisdom to a child, to a conversation between two adults, each with an important perspective to share. Alicia felt validated in her ability to make good choices and her mother learned a great deal about herself and the world. Both felt heard and both felt that this would be the first opportunity of many to exchange their different views. If we open ourselves up and take the opportunity, we can learn much from the decisions our children make.

Loyalty versus Opportunity

Another major change in the workscape is that loyalty between employers and employees in both directions has diminished. No longer does it necessarily make sense to stay with one company and work up the chain of command. Companies come and go and get bought and sold. The route to success is more likely found moving from promotion to promotion in whatever company offers upward mobility than staying put in one corporation. As this differs from previous eras, intergenerational differences on perceptions of career paths and social mores too can cause friction. Fred, a seventy-four-year-old retired furniture executive, advised his son, Jason: "Join a good solid company and stick with it. I started as a floor salesman and look at how I rose through the ranks to senior vice president. Work hard. Be loyal, stick to one company."

His techie son Jason, age twenty-seven, responds: "Dad, are you kidding? Enron failed, the blue-chip companies look anemic, hi-tech firms come and go. I am not sacrificing my life for any one employer the way you did. I am going to look out for number one, for me. All the career books tell me I will work for many companies and that the way to get ahead is to change jobs. With all due respect, Dad, you are out of date." Fred is disappointed that his son is looking at a short-term job. But, clearly, dad is out of date. His advice is unrealistic. The economic situation in the early 2000s is vastly different from that of the predictable 1950s, 1960s, and even the 1970s, when Jason's parents were starting careers. Job insecurity is now a fact of life for most adults. The fear of layoffs, downsizings, and mergers is very real. It is unlikely that our children will be in one job with one employer for the rest of their lives. A U.S. Bureau of Labor Statistics survey supports Jason's position. Baby boomers born between 1957 and 1964 held almost ten jobs on average between the ages of eighteen and thirty-six.[7] Typically, both men and women held a greater number of jobs earlier in their lives. In addition, globalization and the effects of immigration to the United States are not limiting the number of jobs, but keeping wages lower, putting additional strain on job seekers.[8]

The child's choice may not be the result of contrariness at all, but just a different point on the continuum between short-term and long-term gain than the parents would have made. In all the cases in this chapter, the children made well-reasoned decisions. However, their conclusions were contrary to the ones their parents would have made. Each was analyzing opportunities through the lens of his or her own age and needs. Before judging, the parents could have noticed their children's creativity and motivation to create a meaningful life. Had they looked at their negative judgments first and examined them, they might have turned them around into positive pictures of themselves and their children. The children might have approached their parents by explaining their reasoning and laying out the benefits of their decision and the way they arrived at their conclusions. They could acknowledge that adults can disagree respectfully without negating the merits of another path. Over time both parents and children can help each other by reminding each other that by sharing their own feelings and thinking before they take umbrage, they can reduce cantankerous outbursts. Each small success in this regard can be called upon as evidence that the parents and children can communicate.

Questions:

- List all the times in your child's life when you thought you had everything figured out and something changed.
- Does your child accuse you of controlling his or her life? When?

- In your opinion to what extent should parents be involved in their children's lives?
- Do you ever discuss one subject and your child brings up another subject from the past? When does this happen? Why? (If you can't figure this out, describe the situation and ask for someone else's perspective.)
- What can you learn from looking at your children's lives that might apply to your own life?
- When you need more information to understand one of your children's decisions, how do you ask for it?

5

REFILLING THE NEST

K ids come home for a variety of reasons: for short visits, for holidays, for refueling between school and jobs, and for longer stays to save money or because they are down on their luck. Each of these events requires the parent and the adult child to redefine their dynamic. Often the reunions are fraught with anxiety. Nobody knows which of the old dramas will be played out or whether the family members will be able to learn new roles. The old dictum "You can't go home" is true. Once at home, your kids find they have changed, all the people they left behind seem to have changed, and even the physical space may have changed. Perhaps equally disconcerting: on the surface so little has changed when so much has happened to them in the interim. There is a disconnect between the expectation that their home as they remembered it will be waiting there unchanged, and the reality of what they find there. Even the most independent adult child will often fall back into old roles—one minute relying on others to do what they do for themselves when living independently, and the next moment being totally self-sufficient. On the flip side, the parents, whether out of love or habit, often automatically revert to their parental ways, for example, nagging an adult child to do something, when the adult child is responsible and mature enough (or, should be!) to follow through without reminders.

For the adult child, the moment of reentry is tough. It feels like everyone wants a piece of them. They have been their own bosses and now it feels like the whole world needs them or wants to talk. The people who are living in what was their home are treating them with familiarity. All the inhabitants think they know the new entrant, but they know the person who left, not the one who just entered. They are different in subtle ways, ways that they know, but cannot explain even to themselves. They have seen and experienced ways of living different from the family. They may be critical or they may be thrilled, but they watch every interaction through new eyes.

You, too, have changed. You have filled the void created by their absence with others, or with activities, or with time for yourself. The child needs to nuzzle back into your life. You treat them as you remember them, but there have also been subtle inexplicable differences in you, and you may not be able to drop everything to greet them with the love and adulation they remember. In addition, you may have changed their room into a den or a study. Even the world outside the house may seem altered, especially if their friends are no longer around.

Just as the adult child is astounded by what he or she finds upon returning home, you too are surprised by your reaction to the homecoming. You anticipated the event with intense feelings. You may have pictured how you would talk until the wee hours, sharing everything that had transpired in the absence, only to find your child say, "Hi," drop his or her things, and run off to see friends. Or you may have dreaded the invasion of your time or space. In either case, or all the cases in between, their return was different than its prospect. Particularly in short visits, everyone at home expects the returning one to be ready for interaction upon arrival. There is no allowance for the transition. Yet, your child may be exhausted because of jet lag or the chaos of leaving work and home. Cell phone and computers both help and hinder the situation. Without them our kids might not be able to visit at all because a work assignment is due or a friend needs immediate advice. However, we all risk being so wired to these technologies that it feels like our scarce together time is spent in cyberspace. Just as we need to be aware of the advantages and disadvantages of technology in maintaining our connections, we need to be adaptable and understanding to facilitate a successful reentry.

Both child and parent need to be cognizant of the changes in the self, others, and the environment.

Whose Space Is it Anyway?

Though not simple, the easiest of the three to negotiate is a change in the physical space. Children's expectation that parents will be available often turns into expecting housing to be available. Some adult children have strong attachments to their childhood rooms and homes, even if they live miles away.

When the parents decide or are forced to sell the family home, the child may be upset. The decision to give away money or furniture or to sell their home anytime or any way they want is clearly the parents' prerogative. However, parents can save themselves lots of aggravation and their children lots of disappointment if they discuss and explain their rationale with their children. Many of us will face this conversation. The Del Webb Corporation survey conducted in 2003 found that 36 percent of boomers plan to move when their children leave the nest.[1] In families where the lifestyle has been more authoritarian, it may feel demeaning to share decisions with one's children, the more so if the reasons for selling the house are reverses in fortune. Life does not always go well, and one has to be flexible and manage. Whatever the reason, this is an opportunity to help your kids make sense of their nostalgia for their childhood. Let your children know that you understand their attachment to their home and you believe that they can understand why you are moving. Share your own feelings both good and bad about the move.

Of the 36 percent that predicted they would move, about one-third considered moving more than three hours away. If you relocate to another town, your kids do have a stake in the matter. They will no longer have a place to stay when they visit friends—and friends may be a key lure for home visits. This is a loss to them, even if not a big enough loss for you to change your plans. You might suggest they come home to see what "stuff" they want or you invite your child to say goodbye to the old house or take a moment over the phone to remember the good times in that setting. These memories are the capital of current and future warm feelings. Maybe later you can include them in a welcoming party in the new place, so that some of the warmth that makes a house a home follows to the new location.

Smaller changes in the home, too, can touch off intense feelings. The Del Webb survey also revealed that 44 percent of baby boomers who moved wanted a smaller house, mostly for easier upkeep and maintenance. Sometimes during this downsizing, the "shrine" of the adult child's youth may not make the cut in the new house. Marilyn, a sixty-two-year-old mother, told me that her son, Michael, age thirty-nine and single with a responsible job as a regional sales manager for a textile company, "was upset when we changed his room into a den even though he moved out ten years ago. He told me I was kicking him out of his home. I think he not only wanted the place to be kept as a museum for himself, but he also expected to inherit all the furniture. I was surprised because he was so mature and had lived on his own for years." Here we see a conflict between Michael's mature self and his childhood self. Marilyn is surprised by her son's reaction. She viewed the room as hers to do with as she wished. By not warning her son in advance, Marilyn missed an opportunity to share what was happening to her as well as a chance to reconnect with Michael. They could have laughed about some of his treasures and reminisced about some good times. She might have asked him if there was anything special he would like her to save that did not take up much space in her new, smaller place. Or she could offer to keep his favorite poster and put it up when he returned.

Moving out often happens in stages. The first may be the physical move, and the last is the emotional. None of us completely understands our emotions and frequently material goods become substitutes for strong feelings. Much like the little child's teddy bear or blanket, objects can take on intense meaning. Michael was unaware of his emotional connection with the space in which he had grown until his mother took it away. He may not have really wanted to inherit the furniture; he just wanted to hold onto his memories a bit longer.

The disposal of material goods can feel like throwing out one's past, and planning for such an event can mitigate much future tension. For eighteen years, often more, that home was the family home. The kids may be living elsewhere, but still think of your real estate as theirs. They come back as a combination of resident and guest. In your mind, it is now your home, your culture; logically your children should be the ones who must accommodate. The difficulty arises when they feel that because the home used to be theirs, it still is and they can lead their own lives in it as they do outside. Be prepared, as the discussion itself is often quite tense and when you insist that your choices prevail, it can lead to conflict. Conflict is not all bad. It is an opportunity to discuss your differences.

The difficulties of refilling the nest encompass more than just material goods. We know our children may be out until all hours, that some will use illicit substances, and that they sleep and even have lived with a significant other. Some of us do not want or allow these activities in our homes. In the process of setting rules for their new role in their previous home, children often accuse parents of hypocrisy. And hypocrites we might be. We have a choice: pretend these things are not happening or we can confront them head-on. "I know you do ecstasy in your apartment, but as you know, I don't feel comfortable with those activities and they are not allowed in my home. You know I fear substances will hurt you and that I have been brought up to think that some of your other activities are wrong. I cannot be a part of supporting them. I still love you, but part of being an adult is understanding the other's point of view, including mine."

All these restrictions work better for short stays than for long ones. Whatever the benefits of getting together, they need to outweigh the inconvenience to your offspring. When your child was at school, scheduled vacations marked the times for kids to go home. At work, there are fewer regular markers of appropriate times to visit. Thus, visits themselves are negotiable. Once she or he is established in other space, the issues become less contentious. Home is more a place to visit and less a place to reside.

Short Visits

More complicated than the real estate issues are the human interactions. Holiday reunions are prime times for disappointment.
We are lulled into thinking that the best holiday celebrations are
just like the ones "we used to know." Unfortunately, that bit of
fantasy, however compelling, is way off the mark and may set us
up for more disappointment than joy. Today's families and the
traditions that are developing are unlikely to resemble those of
our parents or grandparents. The divorce rate hovers around
50 percent, and about half those that do divorce get remarried.[2]
Interracial and interfaith marriages are on the rise. Jewish interfaith marriage increased by 46 percent from 1991 to 2001.[3]
Homosexual couples live together openly and raise families.
Increasing numbers of young people are choosing not to marry at
all or to marry later, and almost 20 percent of women over age
forty-four remain childless.[4] Never have we had as many different
kinds of families as we now have. On top of all this, family
members are mobile, often living at long distances from one
another. "Over the river and through the woods to grandmother's
house" can mean an expensive and lengthy trek through multiple
airports.

Some families face the challenges of multiple religious or
ethnic celebrations. Adult offspring may be celebrating different
holidays from the ones they grew up with. Other families incor-
porate a mix of religious and family customs to accommodate
stepkids and second spouses. In addition, most adult children
are in dual-earner families in which there may be little time for
the special touches that may have meant so much to us. Equally,
grandparents are more likely than in the past to be working,
putting to an end the homey picture of grandma in the kitchen
baking cookies or the holiday meal. Meeting these challenges
requires both parents and their adult offspring to recognize and
accept a new and sometimes uncomfortable reality.

Open negotiation and good communication are essential;
neither happens by magic. It is so easy to slip back into traditional
behaviors and familiar roles. But it's clear that as families evolve,
many of the old patterns of interaction have to change. Getting it

"right" is harder when parents and adult children see one another infrequently. They may not have a good handle on each other's lives and obligations. Motives can be misunderstood. Because holidays are markers which recall all good and bad times, emotions are close to the surface. Both children and parents may be afraid that they'll "do it wrong" and that anything they say to try to influence the situation might be taken as overbearing and risks spoiling the holidays, not only for this year but for years to come. Faced with such risk, many families turn to discussing the weather and watching football to smooth over possible difficulties. The holiday becomes a shell of itself: lots of food but no emotional nutrition. There is contact, but no connection.

Handling these challenges in positive and mutually respectful ways so as not to jeopardize the all-important connections with adult children and grandchildren is indeed delicate. Both seemingly trivial issues such as what food to serve, and the more "substantive" issues such as whom to invite, what to celebrate, and when and where to hold the celebration, are really about values, power, and respect. The list of reasons for potential disagreement is endless. Often, these issues mask larger questions concerning violated expectations, long-held or smoldering resentments, and past hurts. If parents and their adult children really want to create close relationships, keeping quiet is a terrible strategy. It may avoid war, but it yields a very cold peace.

Preparing in advance is a far more useful strategy. Take the plunge and share your concerns with your adult offspring! At the same time, encourage them to tell you about their wishes and constraints. Be positive and creative. Some problems can be solved by ingenuity. For example, labeling the drawers can reduce frustration and animosity between orderly and disorderly users of the kitchen. Or each person bringing a dish potluck style can reduce the work so nobody bears the whole burden of preparation. Perhaps, try to discuss the schedule so that you establish the timeline for the home visit. Say, right off the bat or in advance, "I'd really love it if you could set aside some time for just us as a family to be together this weekend. Dinner would be my first choice, but I am willing to consider other options."

Assume good motives, not bad. It's nobody's fault that there are conflicts. For example, when your daughter tells you that she won't be able to make it home for Thanksgiving dinner after all, don't assume she is saying, "I don't love you." Before getting paranoid, find out the reasons for her change of plans. She may be just as sad about missing the holidays together as you are. Listen with your eyes, your ears, and your heart. These are adults with multiple obligations. They may need to please in-laws, ex-spouses, their own children and stepchildren, as well as others in their lives to whom they have responsibilities. It may be a time to create new family traditions, ones that better reflect the reality of today's complicated families.

Elizabeth's father-in-law insisted that all four of his children be present every year at Christmas dinner with their significant others by their sides. This was the only family reunion of the year and as far as he was concerned there was no room for negotiation. He had no regard for the feelings of the other side. He would not invite the in-laws. He fumed when his children suggested they go to their in-laws every other year. He was enraged if his children arrived late or left early to visit others. When Elizabeth called her own mother, Samantha, to tell her once again she would not be home for Christmas, her mother heard the pain in her daughter's voice. She coaxed Elizabeth into explaining. Elizabeth felt trapped. Her father-in-law was absolutely immovable. Her husband knew his father was being unreasonable, but did not dare defy him.

Most of us live in families that are not perfect. Samantha did not want to add problems to her daughter's life. So she suggested, "How about we create a new tradition? The Sunday before Christmas you will come here and we will trim the tree. Your kids will get a taste of the Christmases you remember. I will get to see them and you will be able to keep the other side of the family happy. Thanksgiving, Christmas, Boxing Day. What difference does it make? We just call it the holiday season and find a time to get together to share stories and gifts. There are just too many schedules to coordinate, too many work obligations, too few flights." Not all family squabbles have such generous actors. Samantha could have focused on the selfishness of her daughter's father-in-law. Instead she chose to look at positive alternatives. She was now free to travel or visit with friends on the holiday. The sum is, whether your children are coming home for a short visit or a long time, you may want to set expectations beforehand.

Other families unite for vacations either in a rented space or one that is owned by one family member. There is much to plan ahead. Who pays and for what? Who does the laundry? Will there be family meals? All meals? Or just in the evening? Who cooks? Shops? Who cleans up? Are their rooms their castles, which they can clean or dirty as they wish? What rooms are sanctuaries and to whom? Is the house off-limits or open to guests? Will they pay rent? If so, will it be paid in dollars or services?

Kitchens and bathrooms are classic battlegrounds. Our basic human needs are met there. There is just so much room for animosity. The slobs drive the neat-nicks crazy. They never wipe the counters; they don't put things in the right place. The list goes on. The more spontaneous grab an opportunity to chat and clean later; they view the neat-nicks as anal compulsives who miss the fun of being together. The judgments fly. Even when jobs have been assigned in advance, some family members have higher standards than others. Expect differences and work with them.

Everyone needs to be willing to compromise. This is definitely a situation in which if you are judging or wanting everything to be done your way, it's time to bite your tongue. If, however, you can explain your position without impugning and belittling others, you can speak.

One thing is certain: no martyrs are allowed! No one is allowed to do all the housework. The problem with human martyrs is they expect payment, and no matter what we pay it is not enough. The person who slaves always expects us to be grateful for what we may not have noticed. The martyr usually ends up feeling abused and exhausted. And the other relatives may feel like hotel guests rather than members of the family unit. This leads to disappointment and resentment all around. If you or one of your family members is a martyr, insist the work be shared.

Some families share the work while some share the cost. Some families set up a work chart where everyone has a task. In others, each contributes according to his or her talents; the nursery school teacher does the childcare while the gourmet cooks. The type of system doesn't matter. That there *is* a system does!

And, because sometimes no one knows what the sticking points will be until annoyances arise, setting up a system beforehand for resolving the details of daily life is important. For example, some families choose family meetings, as an adjunct to the devised system. There are innumerable ways to resolve family problems.

Long Stays

Kids moving back after schooling or between jobs is common now. The Del Web Corporation 2004 survey revealed that 27 percent of baby boomers would not let their grown children move back home, while 40 percent anticipated such an event in the near future. Additionally, the survey also found that one-fourth of baby boomers fear they will not have enough money to retire, and consider getting out of debt imperative. Almost 30 percent of the parents said they would charge their children rent. In long stays, all the uncertainties of emerging adulthood are played out in the family home and all the conflicts of short-term visits are magnified.

When Jean finished college, she knew she would eventually go to graduate school. However, she was tired of school, was not sure what field to study, and needed to save for tuition. After working and living with friends for three years she moved home. Ann, her mother, understood her oldest daughter's need to move home. Changing trends in our society practically demand it and about half of young adults ages eighteen to twenty-four, lived at home in 2003.[5] Rents are high, entry salaries are low, and tuition is expensive. Ann understood the need both to speak effectively and to know when to be silent for this reunion to be successful. Before her daughter moved back, Ann welcomed her and acknowledged how proud she was of what Jean had been able to save and that she had chosen a graduate school. She was happy that her daughter's life had evolved. "But," she said to Jean, "we need to talk about what kinds of lifestyle Dad and I feel comfortable having in our home. We need to talk about duties and responsibilities. I want to work out a system that allows you freedom, but also gives us the privacy and life to which we have become accustomed. I don't want to be your supervisor."

For the adult child who lives at home, command-and-control parenting doesn't work. Of course, years of familial history colors everyone's behavior and cannot be ignored. Though it is normal to ask guests their schedule, often adult children see a simple question like, "When are you coming home tonight?" as intrusive and the old teenage scripts take over. For instance, if a parent were to ask whether to keep the front light on, information we see as considerate and necessary for communal living, the adult child might perceive this question as an attempt to gain "control." However, this same question asked by a friend might lead them to respond with the information.

Your returned children may want space to entertain; that could be in your house or at the local lounge. Make clear your expectations. If you need space, if you hate clutter, if you are uncomfortable with the expense of having an extra person in the house, sit down together and discuss these things openly. This is a two-way street. Tell what you expect and invite your returning child to do the same. Work out all the details you can think of. Agreeing together about "rules of the house" before your adult child returns may be key to preventing every out-of-place coffee cup, shoe, or T-shirt from becoming a cue to reenact past dramas.

Ann and Jean did exactly that. "We then worked out the details: no rent, but all common rooms had to be kept to my standards. She did not need to fold her laundry nor could she leave it in the laundry room. If she wanted a mess in her room, she was entitled to it, but she could not make one in the rest of the house. We just divided the public space from her private space and that seemed to make sense. The public space had to be kept to my standard, which meant no old coffee cups lying around."[6]

Working out the practical details of domestic life can be touchy, but is usually far less controversial than tackling larger lifestyle differences. Any meaningful discussion of critical life issues brings home the point that our children's social environment bears little resemblance to the circumstances we parents confronted when we were young. By the time your children are out of school, they've grappled with the issues of drugs, drinking, and sex, and it's too late to control behaviors. However, clarifying what behaviors are acceptable in your house is reasonable. For example, your daughter may have shared an apartment with her boyfriend when she was working. Whether or not you approve of your child's sexual life, you need to talk about how you feel about such activities on your premises. In return for both sharing space and being willing to at least talk about our children's social context, we can enjoy rewarding, reciprocal intellectual and social companionship.

Adult children who have gone through divorce or a job loss can bring home not only apprehension, but also a sense of failure or inadequacy. The disappointment and pain need to heal. The comforts of home can help. But the risk of regressing to childhood patterns is real, for parents and for the adult child. It is painful for parents to see their child "down" and often they help by offering housing. Housing easily turns into more—more time, more effort, and sometimes more help than either participant wants.[7]

When a spouse loses a job, it can pose serious problems for the family. In 2005, almost two-thirds of two-parent households with children under eighteen depended on both incomes, as opposed to 50 percent in 1986.[8] Gail is a former nurse and a sixty-seven-year-old widow. After fifteen years in Montana, her son Jared and his family moved back East. His wife Barbara had lost her job, then Jared was laid off when his firm was bought by a large conglomerate. They were in financial straits. Gail wanted to help, but did not have much money, so she invited her son and his family to move in with her until they both found work. After a month, her daughter-in-law found an adequate job, though the salary was lower than she had been earning previously. Gail found having her kids and grandkids back in her home was a very mixed bag. "The whole time my son and his family were out West, I wished for their return. Well, they have returned with a vengeance! They are living with me and are very considerate and all, but I had gotten used to my space, and sharing it with four others is stressful. I need to be quiet at the kids' bedtime, and can't get the bathroom when I want it in the morning."

Gail had become used to her single life. She enjoyed not having to compromise with anyone. Living together brought back all the complexities and irregularities of a life that she had left behind. Her fantasy had been of blissful evenings sitting around talking. The reality was hectic nights of homework, bedtime routines, and little time for adult conversation. She could either laugh at her unrealistic expectations or be aggravated by contrasting reality. She knew she would miss her family when they left, but having them around was not quite as easy as she had expected.

Gail was filled with mixed emotions. She was angry that her son was not more aggressive about finding work, but she also felt she should be grateful that she had her children and grandchildren home. Now that they had established patterns of living, Gail was reluctant to say anything, lest it make her family feel unwelcome and make her son feel even worse about himself. Instead of allowing her children to come up with some creative solutions that would make living together easier, her resentments were mounting.

Because they arrived in the summer, her son was unwilling to look for work. The kids were in a new city with no friends and no routine. Then the fall came and he felt it was important to settle the kids in school. Gail agreed this parenting work was important, but as the months passed and her son remained unemployed, Gail became more and more agitated. It was one thing to put up with inconvenience for a few months; it was another if the visit was going to last for an even longer time. It was one thing to help her son; it was another to enable him not to work. More troublesome now were her concerns that her son was shirking his responsibility.

He was clearly depressed, the financial obligations of the family were mounting, and she was beginning to feel "used." She wanted to protect her son, but she felt the time had come for her to take some action even if she might be accused of being meddlesome. She started with the positive. "I am really proud that you and Barbara have brought up such a wonderful family, but I am concerned that you seem depressed and not looking hard enough for a job. I wonder if you should see a doctor about depression." It was not a happy conversation. Jared defended himself. Gail continued, "I know it is hard to get a job in your profession here. There are some free career resources by the government and some community groups." Again, her son balked. Gail continued, "Can I be helpful? If so, how? I am beginning to feel a bit used. I thought you were staying here until you saved money for a down payment, and now you are not making any money. I would feel less taken advantage of if you at least had some money coming in." The conversation did not conclude pleasantly. However, a week later Jared found a part-time job.

Not all conversations go well, but in this case, even a thorny conversation improved the situation. While Gail was initially silent, other parents nag, making the climate unpleasant for all. Negotiating a departure date in advance and then allowing the younger generation to figure out how they will meet that deadline might allow for a far friendlier stay together. If the adult child is not demeaned or infantilized, slipping back into the old familiar roles is far less likely.

When kids return home, especially under unfortunate circumstances, we need to talk early and often and determine together all the terms for staying. We are, however, still parents and we never completely relinquish our desire to help our children. Parents can never be sure if they are helping a child over a difficult hump—something we all want to do for friends and family—or if they are enabling their children to regress and avoid responsibility. We can only take our best guess. And we need to remember that sometimes we cannot solve our children's problems.

When families reunite they need to talk, compromise, and find ways to enjoy each other just as one does in other living situations in which individuals share space. All roommates have problems that need to be resolved. Now that our children are adults, we are more like roommates. We need to resolve our differences. We can no longer assume we are the rule makers or that we all still agree on the former, familiar ways of living together.

Questions:

- How do you and your child prepare for reentry?
- What are the contentious issues around your holidays? Make plans to mitigate them.

- What issues around space or cleanliness in the home do you have with your children? How can you lessen them?
- What are some of the issues that caused friction during childhood that might flare up again?
- What cultural values of the new spouses or newly acquired experiences of the children might jar with old family values?

6

RELATIONSHIPS

In the old days, parents, usually fathers, picked the person the son or daughter would marry. Fathers sold their daughters for camels, traded their daughters to pay debt, or merged business empires by uniting offspring. Most of us would not want to go back to those days, although when our children bring home someone we deem undesirable the old tradition has appeal. Most American children expect to choose the people with whom they associate with for both brief and lifetime encounters. As educational and work opportunities have increased, so have the opportunities to meet potential partners from different classes, religions, races, and nationalities.[1] Technological changes further expand those possibilities. People meet online. Hundreds of dating sites have emerged and prospered since the 1990s. The Online Publishers Association and comScore Networks revealed that Americans spent over $200 million on online dating services in the first half of 2005.[2] It is easier than ever for our children to pick partners quite different from ourselves and without any input on our part.

Many parents fear such differences. They worry that their children will encounter prejudice or that their own traditions will die. They worry that the cultural gaps will be too big to bridge and the relationships will end unhappily. And they worry that the newcomer will not fit in with their own families.

However sensible, reasonable, or justifiable our concerns as parents might seem, our role in this decision is secondary. Adults bear the consequences of their decisions, and these children are adults. Parents can talk, can share experiences both good and bad, but cannot force their adult children to listen, let alone to make the decisions they would prefer.

Susan had dated Sam for more than six months. They had met at work several years before, but their racial differences made each hesitate until, to quote Susan, "it just happened." They were both financial analysts at an investment bank. Neither told their parents at first, but as their relationship became more serious, Susan explained to her otherwise liberal dad that she was dating an African American. She talked about Sam's wit, his brains, and his kind manner. She was astounded by her father's reaction: he was upset!

Susan's dad had been active in the civil rights movement and was a firm supporter of equal rights. He had often described himself as "color blind," and certainly he had never hesitated to befriend, hire, or fire anyone because of his or her race. Yet when it came to his daughter, he did not want her involved with a black man.

Her dad was not sure if he was bothered because he had witnessed the discrimination and hardship they would likely face or because he knew the babies would not look like him. He could not even consider the fact that he might harbor some prejudice. He could also not bring himself to marvel at Susan's openness or express some understanding of how hard it must have been for Susan and Sam to come together after years of seeing the other as taboo. If he had, Susan and her father might have been able to talk about this new relationship.

Sam faced similar difficulties in explaining his relationship with Susan to his own parents, who had been active in the black power movement and did not approve of their son marrying "out." Each family rejected the other. Rather than be forced to declare allegiance to one race or the other, eventually Sam and Susan simply avoided the topic of their relationship with their families, and made the decision to marry without their parents' input.

This decision surprised both families, but prompted them both to change their behaviors. Sam's family invited Susan to their home and to activities in the community so that she could see and feel what it was like to be in the minority. They wanted her to understand their culture. Meanwhile, Susan's father reflected on his own beliefs and apprehensions, and realized how much he had expected a son-in-law like himself. He decided that if Sam really loved his daughter, then he should at least get to know Sam. At their wedding, Susan's grandfather, who had fled South Africa because of racial strife, greeted Sam's family warmly and began the process of bringing the families together with a toast: "Congratulations, you two are part of the future. The whole world should be color blind!" The grandfather's reframing of the marriage was the real beginning of the reconciliation of the two families. Both families would eventually come to see they were actually quite similar in their politics and their desire for their children to be happy. It would, however, take many shared experiences and family events before the families' emotions would catch up with the grandfather's ration.

Eventually, by focusing on their commonalities, these two families were able to share their children's joys. By supporting the marriage, these parents were able to reestablish their close bonds with their children and eventually to enjoy their grandchildren. Because Generation Y has grown up with images of multiracial and multiethnic icons such as Tiger Woods, Mariah Carey, and Barack Obama many are more comfortable with mixed-race relationships than are the parents.[3]

Interethnic Relationships

Even in many first-generation immigrant families, children choose their own partners with or without parental approval. The individualism predominant in the United States trumps the most long-standing social mores. Parents may resent and may be a bit jealous of their children's assumed right to make autonomous decisions, since that possibility had not existed for them. Wen, a forty-eight-year-old first-generation Chinese woman, explains: "When my daughter, Cynthia, became engaged to a Caucasian, I thought she was rebelling against me and denying her background. After talking with my Caucasian friends, I came to realize that when she made the decision to marry George, I was not on her mind. She went to college, met a wonderful boy, fell in love, and married. She is still Chinese and she still loves me. She just grew up in a country where freedom of marital choice is allowed. That is very different from the world I grew up in." Her daughter explains: "When I met George, I knew immediately he was the guy for me. He cared about family, he was hardworking, and he was kind. I dreaded bringing him home to my parents. I knew they'd throw a tantrum and tell me I was an undutiful daughter. I was torn: Was I a better daughter if I hid it from them? Or was it better to be honest right away?" In many societies, including Wen's, duty trumps individual choice. Cynthia and Wen were caught between cultures. Wen dutifully had married as she was told. She knew her daughter would choose her own husband, but she expected Cynthia would at least seek her approval. Had Wen known that 25 percent of Asian women in America are married to white men, she might have found some comfort that her daughter was not a renegade.[4]

What troubled Wen has nothing to do with George as a person. Wen worried that George's family would not welcome Cynthia as she deserved, that they would not recognize the value of her culture and traditions. They would see as drawbacks the attributes of filial deference that Wen worked so hard to instill in Cynthia. At the same time she feared her Chinese friends' reaction; she thought they would find George too modern and too brusque. He might argue with Wen. She also had reservations about her own ability to find common ground with George's family because her English is not flawless and her formal education limited. Wen knows that there are subtle, yet major differences in her culture from that of mainstream America. The more obvious ones are different annual celebrations like the New Year and the New Moon holiday. The more subtle ones have to do with an emphasis on family duty versus individual self-development.

Such uncertainties draw on a long history of discrimination by both Caucasians and Chinese. Neither community has been particularly welcoming to those who marry outside. George's kindness and respect for tradition enabled Wen to accept him, but she still doubts that love can conquer all. She fears her grandchildren will be misfits, accepted by neither community, despite the fact that in 2005 there were over two million interracial married couples, a huge jump from the 651,000 in 1980.[5] The U.S. Census reported almost four million people of mixed race in 2000, and almost five million in 2005.[6]

When cultures differ, there are additional layers of complexity. Both sets of parents face someone other than the person they would have chosen for their child. Perhaps this is different only in degree from the meeting of any two more similar sets of prospective in-law parents. It is usually tense, uneasy at first, requiring effort on everyone's part. Neither set of parents expects to have to make the extra effort involved in interacting with someone from a different culture. However uncomfortable the initial meetings are, all the players can mitigate tensions by learning about each other, their customs, and their histories. They can talk with one another and discover what they do have in common. Small efforts go a long way in showing that one is willing to learn, but is not always easy. If parents want to reduce tensions, then it is their job to not create further difficulties. Over time, if both sides want to, they can adjust to seeing each other as individuals and the relationship can improve, though it may not be perfect. Mutual jokes, yearly celebrations, and shared experiences all can combine to create a new more comfortable setting, if both parties are willing to make an effort. It might, however, not eradicate all difficulties.

The Single Life

Other parents are concerned that their children will never marry. Pat, a sixty-five-year-old suburban, professional mother, relates: "My daughter is thirty-nine and has given up on finding Mr. Right. When I was growing up, such thinking was incomprehensible. She no longer talks about dating. She just plans to live alone and enjoy her work. But I worry about her. I wish she had someone to look out for her and to share her life." Pat's worries have less to do with Belle's singleness than with her own fear that Belle will be alone. Pat sees Belle's married and dating friends and worries that Belle will be excluded from a "coupled society." She also worries that, as her own life draws to a close, Belle will be left alone and unprotected.

Belle, her highly accomplished lawyer daughter, counters: "I know my mother is worried about my getting married, so I don't even talk to her about my social life. As soon as I turned thirty she thought I was an old maid, but half my friends aren't married. I don't know if I will get married, but I just can't bear the questioning and the panic in my mother's voice when the subject comes around." Belle's anxiety may be based on her own fears that she may not find a mate, or that she is failing her mother, or that as great as her career is, it does not fulfill the need for human companionship. Or it may be all of these things. Although Belle appreciates her mother's pride in her accomplishments, when her mother asks about her social life, Belle hears that her single lifestyle is not good enough. She shuts down because she does not want to confront her own anxieties that her mother's questions inflame. The "adult" Belle wants her mother's support and validation. The "child" Belle feels her mother's disappointment and concern, warranted or not, and reacts by cutting off communication.

Viewed from the outside, Belle is a successful professional, able to protect and take care of herself. A romantic partner could enhance her life, but she doesn't need a caretaker. For many professional women today, a spouse is not necessary to build a social network. Many married couples live bi-coastally and thus have time to socialize with their single friends. They take advantages of opportunities to travel even if the spouse is unavailable. The Noah's ark, two-by-two social life, while not dead, is only one form of socializing now. Belle can make a very nice life with other unmarried friends, but also with married ones. But these are more recent developments that Pat understandably doesn't see as approaching the stability of marriage.

The U.S. Census Bureau shows that Belle is part of a cohort of thirty-somethings in which many are single. For many reasons, including the shaky job market, adults delay marriage, and many decide not to start a family. The median age of first marriage in 1960 was twenty-two for males and twenty for females, but the median age in 2003 was twenty-seven for males and twenty-five for females.[7]

Pat assumes that Belle wants a partner but will never find one, while Belle assumes that her mother sees her single status as a failure. There is no easy solution. Belle may never marry. Whatever their respective feelings about it, Belle and Pat must find a way to communicate their thoughts and emotions without offending or shutting down. It may be up to Pat to come to terms with the idea of her daughter staying single, and then approach Belle and tell her daughter that although she had hoped for a son-in-law and perhaps grandchildren, she understands that it is not her decision; she simply wants to understand her daughter's feelings. With that promise of listening without judgment, Belle might be more inclined to share her own thoughts and concerns.

Cohabiting—Different Sexes

Serial monogamy is another troubling issue for some parents; their child lives with one partner, only to get disillusioned, move out, and then move in with another. To parents, it seems that their child fears making a commitment. Most adult children don't see it that way: this lifestyle is acceptable in the culture of their generation, and for many it simply makes the most sense at that point in their career, relationship, and life. There were five million unmarried-partner households in 2004.[8] For some, "try before you buy" is a sensible choice in an era of unsuccessful marriages. It provides a real testing ground for the relationship. Some parents find this commendable, while others decidedly do not. Like it or not, many of us are dealing with children living with unmarried partners. In a sense, we are all immigrants in each other's generation.

Regardless of what the statistics indicate, many people find it unacceptable for men and women to live together before marriage. For parents, difficulties revolve around both seemingly trivial and substantive issues. Some matters, like whether to invite the latest or the long-term, "para" spouse to a family event, may seem trivial. Whether or not your child believes this is the "right" relationship is substantive. If parents don't ask about inviting the significant other, they could miss an opportunity to discuss the more significant and personal dimension of the relationship itself. The trivial can be enlisted to facilitate the important.

Cohabiting—Same Sex

Sometimes our children choose a partner of the same sex. Fine, charming, and bright as this partner might be, she or he is not what the parent anticipated. Some parents are pleased that their child has found happiness and has a caring companion with whom to share life. Others are happy that their child who was unsettled has changed and now feels comfortable with him- or herself. One conservative businessman said: "Listen: my son used to be depressed, didn't have any friends and stayed by himself in his room all day. Now that he's come out, he's happy and talkative; he has lots of friends and he's socializing all the time. I'm just glad he came out. As long as he's happy, that's all that matters." Other parents are so overwhelmed by embarrassment and disappointment that may be deeply rooted in their religious beliefs, their psychology, and their fundamental moral reasoning, that the journey to acceptance is incredibly difficult. They genuinely fear that their child will go to hell or is doing something terribly wrong. Those who cannot adjust risk losing their children. The grief for both generations can be profound. Coming to terms rarely is as simple as knowing the facts, as it involves questioning everything the parent has believed to be true about life and values. The parent is forced to confront difficult choices—sometimes even feeling they must choose between their communities and their children. And the parent may resent feeling forced to investigate issues they never would have chosen to explore. Parents who manage the often agonizing process of overcoming their disappointment and fears can find unexpected rewards in an expanding universe of options.

Many parents find that educating themselves about the latest thinking concerning homosexuality helps them adjust to this unexpected turn of events.[9] Often they know little about the relationships of same-sex couples and are focused instead on the fear that their child will contract HIV-AIDS, forgetting that this is also a risk in heterosexual relationships. They may not know that since the 1974 edition of the Diagnostic and Statistical Manual of Mental Disorders (DSM-II), a handbook used worldwide by mental health professionals who diagnose diseases, homosexuality has not been listed as a disorder. For some the knowledge that 600,000 Americans are living with a same-sex partner helps them accept their child.[10] Many find comfort in support groups such as Parents and Friends of Lesbians and Gays (PFLAG) and other organizations easily found on the Internet. Others let the siblings lead, since the younger generation often has more accepting attitudes toward gay and lesbian people. In other families it is the siblings who judge harshly, and parents can ask these siblings to be more understanding. Friends can be a great support here also. Some parents find that meeting the partner helps to see their child's relationship as a whole with that partner. It is easier to like a person we have gotten to know than to deal with an abstract image we expect to dislike. If that person makes your child happy and is kind, that fact may help you enjoy him or her.

Painful though it maybe, those gay children who allow their parents a chance to adjust to the unexpected disclosure of their sexual preferences without judging them harshly may facilitate parental acceptance. Parental mourning of the loss of their own expectations may be as much a part of their initial reaction as is disapproval.

Since an aspect of parental concern about same-sex relationships is that their children will be pariahs in society, comfort can be found in the growing legalization of gay relationships. In 2000, Vermont became the first state to grant civil unions—the ability for same-sex couples to have legal rights and responsibilities that mirror those of married heterosexual couples. Between 2000 and 2002, Vermont granted 10,572 civil unions, about 15 percent of which were to native Vermonters and the rest to out-of-state couples. In 2004, Massachusetts became the first state to legalize same-sex marriage.[11] By mid-2007, about 10,000 Massachusetts same-sex couples had married in that state. Connecticut, New Hampshire, and New Jersey also have passed civil union legislation. More and more companies are granting employment benefits to same-sex couples, easing the economic difficulties they have faced in the past. Over time, society has become more accepting and supportive of gay and lesbian people and of other sexualities. Parents who include gay and lesbian children in their lives find that after the initial adjustment, they can still enjoy the same things they used to enjoy with that same child and with the partner. After all, sexuality is only one part of our beings. All the things you loved about your child before learning he or she is gay are still there to be shared and savored.

Approval and Disapproval

Most of our offspring would rather have our approval of their significant others than not. Parents who disapprove are in a quandary. Should they honestly let their children know their thoughts? Or should they treat whomever their child brings home as a guest, if not a future relative? And more generally, is there a specific role for parents in an adult child's personal life? All the complexities and ambiguities of the parent-child relationship are wrapped up in these questions. In the United States, adults form their own bonds. These are personal choices, private matters. However, parents do have a stake in their child's choices. The person their child brings home may one day become a relative who will help them out in times of ill health and maybe even choose their nursing homes. And they will become the parents of their grandchildren.

Maggie and Morgan started going out when she was the head drum majorette and he was the lead trumpeter in the high school band. He was in all the honors classes, she was in none. Jane, Morgan's mother, met Maggie at the big Thanksgiving football game senior year. Her treatment of the girlfriend her son brought around sets a poor standard. Jane made no bones about her disapproval of Maggie. In Jane's view, Maggie was not smart enough for Morgan, and her grammar was appalling. Maggie and Morgan stayed together, though they went to different colleges. Throughout all the years that they dated, Jane's criticisms never stopped. Maggie was cheap-looking, she did not hold her fork correctly, and she would do nothing but inhibit her son's career. Maggie was just not good enough for her son. They broke up for a short period while he was in law school and she was working as a nursery school teacher, but found they really wanted to be together, and soon got married. Jane tolerated the wedding, but showed little excitement. Eighteen years later, the marriage is strong, with three lovely children; all five are close to Maggie's parents. But Jane barely knows her grandchildren who live fifteen minutes away, and is deeply saddened by the lack of contact with them, and their parents. Maggie is cordial, but cold. She is still hurt that her mother-in-law found her lacking.

Politeness always affords protection. You never know when your child will bring home his or her life partner. You risk long-term relationships by not treating each with respect and normal etiquette. It is not easy to be both welcoming and discouraging of relationships you don't think are good for your child. We fear civility will be taken as approval. However, one can be cordial without being either cold or encouraging. Graciousness allows us to get to know a potential relative. It enables us to learn about the new person in our child's life without interfering. Perhaps our first impression was wrong. Or, perhaps, the person is worse than we anticipated. In either case, keeping an open door and an open mind will give us more information. Prejudging will not. And initial openness and politeness allows the parent some benefit of the doubt later it if does become necessary to voice serious doubts about a partner.

Parents can find ways of expressing their concerns that are sensitive and respectful of their child and true to themselves. Doris, age twenty-six, was dating a thirty-three-year-old man who hopped from job to job but had big plans. Troy dreamed of becoming a developer one day, but to Doris's parents he was a dependent guy with no job, no prospects, and not much else to recommend him. Doris, on the other hand, was smitten: "Troy is so exciting; he is starting his own business. He is one talented guy. He doesn't have time for the mundane material things in life. He lives simply." Of course, no one can know whether Troy is the next great real estate tycoon who will turn slum housing into fashionable living, or a guy living in a fantasy. Doris's mother Marie sensed that she was not going to change her daughter's opinion of Troy. Instead of shunning Troy, she invited them to her home and noted their interactions. She did not criticize, but she commented on what she observed in the relationship. "I notice you and Troy seem quite enamored with each other. I know he has great hopes to become a success and I hope he will. One concern I have, though, is if it takes a long time or if things do not work out for him, how you will ensure your financial future?" Marie accepted their relationship and acknowledged Troy's ambitions before she asked about what bothered her.

When a year went by and Doris was still supporting Troy, whose plans had grown increasingly vague, Marie used a different approach to relay her doubts. She mentioned a book she was reading in which the main character was a person who was selfish, would get his needs met, but would not cater to the needs of others. Six months later, Doris broke up with Troy, telling her mother, "I realized he was a guy who could take love from me, but not give anything of himself to fulfill my needs." Marie explains: "I did not like Troy from the first because he seemed so self-centered. I feared if I said something directly to Doris it would sour our relationship should he become my son-in-law, so I tried to get her to see it on her own. Maybe I influenced her by discussing the book, maybe not, but at least I felt I had done something to help my daughter clarify her image of some men in relationships." Doris reflected: "I had a feeling my mother didn't like Troy, but she never said so. She let me make my own decision, and I was able to share with my mother why I came to that conclusion." Marie asked questions and framed ideas but did not try to override her daughter's judgment.

The deeply religious find it especially difficult when the child's choice counters their creed's dictates. Some see those choices as a painful rejection of the life lessons they have tried to instill. Many see such choices as disobeying, not merely parents, but God. Some parents resign themselves to severing or curtailing ties to someone they perceive as a disobedient child. Doing so likely inflicts great emotional cost on all. Others struggle to continue to accept their child, if not his or her choice. They do so despite their strong religious convictions, their real fears that the child is committing a grievous sin, and the evident disapproval of their communities. Often these parents consult clergy. Some are comforted, others are not.

Inevitably, life-long patterns of interaction between parent and child are radically altered. Nonetheless, especially but not only, where sexual preference is involved, the child rarely accedes. From the child's perspective, the life decision was his or her own, engendered by his/her own needs and hopes. In his or her mind it is not a slap at the parents. Though exceedingly difficult, avoid blaming either your children or yourself. Instead use that energy to find an accommodation between long-held beliefs and our children's life choices. Here, as in so many aspects of life, we need to accept something short of ideal, but also short of the worst we fear.

Tables Turned

During the long period when parents and children are adults together, a parent or even a grandparent may remarry, or develop a new relationship, or finally declare a long-held secret of homosexuality. For adult children any of these possibilities can be disquieting. The child feels the same mix of emotions that parents feel when their child develops a significant relationship. In some cases, the children are thrilled that their parents have someone new to care about them. The children feel unburdened. No more worrying about whether mom or dad is lonely. No more having to help with the practical minutia of life. This excitement might also be tinged with a bit of jealousy that the parent will no longer be as available to the child. However, just like parents, adult children may not like the new quasi- or legal family member. The child might find the significant other to be obnoxious, unlikeable, be from an unacceptable tradition, race, or religion, or have the "wrong" values. Three differences, however, jump out in this situation. First, children have never assumed they can control their parent's decisions. Second, when families are tied financially, the children worry about current parental contributions or about any anticipated real or imagined inheritance. Third, in most, though not all cases, the children are not concerned about their parents' progeny.

However, like parents, adult children worry about others' reactions and may not want the parent to bring a cohabitant to their own house, as they have given their own children a strict message against cohabiting before marriage or against homosexuality. They may not want to even talk about these relationships with the grandchildren. Like parents, the children may not have any input into the actual decision, yet find themselves having to deal with a new adult in the family circle.

If you want to keep close ties, you need to be open and honest with your children about your new relationships. Together you need to negotiate the rules of engagement, such as who will be invited to what family events and under what circumstances. You must discuss the financial implications, though you have no legal obligation to do so. For many parents, discussing personal and financial matters with children feels wrong and intrusive. However, now that you are both adults, if you want to remain close, and show that you respect your child, you must share your life and major life decisions, just as you would like them to share. Adult relationships must be mutual. And you must, if visiting or staying at your child's home, recognize the role and authority reversal.

Knowing how it feels to your child can help you in your discussion. As one young adult said:

> I think the biggest part for me was the feeling of role reversal—that as the "child," I'm supposed to be the one having relationships and getting my heart broken and making bad decisions. It's sort of an uncomfortable feeling seeing your parent that vulnerable, on the roller coaster of love, and it breaks the bubble of the invincible image that we all wish our parents could be. Also, sometimes it can feel like your mom or dad changes a lot when they're with this new person and takes on a different personality and lifestyle. This can be for the better or worse, and sometimes you feel like you lose the parent in a way because they act so differently. Little things like stocking food that the new partner likes in the house that wasn't ever there before can feel like an infringement on space of which you feel part ownership. Additionally, when your mom or dad is dating someone outside of the house, it is a completely different ball game from when they start living

together. The "clashing of cultures" starts all over again and you have to negotiate the new 'intruder' even if you don't live at home.

Even harder for adult children is when the parent develops a new relationship with a child, as when they adopt or become a step-parent. This is perhaps the only time that the oxymoronic phrase "adult child" is truly appropriate. No matter the adult child's age or stage of life, he or she is suddenly competing for family resources with another or many others. Sibling rivalry can rear its ugly head. Parents who are in the active supervisory parenting stage may have less time to play grandparent. In order to keep peace in his or her own home, the second-stage parent may now need to divide his or her time, and it might not be divided evenly due to geography or personal preference. Inevitably there are rifts. Putting effort into helping all the families know each other is one strategy that can help. Openly talking about how you plan to negotiate the new family complex is well worth the effort. Otherwise, adult children can feel abandoned.

Whether it is the parent or the child who is entering a new relationship, it disquiets the parent-adult child bond. Tending to each other's feelings is essential.

Questions:

- What kinds of coupling in this chapter are relevant to you and your children?
- How do you continue to try to protect your children now that they are living independently?
- What have you done to talk about your children's relationships? If the discussion has not gone well, what can you change?
- What negative judgments have you made? Try reframing these judgments in a positive way?
- What issues do you have with your child that you cannot change and must accept?

7

WEDDINGS

In ancient traditions, some of which continue to this day, weddings took place at emerging adulthood and welcomed two children into the adult community. The wedding was a public union, agreed on and planned by parents who might have studied the relevant stars and planets, considered financial situations, and relied on the matchmaker to find and negotiate the marriage contract. The wedding joined two families and formally granted the couple permission to begin a new generation. These festivities have been around for a long time in many societies, virtually all put on by the parents, often at great expense. Traditional weddings are filled with ceremonies that either honor the parents or demonstrate the importance of their involvement. In traditional Jewish weddings the guests dance a *Mezinka* around the parents when the last child marries. In traditional Chinese weddings the groom's family welcomes the bride to the family and the bride serves her new father-in-law tea, addresses him as an "esteemed old father" and thus elevates his status. In villages in Muslim countries the groom's family gives *Shirbaha*, that is, money, to the bride's family. In Iran, *Khastegari* precedes the wedding, that is, the groom's female relatives go to the bride's house to inspect her head to toe and learn about the educational and financial status of each member of her family.[1]

How different things are now, in the United States. The only function that American weddings universally continue to mark is the union of two individuals. In the Western world the parents are rarely involved in arranging the match. The younger generation long ago claimed that right. Today weddings generally belong to the bride and groom, who no longer ask parental or institutional approval to start a family.

The Planning

Planning weddings can bring out the worst in everyone. For some, weddings embody outmoded traditions that seem to relate to another time and another place, and for others these traditions are crucial. Traditions link us with the past, yet each decision in this highly emotional context can evoke an uncomfortable confrontation between the old and the new. Weddings used to join two different families with a set of obligations and responsibilities. Now they join the couple and the parents with vague and often conflicting notions of what the obligations are. The in-laws may never see each other again and may feel no responsibility to one another; or worse, one set of in-laws assumes there is a relationship and the other assumes only the children are related.

Everyone involved in the wedding—the bride, the groom, the bride's parents and the groom's parents, and maybe even the siblings, the grandparents, and possibly the step-families on both sides—has a vision of the ideal wedding. Conflicting dreams, long-held hopes, and differing traditions clash. For those tied to their ethnic and religious traditions, the planning of the wedding is particularly painful if their children decide to disregard those rites or honor other customs.

Much understanding is necessary if ruffled feelings or worse are to be avoided. There are books that deal with modern weddings.[2] These books can be helpful, and can make suggestions of how to navigate new families and new customs, but they cannot simplify or tone down feelings.

One may wish that the old saw that a wedding is an event for two people—the bride and her mother—were true. It would keep things simpler! As it is, though, every detail is open to negotiation. And there seem to be countless such details. Where should the wedding take place? What type of ceremony? How many guests? Who should be included? What should be served? This is but the beginning. Just go to one of the many wedding-planning websites to get a fuller sense of the potential myriad of detail to get involved in or avoid. Stress can accompany each decision.

Who Pays?

Good question. Among some ethnic groups, the bride's parents pay for the wedding, in others the groom's. Today, in the United States, there seems to be no rule: the two families may split costs evenly, or the couples pays, or even the guests. "Who pays" may or may not imply "who controls." The once-golden rule, "The one who pays, rules," may also be a thing of the past. Yet some parents who are paying for everything feel justified in taking charge of the celebration and the guest list. Maybe the parents state the amount they can or will pay and leave the rest to the children. Some engaged couples want to have input in every aspect, from the guest list to the venue and all that occurs in between. Still others cannot be bothered and want no control at all, that is, until they do not like the decisions made! Navigating the shoals of all the parents' expectations—who themselves may be at odds—and the couple's requires negotiation and enormous tact. Parent and child are not only pleasing themselves, but also the child's future spouse and in-law family. And, the bride and groom are often walking a tightrope when the customs of one family are in conflict with the customs of the other.

Wedding Travel and Other Details

When Charlie and Lisa, both twenty-five, announced their engagement, their parents were thrilled. The kids seemed well-suited, and both had promising futures. Charlie's parents offered to pay for the band and the liquor, and Lisa's offered to pay for the food. Everything was going well until the couple wanted the wedding at the charming lodge in North Carolina where they had met. Both families objected. Lisa's mom said, "I know that seems ideal, but it is a five-hour drive from the nearest airport. It'll be hard for guests to get there." Charlie's dad continued, "As I recall, the space is small, fits maybe 75 to 100 people. We haven't made our lists, but I bet between us all we plan to have more than that. My brothers and their families alone are forty-five." Charlie and Lisa were upset. The small romantic event they envisioned was about to be co-opted by their parents.

Some version of this scenario is inevitable in most weddings. Each person's vision of the perfect day interferes with the logistics of the wedding. Charlie and Lisa's parents see the wedding as a chance for a family reunion which is quite different from the intimate event the couple has in mind. Anger and strife could easily follow, unless all parties explain what they each want and are willing to compromise. Perhaps with the right explanation Charlie and Lisa will understand why it's so important to their parents that the aunts and uncles be present. Perhaps the parents will suggest a romantic honeymoon at the lodge after the wedding or even give a weekend stay as a gift. Peace and harmony are attainable, but not without open discussion.

The Ceremony

Regardless of who does it, planning the ceremony can open another set of issues between the parents and the couple. Customs like the father "giving away" the bride may seem anachronistic. Some brides don't have fathers, and some grooms never asked the bride's dad for permission. And in some families this was never part of the traditional ceremony at all. In feminist families the mother may want to join the dad. And, of course, each side of the family may have differing long-held dreams for this one detail. Other customs like dressing the bride, who may be pregnant or already a mother, or may have lived with one or more boyfriends for several years, in virginal white may seem ridiculous. The color of the bride's dress may be a sticking point in other regards. In Asian cultures the bride wears red, signifying good fortune.

With so many couples divorcing and remarrying, family structures that were once rare are now commonplace. There are stepfamilies, blended families, single-parent families, cohabiting families, and on and on. Each family type presents certain challenges and most are not solved by traditional marriage customs. How you acknowledge multiple parents on the invitation, who stands where, and what we call each participant are not easy questions. They can be minefields, and the repercussions of these decisions can reverberate through the years. Each person has strong feelings about how to honor the other participants in the wedding. Some want an "ex" completely obliterated, others want him or her to share a position of honor. Some couples may have his, her, or their children present. Creativity and negotiation are in order here, too. Maybe the children design the wedding they want and the parents have a party after or before. Maybe the parents just accept what the couple wants. Each family must decide. Fortunately, there are as many options as there are family configurations.

Negotiations around such seemingly trivial matters are training grounds for negotiations around the bigger issues the future inevitably holds. Here the parents and the nuptial couple begin to work out their future relationship. Your own adult child is making a formal link to a partner and that partner has her or his own family. English has no word to describe the relationship between in-laws. We use awkward phrases such as my daughter-in-law's father, unlike *machatunim* in Yiddish, *khnami* in Armenian, or *consuegros* in Spanish where one word names this relationship. This lack of vocabulary reflects real ambiguity. There are no longer rules, and every permutation and combination of everything to do with the union depends on one's degree of flexibility and one's traditions. In fact, in weddings we see the seeds of the complexities of the future. Obligations to parents, siblings, and other relatives are vague, and each party involved may have a very different conception of what those obligations are.

Henry had been Melody's stepdad since she was three. She had lived with him and her mom, and spent a week or two in the summers with her biological dad. Henry loved Melody and thought of her as his own. She had been dating Tom for six years and finally a wedding date was set. On a visit, Henry said to her, "I wonder if you are concerned that having a wedding might be complicated. Would I walk you down the aisle or your father?

I just want you to know that whatever you decide is OK with me. I know you love me and I want this day to be wonderful for you. This attitude contrasts sharply with that of another stepparent: Mary Cate, Melody's stepmother, had married into the family when Melody was in her teens, after her parents had amicably separated. Mary Cate contributed half the family income and had been generous in paying for part of Melody's college tuition. She and Melody liked each other and spent time together. When Melody announced her engagement, all her parents offered congratulations and were truly happy. Mary Cate and Melody's dad had agreed that they would pay for half of the wedding.

Plans for the wedding were going very smoothly until it came time to design the invitations. When Mary Cate learned that her name would not be on the invitation, she was deeply hurt. She lashed out, "If you expect any money from your dad and me, my name must also be on the invitation." She set conditions specific to paying for the wedding, but behind her tone and message was her need for reassurance that she was important in the family. As outsiders we might think Mary Cate's behavior is self-centered. And in a certain sense it may be, but it is also a manifestation of her own deep, and very real, needs.

Even if Melody and her biological parents had given logical reasons why Mary Cate's name should not be on the invitation, they would have missed the more important issue: Mary Cate felt not only that she deserved some special role in the wedding, but she also wanted to feel a part of Melody's life. If Melody had anticipated this, it would have been an opportunity to reassure Mary Cate. Maybe Melody could have suggested another way to recognize Mary Cate in the wedding. Unless these wounded feelings are attended to, they can damage the parent-adult child relationship for a long time. Melody's dad will feel caught between his wife and his daughter, and Mary Cate and her stepdaughters' warm relationship will have cooled.

Of course, it is always wise to brief family members in advance about any potentially delicate wordings or moments. However, even the most insightful people cannot possibly know what particulars will trigger past hurts and insecurities. Weddings seem to bring out underlying insecurities and jealousies in us all. One would wish that all family members could be forgiving, or at least ignore the failings and focus on all that is sensitively done. That, sadly, is often not the case. Unexpected reactions to wedding details are part and parcel of the tension surrounding the huge changes that weddings signify. Listening hard for the meanings behind the details is really difficult but also is really worthwhile. And, when despite all good intentions, someone feels slighted, apologize and work hard to prevent the eruption of the moment from ruining the event or your future relationship. If that person refuses to accept the apology there is little one can do, except know you have tried the best you can.

Expectations from relatives and close friends multiply the pressure. So many people expect to be invited to the wedding. If you are given a limit to the number of guests, you have to soothe the feelings of those not invited. You may feel embarrassed that you cannot invite a friend who invited you to his or her child's wedding. It bothers you that your children do not understand that you will need these friends as your children form their new families and that the wedding is also a significant celebration in your life. You do not want to distance the people you will need in your next phase of life. The reality is you may not have control of the guest list; thus you may need to make the embarrassing calls to friends and family members to let them know how much you would have loved to share this great moment with them, but you cannot. For those who come from cultures where weddings are the adhesive that keeps families together and a way to honor the relationship with an invitation, these calls can be particularly difficult. Sometimes, explaining the intricacies and expectations of your social networks to your children without pressuring them to invite all your friends to their wedding can lead to innovative solutions. Perhaps they would be willing to attend an informal gathering you create to enable your friends to meet them. Maybe they will send pictures or writings to the people who are meaningful to you. This lessens the sting of the rejection your friends and family members may feel. It also gives you an opportunity to include the couple in important but subtle details of your life.

Invitations to pre-wedding festivities can alienate the most devoted friends and family members. When families and communities lived close by, attending showers and bachelor parties was easy and far less expensive than it is now. It is easy to be hurt when friends and families do not come to your events; only an understanding that life is complex and filled with multiple obligations can mitigate the upset. Placing one's self in the other's shoes is a skill that will help in all the couple's future relationships.

Parents may not be included in long-awaited moments. The bride's mom may find that she has not been invited to help her daughter pick out the wedding gown. The bride's fiancé or her friends or even her children or future stepchildren may be the ones approving the couture. Prospective husbands often weigh in on gift registry decisions that either the bride or her mother might have thought were exclusively within their own purview.

The wedding for some parents is a relief from the responsibility of caring for their child. For others, the focus on the particulars of the wedding and all the folderol around it are a distraction from facing their fear of losing their child to another family or facing their own new stage of life, one in which their children have primary loyalty to someone else and in which they must redefine their own relationships. All life's tensions are magnified to the extreme in the preparations for this one day because the details are proxy for all the changes that are about to occur. Thus, every detail of the wedding is fraught with significance beyond its face value. Each decision can lead to war if one doesn't sort out one's emotions from the particulars.

On the other hand, every decision is a chance to learn about each other and to compromise. Sometimes the differences are huge, sometimes trivial. Sorting out major from minor is no small task because often we confuse the familiar with the correct. Cultural conflict, whether between generations or countries, is often based on this confusion. We all tend to assume wrongly that what we know is the way things have to be.

These discussions, sometimes debates or arguments, are not about unimportant details. At best, they are about social change and social policy within the new family. Through the minutiae, families sort out their quite different views about the purpose of the wedding. For the couple the event is a celebration of their love and commitment. To other family members it might mean something else—an important way to solidify business and social contacts, to honor elderly relatives and family traditions, to keep the extended family together, or even to show off what a great kid they have raised. To the couple, this may seem absolutely out of order. To the parents, who remember other such weddings, the bride and groom seem utterly naive. Two generations, and sometimes three, have individual visions of a lovely day. Unless they discuss and work out their differences, all risk ending up disappointed.

It is truly a time to say goodbye to your fantasies. Whatever your dream of a wedding is, you need to modify it to accommodate the others with a stake in the union. Parents can exacerbate this stressful time in the couple's life, or they can strive to ease the tensions. Starting with a conversation about the purpose of the wedding is a way to begin. From there, compromises can be developed. Each of us, and no one else, understands the sensitivities of our individual social relationships. So this is a time to listen to each other, ask, talk again, and listen again! There is no right answer. But there are lots of wrong ones, ones that trample over the feelings of others, ones that create hostility and resentment. Minimize these by asking why someone has a specific preference and together explore other ways to accommodate them.

Whether in legislatures, community groups, or families, an argument about material matters often really is about who has the power. For example, it may not matter in the larger scheme of things what color the napkins are, but who makes the decision does matter. Whatever the ostensible subject of discussion, the real issue is sorting out roles. The difficulty in planning weddings is figuring out the issues and emotions that underlie the minutia. We need to be very honest with ourselves about why we feel uncomfortable about a specific arrangement and then try to share that discomfort. Only then can we find solutions.

For example, you may have been firm about not wanting any liquor at the wedding. You fear old Uncle Milt will tipple a bit too much and become obnoxious if it is served. But if you could assign someone to "mind" him, you might be more comfortable serving liquor. Sometimes our own insecurities are at the root of the problem. We worry that others will think us ungracious or inadequate.

In this case, review your friendships, or your own insecurities, not the wedding plans.

Intermarriage

When the participants come from different religions or cultures, tensions can be enormous. Religion and culture can determine key elements of the wedding ceremony. When these differ, out the window go your dreams of a ceremony that is exclusive and meaningful in religious or cultural terms. Your children may try to make both families feel comfortable by having clergy from both religions officiate or they may decide to have no clergy present. You may find either of these ideas abhorrent, or you may think they are both lovely gestures. In either case, you can graciously explain your position, but do not be surprised if your children choose a different ceremony. You can explain why religion is important to you, but you cannot force your children to feel the way you do. Religious beliefs are paradoxically both communal and personal. You may focus on the communal, they on the personal. That is, you may think it is important to be part of a continuing history or of a community and to submerge your individual needs and beliefs to those of the group. Your children may emphasize their own personal theology. The minds may not meet. Adults can and will differ on the weight they put on the need for collective engagement versus individual fulfillment.

Whether your child is marrying someone of another race, religion, or of the same sex, or if your child is marrying a spouse who comes with a ready-made family, learn about the individual they have chosen. Reading about the other religions or cultures or attending the services or celebrations of these other communities can help reduce the strangeness. Talking with others who have experienced intermarriage or other marriages that initially made them unhappy can be useful. Talking to other parents or professionals can help parents become more comfortable with their child's decision. Although our children might not realize it, we too need support for this major life transition, and any way we can find it is helpful to us in building bonds.

One enters a new culture when one enters a new family.[3] Just as one needs a guide in a foreign country, you need a guide into the new culture your children are creating and into the culture of your in-law child's family. This is true if your children are marrying someone from the same demographic, but even more so if they are entering a family from an entirely different group. We enrich ourselves as we become sensitive to the decisions, customs, and values of others. At the same time, we may have to live with our own disappointment. Breaking the ice is the first step, and focusing on commonalities is a wise way to do so. All of us are human, so even the family that appears on the surface to be most different from yours has something in common. Calling on the skills we use in business or daily life can be helpful. Finding common interests is the task of any conversation with a stranger. Turning the comment, "You're from Pittsburgh," into a conversation is an art based on asking open-ended questions, such as: "So, you're from Pittsburgh. What's it like there?" Then start talking about the children; ask what they were like when they were young. This is the subject you have in common. You both ultimately want your children to be happy. Once you have established an initial rapport, you can begin to learn about each other's customs. Remember, you and the other parents have the same goal: to create a family which will share joys and help each other in crises, a family that can work out difficulties. Even when a family is ostensibly like you in terms of demographics, you may feel you have nothing in common. Focus on the universals, the desire to love, to raise good, loving children, to have peace in the home. We often find extraordinarily wonderful people under facades that we initially shunned. Each family has different prescriptions for living their lives and different methods of interacting. The children are our guides in how to communicate with this new family.

Before the wedding, it seems that every minor thing that happens on that day will be noticed and remembered in full detail by the guests. I have been to weddings in the most lavish settings with food galore and a sixteen-piece band, and to weddings on hilltops with one glass of wine, no food, and music supplied by the voices of the attendees. Virtually all of these weddings have been glorious. A bride and groom who seem well-suited and are committed and kind to one another make a great wedding. The rest is inconsequential. Few will recall the pitfalls; more often they become humorous memories. Spend the day enjoying the couple.

However, the feelings surrounding each detail do remain important. Because lives are built on details, we spend energy discussing them and may overlook the more elusive but very real emotions involved. If you are stuck in your own vision of the perfect wedding, failure is certain. Like the open-ended questions I just mentioned, your vision of the upcoming wedding should not be filled in with your notions before it has even taken place. Leave some room in your mind for the unexpected, the unfamiliar. Everyone involved in the event has had to compromise. Probably some will be more pleased than others. But the process can set a pattern of relationships among the three families: yours, your children, and their in-laws. You have years ahead of you to work out all the little details and to figure out how your families will intertwine. The wedding is the first of many events you may share as an extended family. Some of these may be easier or more successful than others, but certainly focusing on the positive will help you all.

Questions:

- What are your memories of your own wedding, and how do they influence your dreams for your child's wedding?
- What is your image of a dream wedding for your child?
- What is theirs?
- What do you expect your role in your child's wedding to be?
- What kind of relationship do you expect to have with your children's in-laws?
- Do you see the wedding as your celebration or your child's, or what mix of the two?
- Have you ever befriended someone from a different religion or culture? How did your friendship develop?

8

GRANDPARENTING

Increased life expectancy has increased life's opportunities. At the beginning of the twentieth century, parents felt blessed to see their grandchildren born; now many parents can expect to see their grandchildren married. Some even get to enjoy great-grandchildren. It used to be rare for a person to undergo big life changes after fifty. Now, fifty is the beginning of new opportunity, a time for education, for travel, and for learning new skills. It's not uncommon to hear, "My grandmother is going to Italy for her eighty-fifth birthday!" or, "My grandmother and I are graduating from college together this year!" This generation of grandparents is rewriting what being "old" means. We can be involved with our grandchildren and with our children's parenting experience in an endless variety of ways. We can be exciting role models as we share experiences with the two younger generations and demonstrate that we can continue to grow and learn.

Our children grow as parents and as our grandchildren age. Each new stage of our children's growth and our grandchildren's lives requires new ways of interacting. With newborns, parents may want to exclusively control their child's environment; as grandchildren age and as more arrive, parents become more willing to let others take care of the older children in their own way. Thus, in the grandchild's preschool years, we support our children as they parent. During the school years, if we are fortunate to have good relationships with our adult children, we may take our grandchildren for overnights or even expanded visits during the summer and school vacations. This is particularly heartening to families who are geographically dispersed. Grandparents can travel with their grandchildren or keep them during the summer or when school is out. A whole new industry has sprung up around multigenerational family adventures. *Harvard Magazine* reported that Elderhostel, Inc. offers more than 400 intergenerational travel programs.[1]

As infants, our grandchildren may forget who we are between visits and scream at us like strangers, but over time, they will see us as part of their lives. And as adults they may willingly visit us just to chat.

Just as there are many stages of grandparenting, there are many ways to become a grandparent. Some become grandparents the old-fashioned way: their children become parents. Others become grandparents after their children have assisted reproduction, which can involve in vitro fertilization, surrogacy, or sperm donation. These are decisions that only the couple and their doctor can make.[2] Some parents cajole and beg their children to reproduce—or to stop reproducing. This only causes tension. No child was ever conceived from parental pestering. Infertility is a deeply personal and private matter, an area fraught with emotion that parents enter by invitation only. Some couples hoping to become parents talk easily about the whole process, others keep the topic to themselves.

Some people become grandparents when their offspring adopt. Over the past decade or so, the number of adoptions in the United States has remained fairly steady at 120,000 per year.[3] This is a huge jump from the 50,000 in 1944. While the U.S. population grew 118 percent during this time, the adoption rate increased even more, by 140 percent, from 362 per million people to 399 per million.[4] Many of those adoptions were by single parents. In the 1970s, only about 1 to 4 percent of adoptive parents were single, but that number continues to steadily increase.[5] In 2007, the U.S. Department of State reported an increase in international adoptions from 7,093 in 1990 to 20,679 in 2006.[6]

Some grandparents worry they will not be able to love a child who does not carry their genes or who looks different from them.

Worry not: nature has made babies winning, and they will win you over if you open your heart. Loving a child is an interactive process, and fortunately most babies reach out.

Not all adoptions are of babies. Adoptees who are older or who have emotional disabilities may take longer to adjust to all their new family members, and some never will. A grandparent can try to reach out, be loving and helpful to both child and parents. Criticizing either parent or child for the length of time it takes for everyone to adjust to each other is rarely helpful and can only add to the difficulties.

When your child marries or cohabits with someone who already has children, you may be invited to be another grandparent or you may be relegated to a more distant status. Ask your child what role he or she thinks best for you to play. If your adult child is crazy about the child that his or her spouse brought and you are not, it can feel awkward, particularly if you don't love the spouse or partner. However, making the effort to find some qualities in the child to which you can relate and focusing on them can help. It also helps if you can find some activity you both can enjoy together. It may be hard not to play favorites, but grandparents can and should have hearts big enough for all. If you bring gifts for one, bring gifts for all. If cost is a problem, buy less expensive things or give your time. Of course troubles will arise: the bitter ex-spouse may try to create problems, the stepchildren may not get along with the biological children of the new couple, or the children from his first marriage may not like the children from her first marriage. These problems require the family to work together over a long period of time. Take a long-term view and don't get discouraged. The grandchildren did not create the situation they are in and we cannot blame them. Our job as grandparents is to not add to family jealousies. We must try to help every child by giving each child the time or attention that she or he needs.

Many parents whose children choose not to reproduce are disappointed. Sometimes you can mitigate those disappointments by making changes in your own life, just as Bonnie did. Bonnie, a retired real-estate agent, relates:

> My son is married, but he and his wife have no interest in having a family. My other son appears to have no intention

of marrying. When I was growing up, such thinking was incomprehensible. So here I am hoping to have grand-children and pretty sure that it will not be in the cards for me. I have always fantasized about taking the grandkids to the park. I have to accept that I may need to substitute other people's youngsters for my own flesh and blood. So, when a colleague of mine and her husband asked if I would be a surrogate grandmother to her child, since her grandparents live on the other side of the world, my hus-band and I decided to take this role seriously. We go to Grandparents' Day and Halloween celebrations at her school, and we babysit.

This creativity benefits everyone. Bonnie's children no longer feel pressured, and Bonnie and her husband enjoy the pleasures of grandparenting. And the surrogate grandkids get the visits and wisdom of grandparents.

We don't have to wait for others to make us grandparents. If we choose, we can emotionally or legally adopt our own grand-children. We can use our grandparenting skills by joining mentor-ing programs or volunteering to hold sick babies in hospitals. By whatever method those babies come, enjoy them, love them, and the rewards will be enormous.

Sometimes our grandchildren come before we consider it proper or by methods of which we do not approve. Women are having babies outside of marriage, and even outside their own wombs. Gay dads have babies via surrogacy. Many women are choosing to have children alone rather than forgo the joys of motherhood. In 2003, over 500,000 women over the age of twenty-five gave birth as single mothers.[7] Some parents are con-cerned about problems they think their child and grandchild will face in such circumstances. Or the parents may worry that their child being a single, gay or lesbian parent will reflect badly on them. They may also be concerned that the arrival of a baby to a single parent could mean greater demands on them for help and support. However, there is far less stigma to being single than in the past, particularly for older women, and gay and lesbian par-enthood is becoming more common. Many successful families do not represent the traditional husband and wife, 2.5 kids and a dog scenario. The 50 percent divorce rate suggests that being married doesn't always keep parents together anyway.

The law gives adult children the right to manage their own bodies. Although parents can legitimately worry about disease, pregnancy, and moral rectitude, by their twenties most of our children have made their own decisions about how to use their bodies. Parents are not disinterested parties, but they do not control the decisions of their adult children. They can, however, choose to be involved or not with the results of their children's actions.

When religious convictions intervene, it is especially hard for parents to keep both their ideals and their connections with their children. Self-help groups and knowledge of the mores of our children's generation help some parents. Facing our own disappointments and finding other ways to fulfill ambitions can offer solace.

Lynn and Richard are members of a tight-knit Protestant community in which premarital sex and abortion are forbidden. Their daughter Prudence had gone away to school and remained outside her community to build a successful career in human resources. At twenty-nine, she became pregnant. She did not have a husband and did not wish to marry the baby's father. Her parents recalled:

> At first we were horrified when Prudence said she was going to have a baby despite our church's injunctions against having babies out of wedlock. My daughter had made a mistake. We were distraught that we had taught her the church's teachings and could not believe she would do such a thing and embarrass us so terribly in our community. She had a good job and had planned to go back to school. We thought she had ruined her life and were humiliated. But when the baby came, I remembered that God said to love. So, we started loving. We are still bothered by the circumstances of his birth but we love our grandson and think God would want us to forgive our daughter.

After Prudence's parents disentangled their own emotions from Prudence's actions, they were able to love. And in Lynn and Richard's church community, Prudence's action was not seen as evil. One aspect of a pluralistic community is the demonstration that there are many ways to live. Unless they live in a bubble, TV and the Internet make it virtually impossible for our children not to realize there are many paths to happiness. Prudence's life may not be ruined, but may take a different path from that either she or her parents envisioned. Prudence made a decision. Now it is up to her to make the best of that decision.

"Prudence is a good mom and is managing well, so we just help out when she wants and when we can," Richard admitted. "Her home actually has fewer conflicts than I see in the homes of some married children. However, truthfully, we still worry about her soul."

Not all of us would use Richard's theological language to express our feelings, but the process is quite the same. The parents focused first on themselves—their disappointment, their sense of betrayal. Then they moved on, seeing the positives—the baby, the steadfastness of their daughter as she endured the terrible remarks of the church community, and the difficulties of single mother-hood. Finally all of them focused on forgetting the past and look-ing toward the future. The parents discovered that their daughter was strong and a good mother. Dire predictions of a ruined life did not come true. Yes, life was hard for her as a single parent, but Prudence managed like so many others to work, have friends, and enjoy her baby. This scenario could have ended with the parents losing both their daughter and grandchild. The parents could have abandoned, or been abandoned by, their community. Instead, they worked to make their community stronger. Prudence could have failed to find the strength to be both mother and worker. Worry alone would not have helped Prudence, but her parent's caring support could have been one of the factors that helped build her life. We cannot choose the drama of life in which we play, but we can create our part in the play.

One way parents can deal with their children's choices is to accept that we are not omnipotent. While we would love to pro-tect our children from all discomfort, at some level we all know we cannot. We couldn't do it when they were young and we cannot do it now. When we have children, we become hostages to fate—theirs and our own. Knowledge of our own impotence is one of the most difficult to accept.

Some grandparents become the backbone of their families. Thousands of grandmothers in the United States are now raising grandchildren for parents who are unable to care for them, a situation that has attracted a spate of public concern, media attention, and academic research. The U.S. government maintains a website, http:www.usa.govTopicsGrandparents.html, to offer assistance to this growing demographic. The importance of grandmothers in the survival of the species has been documented in *Nature Magazine*. Mirkka Lahdenpera and her colleagues at the University of Turku in Finland found that after reviewing records from eighteenth- and nineteenth-century Finland, people whose mothers were alive gave "birth to more offspring and raised a higher portion of those offspring to adulthood."[8] The value of grand-maternal participation in our era was noted in the *New York Times* on November 5, 2002. An article titled "Weighing the Grandma Factor" reports that an active maternal grandmother can mean the difference between life and death in subsistence cultures. With parents spending more time at work, with more single mothers, and more mothers unable to care for children because of addiction or illness, the value of grandmothers to families and to our society increases.[9] The benefits exist even with grandparents who don't babysit on a regular basis. Some grandparents fly in for emergencies or when the parents have conflicting business conferences.[10] And with instant communication, the parents and grandchildren hear from and "see" distant grandparents frequently. Their presence can be felt.

For some grandparents, grandparenting is all fun. We coddle our grandchildren, we play, we watch the squirrels finding nuts, and we watch the sunset together. We return the children to their parents when the whining begins or when homework time approaches. This recreational grandparenting is satisfying for all concerned. Helping out our children and celebrating the growth of their children is a sure way to build positive feelings.

However, others find grandparenting stressful. The kids invade, take over, make messes, and generally disrupt our daily routines. If we want to strengthen the bonds with our children, we need to find ways to enjoy their children. Those who hate messes should take the grandchildren outside, or visit the grandchildren in their home. That way they can leave when they become stressed. Though not always possible, those grandparents who find it difficult to cope with several children can visit or invite one grandchild at a time. Unless we connect with the most important aspect of our children's lives, their childrearing, we are unlikely to build a close relationship with either generation. Anything we can do to be helpful and reduce our children's burden is sure to create goodwill. Life is complex. Parents make trade-offs between work and home, between paying attention to friends and family, between themselves and their children. Each of us will make different trade-offs. Judging the trade-offs others make is unfair, as we are not dealing with the full information of the other persons feelings and circumstances. Providing twenty-four-hour care, managing a home, and—for many, both parents working—is a really tough job!

I repeat, anything grandparents can do to make the parent's job easier is a gift. Sometimes that means not even interacting directly with the child, but cleaning the kitchen or going shopping for the parent. But even such helpful assistance has its pitfalls. If we attempt to take over and do these most personal of tasks without permission, it may be insulting and demeaning. Some like having guests put their dishes in the sink or even the dishwasher; others find that it ruins their system or infringes on their sense of graciousness. Now it is we who are guests in our children's homes. We cannot assume that the help we offer is useful. We find out that it's useful if, when we offer it, the response is gratitude—not platitude. With the first child, parents may want help with the household. If so, the grandparent's job is chief cook and bottle washer. Other parents are terrified that they will harm their newborn, and so all they need is reassurance that what they are doing is OK. In this case, the grandparental job is to be a calming presence. Having a newborn is stressful, and grandparental needs must come third, after those of the infant and the parents.

In a sense, when a new baby arrives, it feels like the parent-grandparent relationship goes back to the parent-dependent child relationship. The kids lead, we follow, and their needs come first—but there is a subtle twist. In this case, they have taken on huge responsibility and this shift is temporary. Crises always shift roles; the cleverest among us know how to skillfully maneuver the changing ground by moving back and forth between being an equal and a minor player. We know we will have realized an adult-adult relationship with our kids when we and our children can go back and forth between dependence and independence. Parents and children caring for each other in times of need is a worthy goal. This reciprocity keeps our relationships flourishing and growing. Hopefully, we have many years to recalibrate the relationship. Our nuclear families required hard work to build, and so will our extended families.

The way to enjoy grandparenting is to relax, to stop judging, and to realize that there are many ways to bring up healthy considerate people. In 1967, my husband and I headed to Western Samoa for the Peace Corps. Every morning, a Korean friend and I would explore the island with our infants in their strollers. One day she asked me, "Why are you Americans so cruel, you make your babies sleep alone?" So much for the American dream of a house in the suburbs big enough for each child to have his or her own bedroom. This was my first encounter with the notion that what one person thinks is wonderful childrearing, another thinks is a disaster. There were many more, but this story has a moral for any grandparent. Feeding, clothing, sleeping, toilet-training—all the basics of life—are the areas where parents not only show their love but also attempt to shape their children. Most of the minutiae of child-rearing that we worry about just doesn't matter, or if they do, they matter in ways we can't predict. We all know siblings raised in the same family who are completely different, in spite of having been raised with exactly the same rules and treatment. Each generation puts its own stamp on its children, just as each culture does, but we cannot assume that our way is the only way, or even the best way. Looking at the good motives in child-rearing goes a long way in allowing our children to raise their children in their own ways, just as we wanted to do with ours. Because there are many systems of child-rearing that work and work well, grandparents should intervene only if they see abuse or neglect, or if they are asked to. Many grandparents are disturbed by their children's obsessions with safety or food fads. Maybe their kids are neurotic, maybe they desperately want to protect their children. In most cases, our kids love their children and are doing the best they can. And in most cases, their child-rearing is fine. Our job is one of helper, cheerleader, and shoulder to cry on, or ear to listen. We are well-advised to set limits on what we are willing to do. We can add continuity to the family and links to the past, but we cannot freeze the new family in our old ways. That is why it is important not to criticize, and even more important not to judge. Understanding context can help us be less judgmental.

Maureen's son Ryan and daughter-in-law, Molly, slept with their infant son, Jake, every night. They were part of the co-sleeping movement so popular now.[11] Maureen felt this was bad for the child. He might suffocate; he might never be able to lull himself to sleep. She told herself she was not intervening, but gave her children subtle hints like, "Don't you think you would get a better night's sleep without Jake in the bed? Aren't you worried you might roll over on the baby?" Finally, Molly blew up at her. "When you had little ones you were home with the kids all day, you could snuggle them anytime you wanted. I work all day and I need this time to be close to my child." Our children hear the deeper messages—the meaning behind our words, our anxieties, our disapproval. Maureen learned that her children were raising families in different circumstances. She stopped judging and instead started asking herself questions. "Do the things that bother me about the way my children raise their children really matter? Are they dangerous? If I think their actions make life more difficult for my kids but they are willing to pay the price in lost sleep or tantrums, why should I care?" In cultures all around the world infants sleep with parents and eventually manage to separate. Jake will eventually sleep in his own bed.

First-time parents may be completely controlling of every inch of the child's environment, but less so with their second child, and if they go on to have a third or more, the workload is so great that the parents are more likely to accept any help at any time or place. As our children learn and gain confidence in the multiple tasks of parenting, they are able to be more flexible. So as a grandparent, be patient and, if you will, "bide your time," your child's rigidity may fade over time. Some of our children's rigidity is a way to make order in the foreign and chaotic world of parenting. Initially many grandparents find their children ridiculously overbearing with rules and regulations, or ridiculously accommodating to the baby's needs (some would call it overindulgent). Over time, grandparents can relax and see that their grandchildren are growing well; many different methods can turn out a great kid, and grandparents can play a role in their lives just by mailing cards or pictures and offering emotional support. Many of us will see our grandchildren grow into adults. Those of us who have remained involved even if we were not comfortable with babies or young children can shine as grandparents of teenagers or adults.

Discipline

One of the biggest annoyances and fears for grandparents are grandchildren who are "out of control." Of course, one person's definition of "out of control" is another's definition of "spontaneous." Discipline styles fall along a continuum from the most rigid authoritarian to the laissez-faire. Gordon, a winning child of eleven, had done very well in school until fourth grade; in fifth grade his grades started to decline. His grandparents thought he needed some good old-fashioned punishment. His parents felt he needed tutoring. The teacher had said Gordon decoded the words on the page well, but did not understand what he read. Here it is clear the parents have more information than the grandparents. Often how best to teach a given child at a given moment is not clear. Sometimes, mercy and kindness work, and at others strictness is required. Grandparents might want to freshen up on childcare manuals to make sure they aren't expecting more self-control than is age-appropriate, doling out punishments when a tincture of time will cure the child. Thankfully, most of our grandchildren grow up and become calmer!

The real bugaboo between parents and grandparents can be who is in control and when. Children are brilliant "psychologists" and know who is the softie on what issues and who is more rigid. The skill of knowing who will give permission and who won't is useful in business, but very annoying to parents. It is far better not to undermine our children's parental authority, since they are on duty 24/7 and we just come and go. When three generations are together, it is important to clarify just who is the rule maker; it is wise to give the parents the authority.

Sounds simple and clear, but location can complicate the hierarchy. Each generation has a right to make rules in its own home: where food should be eaten, where diapers should be changed, and other cleanliness standards. Thus, when you are in your child's home, your child's rules apply. When they are in yours, yours apply. If the rules in your child's home bother you, and negotiations and discussions go nowhere, you can stay elsewhere, not visit, or realize the price of admission to this "hotel" is following its rules. Conversely, if the rules of your house are so rigid that the tiny children find it difficult to follow or parents are so nervous they will make a mistake, your children might decide not to visit.

Wise parents talk about their expectations and negotiate a bit around the edges. As guests in others' homes, we try to be sensitive to the written and unwritten house rules. These specific innkeepers are our children. As adults they are in charge of their own territory. As hosts, we do not invite back those who are a problem, unless they are guests we love so much that it is worth the trouble to clean up after them, or put up with their idiosyncrasies. We have the same choices about children and grandchildren. We can talk about how we feel, but they are free agents and, just as we can pick the option of not going to their homes, they may decide not to return. For most of us, living together is no longer a required aspect of our relationship. Even visiting is optional. We all need to be flexible if we want to spend time together.

Even muddier is the question of whose rules apply when the grandparent generation is in charge. Negotiation and understanding are absolutely required! When our children leave our grandchildren with us for short or long periods, they often come to us with a list of instructions so long you would think we had never held a baby before. Some of these directives take little effort on our part and some take a lot. Some are a result of the latest scientific thinking. For example, in our day, we were told to put babies on their sides to sleep; now the mantra is "back to sleep." We do need to follow the instructions of the nursing mother, since her body and the baby's need to synchronize.

Sometimes instructions come with a tinge of guilt and blame. Some children feel that their own parents did not parent them well. They may judge them by today's standards and find them lacking. Or they may feel over- or underprotected. When the caretaking messages for the grandchildren are overlaid with recriminations, the guilt and blame game begins. When you child makes a comment like, "Whatever you do, don't let Gregory go to the store for bread the way you made me do. I was so frightened and much too young to take on such responsibility." This is a signal to let your child know you are sorry for any misjudgments you made as a parent, but at the time the decisions seemed good. Nothing is wrong with admitting your mistakes. This is a chance to talk about your life, about the circumstances with which you dealt. We can't change the past, but we can share our learnings from it and ask for forgiveness or understanding.

As grandchildren age, parents' and grandparents' ideas may not only differ but be diametrically opposed. What food a child is permitted, bedtime routines, and safety issues all can lead to giant intergenerational battles. Be honest about which rules you are willing to follow and why you cannot follow others. It may be that you are only willing to babysit if your rules are observed. If so, tell your children. It may be that you are happy to do whatever your child says. Whatever you and your child decide, the differing rules must be made clear to your grandchildren as well. I know from personal experience that children benefit from occasionally having different environments. For years, my sister and I supervised each other's kids for a week while the other vacationed. The kids soon learned the rules. "At Aunt Judy's we keep everything neat and clean but can eat junk food, and at Aunt Ruth's house we have to eat nutritious food, but we don't have to pick up." Both she and I learned early that one could raise terrific kids using multiple methods. All six kids grew up, now have nutritious eating habits, and know how to keep order in their homes. My sister was hysterical about one item and I another, but both of us cared about all the children, and our children felt that caring. Because we both wanted the vacation, we agreed to suspend our own nuclear-family customs. We knew that for short periods a respite from the family routines could be beneficial. While I did not mind the kids' clutter, for Judy, the nightly pick-up of the toys was stressful and seemed like a useless, endless task; she hated the mess. My sister taught all the kids how to match colors and I taught them how to swim. They all benefited by learning new skills and new ways of living. My kids learned it is nice to wake up to a neat house and to find all the puzzle pieces. I learned that my children would survive with an occasional bowl of sugared cereal. Over the years, I was grateful that my sister taught my children skills I did not have.

Initially, parents are so set on protecting their children that they restrict them; over time they are forced to loosen up. When they send their children to school or day care, they have no choice but to obey new rules. Understanding and remembering the love and nervousness that goes into setting rules can help grandparents be more patient. You can set your rules, but again, just as your child may choose one school over another, they may choose not to leave the children with you. When it comes to safety, this parent generation is fierce. Car seats are a must, every time! This may seem obsessive, but there are more cars on the road than when we were young parents. Car seats are also now required by law in most states. Negotiations around play-date arrangements certainly can feel neurotic to those of us who brought up children at a time when we shoved our children out the door and they played all around the neighborhood. If anything did happen on "our watch," we would hate to feel responsible for the immeasurable harm that might result to our children and our grandchildren. Over the years, parents and grandparents negotiate and the children become old enough to add their own opinions to the mix.

Intermarriage

When your child's spouse is from a different religion or culture, the arrival of grandchildren can arouse distress in grandparents that their own principles and customs will not be continued. The birth of children seems to magnify the distance between cultural customs. In the abstract, it is comforting to believe that each culture brings up children in a worthy way. However, when our own grandchildren are subject to the customs of another religious or ethnic culture, it can strike at our core.

Male circumcision, while very meaningful to Jews and Muslims, may seem barbaric to Christians and Hindus. If you believe that unless one is baptized they will go to hell, it is terrifying to have a grandchild who will never undergo this rite. Most religious leaders tell the couple to choose one religion and stick with it so as not to confuse the child. This feels fine if your religion is the one chosen and not-so-fine if yours is not. Many couples blend their religious heritages, teach a broad humanistic view, or ignore religion altogether. There is little room for compromise, though there is lots of room to make both sides of the family feel acknowledged. Sensitivity to the feelings of both sides of the family is in order. One can and must focus on the universals of all religions. All religious systems profess the need for their adherents to be kind, merciful, just, loving, and forgiving. We all hope our grandchildren will become this universally accepted notion of a good person. Although we may have encouraged independent thinking, when our children are not ideological replicas of ourselves, we fear that our cultural or religious line will be broken, and our beliefs and customs set aside.[12] If our grandchildren are being brought up in another religion, or with no religion, this may feel like a real loss. Perhaps your children will allow you to share your customs with your grandchildren, not as if they were their own, but so that they can understand that this too is part of their heritage. Some people take to heart the fact that their grandchildren may be more open to learning about their grandparent's customs, as schools require "family roots" reports or grandchildren become responsible for their own religious decisions when they leave their own childhood homes. But for many, this is little solace.

While we cannot make the religious decision for our children, we can make ourselves and the other grandparents more comfortable. We can educate ourselves about what our grandchild will learn in this new religious tradition. We can ask our children what aspects of their own traditions and culture they wish to perpetuate and offer to help. We can invite the young family to our own religious celebrations, but we may find we have to live with the sadness that our grandchildren will not be fully integrated into our own religious community. If your religion is the one chosen, you can suggest your children include the in-laws in ways that might be meaningful to them. The child, for example, could be named for their other side of the family. If there is a religious celebration, the foods could be chosen by the family whose religious traditions are not followed. Or, a piece of memorabilia from the other side of the family can be included in the ceremony. One can explain the customs and their roots so that the other family does not feel awkward. Being welcoming and including the other family as much as they are willing to be can lessen the ill feelings.

If your grandchildren are being brought up in another religion, or with no religion, this may be a real loss to you and your people. Perhaps your children will allow you to share your customs with your grandchildren, not as if they were their own, but so that they can understand their background and at least be well-educated about the traditions, if not practice them. For many this is little solace, but a bit of pie is better than none. In the early years there will be many uncomfortable moments as parents and grandparents figure out how to choose which holidays to celebrate together. Holidays that once were governed by long-standing behaviors become a source of anxiety. Who will celebrate, in whose home, and how? Education, kindness, and flexibility are all needed even though parents may be sorely disappointed in the result. And it must be kept in mind that whatever small exposure we give a grandchild, we are enhancing his or her knowledge and hopefully his or her openness to learning more about the heritage.

Divorce

If children divorce, parents fear losing their grandchildren. In amicable divorces, you might remain a part of your grandchildren's lives. You will probably need to reach out to the ex-spouse to do so. In bitter divorces, the grandparents can be tainted by the spouses' acrimony. Their assumed loyalty to their own child makes them suspect, and an embittered spouse may try to sever all connections with the grandparents. Grandparents are caught in the bind of being loyal to their child yet wanting to see grandchildren who are in the custody of the divorced spouse. Human relationships are complex and we do our children a favor by letting them know that the divorce is between the spouses, not necessarily between families. Just as parents are advised to assure children that they will still have two parents even after the divorce, grandparents need to make it clear that they would like to have contact with their grandchildren. Though we may be furious and devastated, we need to transcend the parental conflict to try to build a separate relationship with the former in-law. Our adult children cannot control whom we associate with. We can be helpful with in-kind services or if our own child does not meet his or her financial obligations or we can decide to stay out of the situation. Remembering birthdays and holidays may yield no result for years, but there is hope that as the grandchildren age, they may come back to you. Professional aid might be useful to help grandparents sort out their role. Talking with others who have negotiated these shoals can give you creative ideas. Grandparents can reach out; their reaching may or may not be met, but if they ever want to see their grandchildren they must initiate contact, and may need to continue reaching out for years before there is any acknowledgment.

Our grandchildren, however they come, can open new worlds for us as they each develop their own unique interests. Unlike with our own parenting, we can define how much or how little we want to do. We cannot be assured that our presence is wanted or appreciated, but we can try to be helpful. We are supporting actors in the drama of the next generation.

Questions:

- How do you feel about the way you became or have not become a grandparent?
- How often do you see your grandchildren? Do you wish it were more or less?

- Have you asked others how they stay connected with their grandchildren?
- Have you and your children discussed how they would like you to be a part of the grandchildren's lives?
- What do you think about the way your grandchildren are being raised?
- What aspects of your grandchildren's upbringing bother you?
- Do you fear for the safety of your grandkids or do you dislike your children's methods of upbringing?
- What aspects of parenting do you think your children do well?
- Do you share your traditions and values with your grandchildren? How?
- Are your children happy with the way you do this? Are you?

9

MONEY

Confusion Due to Law

The morning my husband turned eighteen, he walked down the stairs and proudly announced to his parents that he was no longer responsible to them. He was a legal adult. He could sign contracts, go to trial as an adult, and make his own medical decisions. His father responded, "And I am no longer legally bound to support you." In this case, both the son and the father were joking, but like many jokes it incorporated key truths. Parent and child were talking about both the personal and the legal realms. My husband was old enough for some measure of independence, a measure doled out by the government as well as by his parents. At fourteen, the government had granted him the right to work at a limited number of summer jobs; by sixteen, he could work at a wider selection of jobs and drive a car, enhancing both his independence and his earning capacity. At eighteen, he was granted all the rights he proudly announced. However, he was not given full majority rights until three years later, at age twenty-one. An eighteen-year-old is on the cusp of adulthood, not really in it. My husband's confusion, and ours, about exactly what constitutes adulthood is based partly on these policies and partly on the fact that legal majority and emotional maturity are very different matters. His father was correct: he was not legally responsible to support his child and, in most states in America, he could, with no legal ramifications, cut off his son financially or use money as a tool to control him.[1]

It is hard to sort financial independence from adulthood, legal or otherwise. One stellar example of both the shift in government welfare policies and the confusion between adulthood and dependence is a 1985 Wisconsin law that requires grandparents of babies born to teenagers to pay child support until the parents, a term usually associated with grown-ups, reach age eighteen. Becoming parents, typically considered an adult act, must be supported as if the parents were children, which in this case they are. And of course, the law makes no allowances for differences in maturity when age is the defining factor.

In an economy where education is necessary for future financial success, one headed for post-high school education is unlikely to be financially independent regardless of their civic rights. Although no longer legally bound, many parents support their children long after age eighteen. Complicating the family relationship further, nothing requires either that the adult child seek or follow the suggestions of the older generations, or that the older generation cease offering them.

Regardless of law, custom, and emotions, a whole series of institutions and regulations tie us together—from colleges to insurance companies to phone communications companies' "family plans." The eighteen-year-olds may be legally responsible for their own bills, but colleges send tuition invoices home, and parents "voluntarily" sign papers assuring that they will pay. Universities ask for parents' financial records before granting financial aid, and landlords may require his or her parents' income information as proof that the young-adult tenants, even those employed, can pay the rent. The colleges themselves send mixed messages. For example, the Barnard College website, presumably addressing students, says, "The Bursar is responsible for *billing each student* for the appropriate charges as well as crediting grants, loans, and payments to the student's bill. When *you receive your bill*, please review both the charges and the payments being credited to insure the amount due is correct." Immediately below, a different assumption is manifest. "There are a number of different payment options *available to families* who have a balance to pay. *Families can make online payments*, credit card payments or enroll in a monthly payment plan [italics added]." This ambivalence of "the student is billed, the family pays," accurately reflects reality.

Many family health insurance plans do not provide coverage for children once they reach the age of eighteen. A common exception is coverage for dependents through age twenty-five as long as they are full-time students. However, about 60 percent of employers who offer coverage do not cover young adults over eighteen or nineteen if they are not full-time students. As a result, over 13 million young adults ages nineteen to twenty-nine lacked health insurance in 2003, according to The Commonwealth Fund. Until these young adults find employment that gives them their own health insurance, many are uninsured and some forgo necessary medical treatment. According to the National Conference of State Legislatures, "recent sweeping legislation has affected the entire age group in some states. In Utah, for example, a dependent may not age-out of health care coverage until their 26th birthday, regardless of whether or not they are enrolled in school. And in January of 2006, New Jersey enacted a law that provides coverage for dependents until their 30th birthday, as long as they have no dependents of their own. At least four states also recognize grandchildren as dependents."

Regardless of legislative mandates, states set the maximum age at which children can be covered under the family's health insurance. Some insurance plans, however, are more generous than others in raising the age. According to Daniel C. Vock, Stateline.org staff writer, "Legislatures in at least 11 states—Colorado, Connecticut, Idaho, Indiana, Maine, Maryland, Montana, New Hampshire, South Dakota, Washington and West Virginia—voted this spring to require insurers to let adult children stay on their parents' health insurance, even after the traditional cut-off dates of a child's 18th birthday or college graduation." That makes nineteen states with such laws now, although the specifics vary greatly. New Jersey directs insurers to keep young adults on through their 30th birthday; South Dakota and Rhode Island guarantee coverage for nonstudents until they're nineteen.[2]

The nation as a whole is deeply divided about the role of money, not only in families, but also in the overall economy. The 1980s, under President Ronald Reagan, saw the beginning of a dramatic shift away from the belief that government should provide a safety net for families and for society as a whole. Instead, the new policies drew on more individualistic philosophies in which families protect and provide for themselves. Politics, a topic off-limits for discussion in many families, is in the end also about how we determine who should get what and when. Politics determines who has the power to make those decisions and in turn who within a family makes what decisions. So, when we talk about politics, sometimes we are talking about economics and other times we are talking about power and influence, since politics is about *what* things are done and *how* things are done. When we talk about money, we often talk about it as an economic medium, but frequently, "money" is a surrogate for class and social status and power. Money is an integral part of the tangled web of issues that we as a society, as families, and as individuals are trying to sort out.

Familial financial relationships are part and parcel of a complex social system. They are founded on emotional connections and traditions that encourage family members to tend and support one another. How much support and from whom is the question that beleaguers both families and societies.

Yet, it is harder to talk about money than to talk about sex.[3] For some of us, finances are very personal and should not be mentioned in polite society or even among intimates. Others don't understand the intricacies of budgeting or household finance, so they shy away from the topic. Different families have different attitudes about spending, saving, and investing. Some focus on the present, some on the future. Some get great pleasure out of spending; others, like the mythical King Midas, enjoy saving. Some are comfortable making risky investments; others put their money only where they think it safe—even if that's under the mattress. Within your own marriage there may be disagreements about money. You may feel free to discuss the elements in great detail with anyone who will listen; your spouse may not. You may feel comfortable with some debt and he may be horrified by any "red." His financially conservative upbringing means that not only is money something absolutely private, but debt is both improper and unacceptable: one should and must live within one's means, period! With another couple, she may find the topic interesting, and want to know how much there is, how every penny is spent and why, and he may find the topic both boring and unimportant. Each of you may feel your own parents' attitude toward money was the "right" one, and, since you came out OK, that's the way it should be done. You two came to the marriage with these attitudes. Once there are children, one may or may not convince the other to discuss family finances with young children. One of you may want and feel comfortable asking your adult children about the financial details of their lives. The other may feel that nuclear family finances are private matters. Further complicating the situation, your offspring's views may differ from those of either of you. In short, individuals have a range of attitudes about money and how it should be handled. Moreover, those attitudes tend to be strongly felt and are often tinged with moral judgments.

When spousal attitudes toward money differ, the partners either work out their differences, agree to disagree, or find the whole subject so painful they do everything in their power to avoid it. The subject is not new. Parents have been confronting money issues with or about their children since the day the children were born. Should you save for their education? Surely the issue arose in the matter of an allowance. In some families, allowances pay for chores. In others, they are a stipend. Sometimes, parents dole out money as they deem necessary—or as the kids wheedle it out of them. As the children get older, you are confronted with deciding if and how you should continue to support your children financially. Perhaps one parent believes that by continuing to support them financially, they will never develop the ambition and direction necessary for success; the other feels that if they are working hard and still cannot make ends meet, you should do everything you can to supplement their efforts.

You can frankly explain the contrasting philosophies to your adult child and together figure out what terms make all of you comfortable. Even if you cannot afford or choose not to provide monetary support, at some point you will be confronted with how much, and what kind, of time or services you should give.[4] Just how much to give is determined by differences in attitudes.

Equity and Equality

Money contributions over a lifetime play a big role between and within the generations. Within the family, money symbolizes a myriad of factors. It can be a measure of success, evoking pride or possibly jealousy. It can be a divisive force that pits one family member against another. It can be a bond that ties, or strangles. Its availability can facilitate family get-togethers; its absence can keep families isolated. Whenever money is given, for whatever purpose, it can inadvertently or otherwise cause rifts and jealousy or gratitude. Thus as parents, we need to think carefully about whether and how we want to equalize what we give our children. When someone becomes ill and can't work, when someone loses or can't find a job, or a marriage dissolves, or one parent is called to armed services duty, parents and adult children often turn to one another for support. For many, emotional and kinship bonds prevail, regardless of legal requirements. In many of America's more recent immigrants groups, even the extended family—aunts, uncles, grandparents—is expected to take care of its own. In others, the financial ties are less strong, but most families feel some obligation to step in when times are difficult.

Parental gifts and financial support can create friction among the siblings. Just as money has many meanings, so does "equality." If, based on their talents, you sent one child to an expensive private college and another to a state university or a trade school, are you treating them equally? Is this fair? In what sense? Do you owe the monetary difference to the child who went to the less expensive school? When one child loses a job and needs financial help, do you give equal amounts to the others? If you take one son and his family on a trip, how do you compensate his siblings? Or need you? Should we maintain a lifelong ledger to assure "equality"? In your will or for gifts given during your life, do you treat your child who has one kid the same as another child who has three? How will meaningful, but not valuable mementos be divided?

The answers to such questions depend on your philosophy and your measurement tools. This may mean deepening your own understanding about yourself and your choices. In finances as in other family matters, explaining your reasoning to all your children, listening to their objections and advice, and taking from it what you think works best for all of you becomes a path to avoid conflict. Taking these steps models how to listen, to advise, and to take from a discussion what applies. It demonstrates that being adults does not mean knowing everything. It means synthesizing all the available information, coming up with a decision, and then making that decision a good one, by dealing with the unexpected as well as the expected results and attempting to turn them into assets.

As they have done so many times before, parents need to decide what equality or equity means to them. When the kids were little you managed to answer at least part of it. If Janie took piano lessons and Joel played soccer, it may never have crossed your mind to compare costs. But at any gift-giving occasion, you knew it would be rare if they didn't compare who got what. You probably planned ahead so you could demonstrate equality in one sense or another. To avoid escalating tensions between the siblings, you need, as always, to decide how you will give whatever your available assets are, now or as inheritance.

As adults, your children may have very diverse financial lifestyles or prospects. One may have more school debt than the other, one child may have more earning capacity; one may live closer so you see his or her needs more; one marries into wealth, while another goes into bankruptcy; one child spends excessively while another saves; one child is strong and healthy while another has a medical condition that prevents the individual from supporting him- or herself. This litany of possibilities corresponds to a litany of questions, or decisions that parents need to consider, choices they need to make. And it is important to consider our children's feelings about all these questions as we make our decisions.

Money for Current Expenses

Transactions, financial and otherwise, between family members have elements of both choice and obligation. The obligatory elements draw on long-standing intimacies and cultural prescriptions. The choice elements are based on believing we are all independent; as individuals we can choose our own actions without regard to others. As I said in the introduction, it is hard to maintain both intimacy and independence. It is equally hard to know how much and when a parent should offer assistance. Many of us want to and some are able to step in when our children are in need, but it is hard to know what real need is. And it is hard to know what to do or how best to do it. Sadly there are no right answers. And, if momentarily you find what feels like the right response, the circumstances or the child will change. Many parents consider the root of the financial need before offering assistance of any type. If the need arises from debt accrued from education they are more likely to help, if they can, than if it is debt accumulated from what the parents consider extravagant spending. Other parents give aid to children when they are working hard in a field that is not financially lucrative.

Ambiguity about money can go on for years. Some adult children go back to school after working for a while; some training programs last so long that they seem perpetual. In either case, making ends meet can be challenging. And some adults are born with or acquire mental or physical handicaps that inhibit them from ever achieving independence. Separating independence from money is always difficult: we need money to survive, but when the money we have is not ours it may come with visible or invisible strings. One can emotionally be an adult but be financially dependent. Most wives used to be; some still are. Doctors train in certain specialties that require twelve years or more post-college. They can be mature individuals, carrying huge responsibilities and often have young families. Ultimately, they will earn high salaries, but in the interim they may need financial help. Others are in families, nuclear or extended, who fund their training, sometimes at significant sacrifice to the parents.

Some adult children fear that asking parents for financial help or advice is admitting their own immaturity and inadequacy. Whether and if the asking becomes embarrassing depends upon the family. In some families, where the how's and why's of financial life are comfortable topics of conversation, asking financial advice may be very separate from asking for money. Liz, a graduate student, had inherited a small amount of stock from her grandmother. At twenty-five, it would be hers to control. A couple of years prior to reaching that age, she looked at the portfolio and studied the stocks' companies. Liz called her dad to discuss the portfolio and explain why she wanted him, the trustee, to consider some alternative investments. He listened and also had some suggestions; together they decided what to do. Sharing advice is not asking for money. It also is not giving an order. Some never ask their parents for a penny once they start earning. Others do not consider themselves a separate financial entity until some mark is reached: perhaps at twenty-one, or when they finish training, or when they marry. Most adult children borrow money for schooling or housing from a lending institution that charges interest; some borrow seed money to start a business. Some parents have the means to pay graduate-school tuitions or lend the money, sometimes at low or no interest. Paradoxically parental money given as a child is starting out, or in a crisis, may provide the boost that allows its recipient to establish financial independence. But both independence and adulthood are different from supporting oneself financially.

Money can be conflated with power, status, or success. It can buy political influence and community adulation, and express great love and support. It can also be used as a weapon of control. Money can bribe a child to study for a particular career, or live in a particular city, or to visit parents. Some parents try to use money to buy their child's presence.

When Maria became engaged, her parents said: "We have set aside $7,000 for your wedding. You can use it for any combination of a wedding or a down payment on a house." Maria chose a simple wedding at home, and planned to use the rest as part of a down payment. When they were ready, Maria and her husband, Richard, found two houses they loved, one in the same town as her parents, the other half an hour away. Maria's parents adore her and want her close by; they said that if the newlyweds chose the house in their town, they would increase the gift. But both Maria and Richard saw this as using money unfairly to influence their decision, a decision they wanted to be their own. What the parents saw as a generous offer, the children felt as control, souring their relationship. When strings are attached to a gift, the gift becomes entangled in a web of obligations, duties, and expectations. The line between generosity and control is very fine and, as in all parent-adult child interactions, depends on the interpretations of each party. Thus, discussions about money must be undertaken and must be reevaluated as things change, no matter how hard it is.

Money can be used for different purposes in different families. In some families there is no money to give. For some parents their role as financial supporter might be the only one they know. They continue to pay because they have done so for so long that they feel this is the only role left for them. Sometimes when we cannot solve our children's problems, or cannot protect them, or when we feel bad about how we brought them up, we give money to assuage our guilt.

When parents provide nonjudgmental, no-strings-attached financial support beyond the years one would expect, it can make obvious just how much the parents respect and will further the grown child's choices. When a child is touched by this generosity, possibly given at great sacrifice on the parent's part, the money demonstrates loyalty and reaffirms bonds. Rita, a school teacher, felt such support when her father, who worked as a librarian, gave her a monthly stipend so she could stay home the first year of her baby's life. Her husband was a graduate student and they had very little money. But her dad was willing to support her desire to stay home though he did not have much excess cash. Of course, not all children, even from the same family, are as thoughtful or grateful as Rita. And not all parents are willing to use their savings for their children rather than for retirement. For many families, choosing between one's own future comfort and a current need to support a child is a very difficult dilemma.

Families differ in their attitudes toward money and each person brings these attitudes and beliefs to their marriages. What one person sees as an act of generosity another might see as an attempt to control or as a means of robbing the recipient of the opportunity to solve his or her own problems. An in-law child might view a gift that seems normal and natural in your nuclear family as a bribe or an attempt to discredit him or her.

Phoebe, a marketing manager for a perfume line, had always vacationed with her parents, who paid for everything. They enjoyed each other's company and the parents were pleased that they could share the opportunities their wealth afforded. When Brian entered the family, of course they included him. Brian had grown up in a family with a very different philosophy of money and vacationing. His parents did not include their adult children on vacations, much less pay for them. They believed that adult children should earn their own money, to build character and teach them to appreciate luxuries. The next year, Phoebe's parents again invited the couple and again they joined.

By the third year, Brian felt that their attendance on the trip was an obligation. He told Phoebe: "I don't like the way your parents plan a vacation, expect us to come, and use up my vacation time. We can afford to take our own vacations, but they make me feel they don't think I treat you as well as you deserve." Phoebe's parents had good intentions. They would have been surprised to hear that their actions were interpreted as controlling. But, had they asked whether the young couple wished to join them, instead of assuming they would, Brian might have seen the vacation offer in a different light. Brian and Phoebe would also have been able to discuss the invitation privately. Brian could have suggested an alternative. He and Phoebe might join her parents for a long weekend and save the rest of their vacation time for themselves.

With any married couple, attitudes and beliefs about money are likely to differ. We cannot assume we all think alike, nor do we always understand our own assumptions. Because the meaning of monetary gifts is open to interpretation, you can inadvertently cause tension in your child's relationship if you insist on giving money or expensive gifts, because your children's spouses or partners may have different attitudes toward money than you do.

All parents hope their children will be law-abiding, drug-free, and healthy. Most parents have dreams that their children will find a "good" job, a "nice" spouse, and have healthy children. Some children are still searching for the perfect job. Some parents want only the most prestigious careers for their children. Parents who can afford it may offer money to pressure a child to achieve, in order to enhance their own profiles. Psychologists have hypothesized that parents validate themselves through their children's achievements. Too often both parents and children are uncertain about why money is given and on what terms. Clarifying the purpose and the terms is essential to prevent hard feelings no matter what the monetary amount.

Ben, age thirty-seven, had worked for years as an architect. He felt stymied in his firm. The design work was moderately interesting, but he had not been given the lead on any project. He was close with his parents; he came home for holidays and occasionally vacationed with them. They knew of his job discontentment. "Mom, Dad," he said to them, "I would like to go to graduate school for a Masters in Business Administration (MBA). I feel it will help my career. I've saved $5,000, but that's only a part of what I'd need. What do you think?"

Ernie and Emily, his financially comfortable parents, agreed. "Not only do we agree, but if you'd like we could give you $15,000." Ben, of course, was thrilled. At the end of the second year of the four-year part-time Master's program, another firm offered him his dream job.

He called his parents. "I was just offered the job I have been aiming for, so I have decided to leave graduate school. Even without the degree yet, I got my money's worth. It put me in a position to get this job."

Ernie and Emily were dismayed. "You took our money and now you are quitting?"

Ben countered, "When you offered the money I thought the idea was to improve my options. I have done that. With my new salary—up 20 percent!—I can pay you back. Opportunities like this come once in a lifetime. I don't want to pass this up."

Ben and his parents all had similar values in many areas. They were all hard-working, all saw education as a route to success, and all cared about each other. But no one made clear whether the tuition was a gift or a loan or what strings were attached. Both sides felt they had authority over how the money should be spent.

The decision whether or not to stay in school was a judgment call. Ben saw the degree program as a means to an end. He knew more than did his parents about his profession, having worked in it for years. He knew this job was a rare find. Emily and Ernie wanted Ben to get his degree, to have a body of knowledge and the potential job security it carried. When they were really honest with themselves they admitted they wanted the prestige of having a son with an MBA. But they also knew more about life. Sometimes dream jobs turn into nightmares, or just don't work out. Ben had asserted his independence and offered a financial settlement. But his parent's disappointment was more than financial. If Emily and Ernie's offer was contingent on Ben's completing the degree, they should have said so. Many corporations pay for classes only if the employee earns a grade of B or better. They could have used this model. The seeds of the conflict were sown in the initial transaction. Had they all agreed in advance whether the money was a loan or a gift and set the conditions, they might have avoided the subsequent confrontation. Ben could still have discussed alternatives with his parents when he got his dream job offer, and they could have reiterated their views and suggested alternatives; perhaps rather than quit he could take a leave of absence from school or attend night classes. Because Ben presented a nonnegotiable decision, instead of provoking a stimulating exchange among adults, the discussion promised to disintegrate into several days of conflict for all of them.

Ben and his parents are not unique. Too often both parents and child are uncertain about why money is given and on what terms. However unfamilial and business-like it sounds, clarifying the purpose and the terms is essential; some even put them in writing. Such clarity reduces the emotional aspects and may prevent hard feelings.

School debt is a major problem for both parents and children. The cost of a college education has gone beyond the reach of many Americans. *USA Today* reports that, although in the 1980s, a student could work full-time over the summer at minimum wage and earn two-thirds of their year's tuition, today's student has to work the equivalent of a year to fund a year of a public university education. The average debt is $19,000, but it is not uncommon for students to leave their undergraduate education over $40,000 in debt from loans. Of course, graduate school adds to this debt, and medical school can leave future doctors with over $150,000 in loans to pay back.[5] This negative balance can force adult children to take a higher-paying, less satisfying job, which then leads to professional and possibly personal unhappiness and dissatisfaction. Worse, it can lead to the pernicious habit of living on expensive credit, which is all too easily available. While the debt belongs to the adult child, such easy access to credit can allow the debt to climb rapidly and force the child to turn to parents to avoid bankruptcy.

Easy access to credit can be harmful to young people who may not possess money management skills. Even business schools do not teach our students how to manage their own money. However, there are many books that teach basic financial skills, such as Beth Kobliner's *Get a Financial Life: Personal Finance in Your Twenties and Thirties*.[6] Even those who do get good jobs are barely able to make ends meet. Rising rents, low salaries, and repaying debt are among the causes.

According to the *New York Times:* "Many children with good solid jobs are barely able to make ends meet. They are working hard and doing all the right things, but are just not earning enough to pay their bills and their educational debt. Parents are subsidizing them. . . . The assumption that financial obligations to children end after graduation from high school or college is going the way of the pay phone."[7] Nationally, 34 percent of those eighteen to thirty-four receive funds from their parents. The new socioeconomic reality is that "paychecks have stalled, housing costs have skyrocketed and credit has become so available as to be dangerous."[8]

Because the young adults are working hard and still not achieving financial independence, parents, even those with minimal resources, are often stretching to help their children. Some families fund only education; others will fund only family outings. Some give stipends, some give gifts at holidays; others buy specific items. Sometimes affluent parents buy an apartment or home as an investment and allow their children to use it. Whether the form of subsidy is a gift, housing, or money the conditions for inhabitance must be made clear or ill feelings can result.

The *Boston Globe* sums up, however superficially, what seems to be happening: "Once upon a time having children was a good investment. But today children are a money pit."[9] Changes in the economy have rendered it difficult for our children to garner the same resources that our hard work earned for many of us. There is unemployment at all levels of the economy; real estate prices have been rising for years. Parents' advice may well be based on out of date information. For many of our children's generation, working one job does not make buying a house affordable. Even two wage-earner couples may not be able to buy a house without help. But when parents' financial support is needed for necessities, rent rather than a home purchase or food rather than luxuries, the emotional content is especially loaded. Yet if children and parents talk only about money and not their daily lives and dilemmas, their relationship risks becoming more akin to that of loan officer and client rather than one between family members. However important, money is only one of the many areas that bind you and your adult children together.

When Roles Are Reversed

Shifts in economic power affect relationships. Sometimes the children are the ones with the money. The great American dream is that children do better than their parents. And for the preceding few generations this has been true. Children of late-nineteenth-century immigrants achieved educations, some completed college, and made a life that was out of reach to their parents. Especially in the years before Social Security, folks made sure their parents had at least life's necessities. Children were expected to maintain their parents in their old age. Some immigrant groups still expect their children to support and take care of their elders. Much of the twentieth century saw the same pattern of the young earning more than their parents. The dot-com boom of the 1990s and the hedge-fund boom of the 2000s have created some families in which young adults have vast fortunes, far more than their parents' wildest dreams. What may have changed is the assumption that those children should use that money to care for their parents. As noted when the parents were the givers, passing money from one generation to the other can be used for control or for support. It can strengthen bonds or damage them. However, other elements enter. "When the wealth between the generations is reversed traditional authority is challenged and cultural change is accelerated."[10] Some parents of wealthier offspring may be intimidated by that wealth and fear the power of their children's purse strings. They may silence themselves, worrying that their children will not support or care for them when that becomes necessary. Others may feel dependent and feel they need to act subservient to their children. They may be ambivalent about their child's success, especially if they don't feel successful themselves, and may envy or resent what they perceive as a luxurious and wasteful lifestyle. Of course, the money alone has not created these difficulties. A lifetime of interaction has. The path to our future relationship begins at birth. Studies show that even when there have been disruptions in societal parent-child interactions, people have managed to overcome these changes.[11]

Walter was a forty-eight-year-old executive. His mother was a school cafeteria worker and his retired father had labored in a factory. They had scrimped and saved to send him to college. Even with every penny they pinched, he could not have attended college without a scholarship. Luckily, and through hard work and determination, Walter not only went to college, but did quite well. He began work at an entry-level position and worked his way up to senior management of a large multinational company. Walter and his wife, an executive secretary, had only one child; they could afford to do things for his parents, and wanted to.

His parents still live in the house Walter grew up in. It is simple and could use renovation. When Walter offered to pay for work on the house, his father said: "No, we're fine, son. This house was good enough to bring up you four kids, we don't need anything," Walter was frustrated. "My parents gave me so much and now they won't let me give them anything." Walter feels his parents were the foundation on which he built his success. He wants to show his gratitude. He feels he shows his parents in a million ways (coming home when he can, calling frequently) that he loves them, but he wants them to share materially as well. Not allowed to do so, he feels cut off.

"When I go out and buy new fishing gear, or go to an expensive dinner, I think the money could be better used to help my folks, but they want no part of it. I am spending money on myself for extras that I could live perfectly well without when I really want to give my parents a more comfortable life. I can afford both. It is not as if I have to sacrifice for them."

Walter's parents may really love their home. It is filled with wonderful memories and full of the quirks and limitations we all grow accustomed to in our homes. They may also feel intimidated by his success, or that it is just not right to take anything from your child, or they may fear they will be indebted if they accept gifts. Or, maybe they feel that Walter should show his appreciation with more love and attention, not material goods. In this case, it feels to Walter that his father is too prideful, too stubborn. One of the joys of parenting adult children is that sometimes they show us the way, sometimes we have to let them take care of us.

Successes are so much sweeter when they are shared with people we care about. Perhaps Walter could initiate a discussion with his parents, letting them know how they would be doing him a favor by letting him replace the heating system; he wouldn't have to worry about them when he travels for work. Then he might mention just a few things that could be done "while the heating system was being installed." In other words, there are ways he could take the initiative, or try to, that might alleviate his parents' unease. And his parents might see that we cheat our children out of the pleasure of giving when we refuse to receive. We cheat them of the feeling of being needed, of being useful, and at times even being appreciated. Refusing gifts maintains the old dependent child-parent relationship. Adults and good friends give to each other; the giving is mutual, though not always of the same kind. To have warm and intimate relationships with our children as adults, we need to allow giving to work both ways. When that giving is only material, the relationship risks turning stale and anemic. When affection has priority, we know we have taught the lesson that it is indeed better to give than to receive. Besides, this is great training for all for the next stage of our lives when we may be infirm and need their support. Each stage of life builds a foundation for the next.

Retirement and the Unforeseen

Complex as the relationship between the parents and children is in normal times, it is compounded when the unforeseen occurs.

Though obviously we don't know what the future holds, preparing for the unforeseen is a necessity, and therefore an important topic of conversation. Some of us have been able to save adequately for our retirement years and others have not. To be fair to our children, we need to be open about our retirement plans and our financial situation, our insurance coverage, our Social Security and medical benefits. How will we support ourselves? Are our resources adequate? In what situation? For what lifestyle? Could we pay for a nursing home? If not, what possibilities can we and they consider? Do we have long-term health insurance? If not, what possibilities can we and they consider?

Most of us fear being a burden to our children, and many find it difficult to talk about this possibility. But, as our children need to anticipate our needs, we need to plan together. Kept in the dark, some of our children will silently worry; others will come forward to ask. Our task is to be honest with them. For some of us, our offspring will need or want to pick up the slack if we face financial problems or become sick or disabled. As adults, our children need to plan for their own futures, and, if they have offspring, for theirs. They need to know how much money we have to take care of ourselves, including our Social Security and medical benefits, as well as long-term-care insurance. Currently, "roughly two-thirds of women over sixty-five rely on Social Security as their primary source of income."[12] Such reliance may have been sufficient when Social Security was in its early years, but since Social Security has not kept up with inflation, the monthly stipends are no longer adequate for most people to live on. Thus individual savings and investments, 401(K) plans and IRAs, as well as employer-based retirement plans (usually defined-contribution plans, as defined-benefit plans such as pensions are becoming increasingly rare), are vitally important to a financially sound retirement. Savings can supplement or substitute for these plans. Sadly, many of us have none of these. And if parents are spending their money supporting their children or their own elderly parents and not saving, they may not have the resources to support themselves in their later years, which can be twenty or even thirty post-retirement years. Average life expectancy for sixty-five-year-olds is now almost another nineteen years.

Thus, awkward and embarrassing as it might be to discuss our financial situation with our children—including any provisions we've made for nursing-home or home care insurance—they need to know our status. Even if our children cannot help us financially, they need our information, as they may be the next of kin making choices for us when we no longer can.

The expectation that children support and care for their elderly parents can often conflict with the needs of our children who have their own families to support. By the same token, it would be good for the parents to be made aware of their offsprings' wishes in many similar situations. Accidents can and sadly do happen, as the case of Terry Schiavo made glaringly evident.[13] She was in a coma, her husband insisted she wanted to be off life support, and her parents insisted the opposite. Disaster in one generation usually affects all three, so openness about financial arrangements and health preferences helps all of us face these possibilities together and to create a plan that will serve the needs of all three generations.

Inheritance

Equally difficult as planning for our infirmity is planning for our demise. While we cannot rule from the grave, we can, through our wills and letters of intent, let our children and grandchildren know how we want our assets divided, whether we have vast riches or only a few mementos to leave. Once again, bringing your offspring into the decision process avoids or reduces conflict. Explain your reasoning to all your children, listen to their objections and advice, and take from them what you think works best for all of you. You do your children a great service by including them. If, for example, you leave your worthless, but sentimentally valuable rocking chair to your daughter, she may be insulted unless you explain why. If you have a son who is a doctor, but choose not to make him the health proxy because you are concerned that his emotional involvement might interfere with judgment, discuss this with him so he understands. The same applies in the case of a daughter who is a judge, but is not made the executor of your will. Doing so avoids imagined hurt where none was intended. Maybe the oldest thinks he should be in charge, or one feels her sibling will protect his own interests above all others. Open discussion in advance can avoid problems. These sessions may not always be comfortable, but they will inform your decisions, and your children may come up with some interesting ideas or compromises which, of course, only you can decide whether to follow.

Oscar, a widower, has a successful small auto parts business. It allowed his wife, who had died a few years ago, to work as a community volunteer and it fed their three children. All of his children were married and had families of their own. Two had done well financially. Oscar decided to leave his company to the neediest child, his youngest, Steve, who had never done well in school, had gotten involved with drugs during his teenage years, and seemed content to work as a sales clerk in his dad's business. Oscar thought the business too small to be divided among the three.

Oscar had the good sense to discuss this with the children before he signed the will. "I thought my children were really close until I offered the youngest the store. I felt he needed it. The others could take care of themselves. Boy, were the others upset!" They said, "You always spoiled Steve. We worked hard, but you made excuses for Steve. He never had to work for his allowance. This just continues the way you always favored him over us." Oscar realized he had opened a can of worms. Oscar explained his concerns about his youngest child and was able to tell the siblings that he hoped they would take care of each other. The children agreed, and decided to consult a financial planner on how to handle the store so that Steve could be helped and the others could get their fair share. More important, Oscar saved himself from leaving a legacy of animosity.

In dividing material possessions, including money, we each define our own purposes. You may choose to leave everything to charity. You may want to transfer whatever wealth you have to your children or grandchildren. Here again all the equity-equality issues we looked at earlier leap to mind. Do you give your child who has one child the same monetary amount as the child with three children? Do you leave more to the child who needs it most because the others have the skills they need to support themselves? Do you make up for the unequal amounts you spent when you were alive? Should you maintain a lifelong ledger to rebalance so your will assures equality? Do you leave everything "even Steven"? Or your goal may be to avoid conflict after you are dead, to avoid divisiveness so as to perpetuate the close relationships your children already have. Some may want to do several of the above. At base, the only surprises you want in your wills are good ones. Discussing your plans and aims with your children goes far toward making them come true.

In doing this, we again model to our children how to listen, to advise, and take from it what applies. We show them that being adults does not mean knowing everything. It means synthesizing all the information, coming up with a decision, and then making that decision as good as possible. Again, here too, there is no right answer.

Although talking about money is taboo in many circles, asking friends how they plan to handle money intergenerationally can be very helpful.[14]

Questions:

- Why do you, or why do you not, give money to your children?
- What are your aims in doing so?
- Is it different with each child?
- What gifts do you feel comfortable accepting from your children?
- Have you planned for your retirement? How?
- Have you written a will and discussed it with your children?
- Have you written a health-care proxy? A living will?
- Have you discussed your savings and investments with your children?
- Have you told them where to find information about how to access the above information?

10

ETERNAL TRIANGLES

Triangles are three-way relationships with multiple and shifting loyalties and obligations. They can be stable and they can create ambiguities and tensions. Clichés about threesomes abound and speak to their prevalence and the problems they create, as in "two's company, three's a crowd." Dramas from Shakespeare to soap operas depict the complexities of such triangular relationships. We have all negotiated numerous permutations of these triangles since before we entered school: you, your best friend, and your new best friend; you, your friends, and your first love; you, your new baby, and the father; you, your second baby, and the "big" sister or "big" brother. As needs and priorities change, affinities shift, with the potential for enriching our lives or for causing confusion or hurt feelings. While these strains are normal, all the misunderstandings that can occur can be exhausting. Triangles can relieve burdens, as when a mother and father share the responsibility of a baby, or they can lead two to team up against one.

As more and more people are added to the family group, the number of possible triangles expands exponentially. I will focus on just a few: the mother-father-child trio; the parent-child-other siblings trio (which may have many players on one side of the triangle); the parents-children-children's kids or friends trio; and the parents-child-in-law triangle. For many families, the parents-biological child or stepchild trio also creates a potentially problematic and complex dynamic. But the same general principles apply to any triangle.

With the arrival of each new person in the family, the joys of a new relationship grow, but so do the complications. It is impossible to avoid the problems that triangles create. We are often hurt because we are not the chosen one. And we are often tempted to let others speak for us. However, because we are social animals, the benefits of other humans in our intimate circles outweigh the complexity of dealing with many different people. The mother-father-child triangle originates with the first child's arrival. In any triangle, each member assumes a role, whether consciously or unconsciously, though those roles constantly shift. It helps to recognize the different roles each person plays. For example, often one person generates anxiety or anger, another inadvertently amplifies these emotions, and the third tries to keep emotions at manageable levels. The first is a "worrier," the second a "catastrophisizer," and the third a "dampener." The roles the individual plays in any triangle also change depending upon the situation. The individual assuming the role of the dampener tries to ease the conflict by smoothing over the problem, but actually she or he merely suppresses it and reinforces the tensions in the group.[1] Sometimes we get frozen in a role. If you find yourself always being the dampener, the one who smoothes over the tensions, you may actually be preventing the other two from resolving their problem. The dampener can facilitate resolution by stepping aside and allowing the two aggrieved parties to talk with each other and come to a resolution. For the one accustomed to being the peacemaker, stepping out of this role can cause some anxiety. You may fear that unless you keep the peace, a firestorm will arise.

Managing the problems that triangles create helps to preserve the unique relationships you have developed with each child. If one person in the triangle brings you a complaint about the third, encourage the other person to deal with the complaint directly. Do not act as an intermediary. It is virtually impossible for one person to resolve a problem between the other two. More often than not, trying directly to change their behavior or relationship will have the opposite effect, making the problem worse. Do not assign motives, take sides, or make accusations. Let the other two work on the problem themselves. You can be a supportive viewer. Getting involved can also make you the focal point of the triangle;

not only will their issue remain unresolved, but they will unite against you. When one person in the triangle has a problem with a third person, then those two people should try to work it out. If two have a problem with one, then choosing the one who is most likely to be heard should speak.

All this sounds simple, but the complexity arises in that sometimes an intermediary is necessary. Sometimes a third person can bring a new perspective, or help the warring parties overcome their pride and begin talking. The art of parenting is knowing when to intervene and when not to. Try letting the others solve any problem for themselves and only then interfere, asking permission to do so first.

Another common pattern in triangles is that two can team up against one. To understand your own role in any family triangle, and to avoid slipping into roles that lead to conflict, you need to examine the interchange objectively, to try to see the big picture. In any triangle, each person's behavior is influenced by that of the other two; moreover, more often than not, one member of the triangle is the focus. There is a tendency for two of the three people to pressure the third to agree. Take a familiar example: a child who asks one parent who says "no" finds the other parent and asks anew. As kids mature, the triangulation becomes more sophisticated. The child knows which parent is most likely to respond affirmatively and learns how to bargain effectively. The adult child can talk to one parent about the other, narrowing in on the characteristics they both find annoying. "Mom is too controlling. Can't you get her off my back?" A wife might say to her husband, knowing he feels the same way, "Can't you tell Cindy to spend less time with her in-laws? We need some attention, too. If I tell her, she'll think I am overly possessive."

Mother-Father-Child

The families of young children figure out how to cope with triangles in multiple ways. Sometimes one parent plays "good cop" to the other's "bad cop," letting one mete out rewards for good behavior and the other give the punishment. Some families divide their parental relationships along subject lines, i.e., "You deal with their schoolwork, and I'll deal with their social lives." In some families, one parent does all the talking and the other sends messages through this intermediary. When the children are young, a united front might have been useful, but now that the children are adults, the roles within this triangle morph to that of three adults each having an equal say in how the relationship works. For many years one parent may have been the go-between for the other parent and the child. This might have helped the family work together, or it might have been a result of a divorce. In either case, it is time to let the child have an independent relationship with each parent. When you step out of the role of mediator and negotiator, that is, dampener, you take yourself out of the center of communications. At first you may feel a bit disempowered or left out. But the benefit is you are no longer responsible for the actions of another person who you cannot control.

If you are feeling "put between," try to talk frankly about this concern with your spouse and your child. Announce your intention to stop old habits in a positive way, without anger, by letting the other parties know you have faith in them: "I know you and your mother can talk to each other and work things out. You don't need me to negotiate for you." The positive side is that you will no longer be the bearer of bad news, and should they want to "shoot the messenger," it won't be you. Paradoxically, by taking yourself out of the center, by being a quiet presence, you will actually be at the center of solving the problem.

Sometimes it is the child who demands the new relationship. Carol divorced her husband Alex when their son Henry was six. Alex only showed up from time to time, paid no child support, was slovenly, erratic in his care-taking of Henry, and irresponsible at work. He was, however, charming and great fun. During his occasional visits, Alex would take Henry to parks and captivate him with a marvelous day of adventure. Carol, on the other hand, was a hard worker. She had been with the same company as a customer-service representative for seventeen years. She resented the fact that Henry was so enthralled with Alex, while she was doing all the difficult work of raising the boy to manhood.

Henry was now a successful adult. He had worked in sporting goods stores since high school and had recently been able to open a store of his own. Carol was so pleased, that she offered to help with the gala opening. Henry really wanted his father at the big event celebrating the opening of his shop. Carol knew that there was more than a 50 percent chance that Alex would disappoint Henry, as he had so many times before. She did not want anything to disturb this day of celebration, and did not want to see her son hurt once again.

She said, "As usual, I am paying. Your father has not given me a penny to raise you. I do not want to see him, particularly on such a momentous day." Henry replied, "Mom, he is my dad; he may not have given me much, but he gave me his genes. I think, as a grown-up, I am old enough to decide who I can have at my own store opening. I will pay for his food!" Carol was taken aback. Henry had forced her to look at the situation in a new way. "I cannot spend the rest of my and my son's life running interference between Henry and his dad. He knows full well that his father might not come through for him. He has stood waiting by the door for his father for hours many times. I guess if he wants to risk the disappointment, he has the right to do so." Carol also realized that she was now free to act as she pleased. She could avoid Alex or speak to him at the opening. She did not have to let him ruin her good time.

Like so many of us, Carol talked about the use of her money when she really was concerned about feelings—her's and her son's. Fortunately Carol realized that money was not the issue. She was filled with resentment. Henry's invitation to Alex felt like a slap in the face. From her point of view, Alex did not deserve to share in the pleasure of his son's accomplishments, since she had both supported and raised him. And Carol did not want Alex to ruin her great moment of pride in her son with his irresponsible ways. When Henry declared that Carol was out of bounds in intervening, she recognized herself in the role of protector and realized it was time to end it. She then saw that while she could not control Alex and Henry's behavior, she could control her own. Carol was freed from feeling responsible for the misdeeds of an irresponsible man. Her son's claim to the right to make his own decisions freed her from her job as go-between. Our children often do force us to change our ways. And, like Carol, we too can find new freedom in ceding control.

Another area of potential conflict exists when one person of the father-mother-child triangle considers a topic taboo. Each person has the right to his or her opinion, but that person does not have the right to censor all conversation. If one family member has the power to stop conversation, other family members may feel invalidated. When one of the members of the triangle says, "It's not important," another member must have the right to say, "It's important to me."

Shannon and Chris had been married twenty-five years. They had three daughters. Chris doted on them, and even after they had grown up, he still thought of them as daddy's little girls. They were all very close. They traveled together, went camping, and the girls came home as often as they could. When Shannon was diagnosed with breast cancer, Chris felt strongly that they should not tell their children. He was devastated. He loved his wife and felt totally impotent in the face of fate. Protecting his daughters gave him a way to still act as protector. He rationalized that this was not a good time for the girls to cope with the news—one was in a new job, another was pregnant, and the third was busy with work and her children. Chris wanted to protect his children from the stress of knowing that their mother was ill and the worry that they might carry the gene for breast cancer. He was also terrified that he would not only have to cope with his wife's illness, but also with his daughter's fears. Shannon did not know what to do. She wanted the comfort of her children's support, but also did not want to worry them. This was her decision to make. She knew that her girls would rush to her side if they knew she needed them and that they would be insulted if they were not told. She also felt that it was infantilizing to try to protect them. They are adults; if her cancer turned out to be fatal, they needed to plan and prepare their own families for the loss. Each daughter needed to have the right to decide whether or not to be tested for the gene. Against her husband's wishes, she told the children. The children were grateful to be included. They supported their mother as she went through chemotherapy and they helped their dad by driving her to doctor appointments. Together they shared the uncertainty of whether Shannon would survive. They liked feeling useful and giving back to parents who had been so good to them. They felt, in short, like adults. Chris in the meantime realized his daughters were grown-ups and his role of protector had diminished. At first, he was genuinely sad; he was comfortable in the role of protector and loved shielding his girls. He found, however, that his girls could now be his partners in dealing with the challenges of his wife's illness. Perceived losses can actually be gains if one can accept change.

The intimacy created by sharing one of life's significant traumas will serve this family well. If Chris were to be widowed, he would now have a closer relationship with his daughters, some people with whom to share his life. Since studies show that widowers have less contact with their children than married men, he has put himself in a position that will prevent him from being isolated. In this case, Shannon not only survived, but with her daughters' support, has felt tremendously validated. Moreover, their relationship was able to evolve to an equal partnership of women who face life's uncertainties together.

It is not easy to change how we do things. If you and your child are in the same or related work arenas, it is fairly easy for the conversation between you to shift to a collegial one, leaving the other parent out. Alternatively, the child may not know how to relate to the other parent with whom he or she has less in common. If you are the one left out, perhaps you could take the lead by discussing your own work, paid or unpaid, or describing a problem and asking for advice. The goal is to do this without anger or guilt. In this, you validate the adult role your offspring now plays. At first your children may seem disinterested, as for years their lives may have been the focus of your relationship. Because many of us couples developed a united front when bringing up children, our children see us as "the parents" and not as individuals. Thus, if they communicate with one of us, in their minds, they have communicated with both of us. If you as an individual feel invisible, it is time to let your differences show. You can both express your opinions and note that they are different. You can pass the phone back and forth so each can talk about what is happening. We all need to learn to think of each other as having multiple roles—as individuals, as part of our family unit, and as parts of other units.

Parents-Child-Siblings

The parents-child-siblings triangle is just as problematic. This triangle gets into trouble on two scores: First, each sibling sometimes feels that their parents treat them unfairly, favoring one child over another. While this perception may not be valid, perceptions determine feelings and attitudes. The eternal struggle between siblings—sibling rivalry, jealousy, call it what you will—does not end with childhood. When I interviewed a ninety-three-year-old woman about her childhood, she said with great indignation: "Sidney was the favorite! He got anything he asked, the rest of us had to share." Among adult children, "unfair" treatment might be seen in spending more time with one child or their kids than with the other, or helping one with a problem and not the other. It is impossible, of course, to be entirely fair. None of us knows what fair is. One cannot measure the fairness of intangibles like love, nor can the measure of relationships boil down to the number of minutes on the telephone or number of contacts per month. It has always been important to acknowledge your children's feelings, to remind them that there may be more to the story than numbers tell. Share your reasoning with your children. Tell them why you do what you do, and ask them for feedback and suggestions on how you might do things differently to make them feel equally loved and respected. Relationships are a two-way street, and no one party should carry the whole burden.

Second, parents can easily become immersed in the crosscurrents of sibling animosities. My advice here is clear and simple. Don't get caught between the sibs! Your children are adults now, and adults need to solve their own problems. You only support the longstanding feuds by intervening. Time to put the family on notice: you will no longer accept complaints directed at or about other family members. Moreover, do not sanctify the feud by keeping the children apart. You can invite all the children at the same time, and if they choose not to come, you will not have become a facilitator of their distancing.

When Leila's children visited individually, they each complained about the others. Travis said he was tired of hosting all the family events and his sister was a lazy good-for-nothing. Tess complained that her brother never paid attention to her children. Leila's response to both her kids was: "I am not interested in who started the problem. I am interested in how you both get together to solve it." Leila abdicated her role as mediator. She let her children know that they had to resolve their own problems. By treating her children as equals, she let them know that they could no longer rely on the old family patterns to work things out. She would not intervene. She also gave the youngest the same status as the oldest. She was modeling the change in familial relationships, by declaring that little sister no longer needs mama's protection.

Eventually, realizing that their mother was not going to get involved, her kids did sit down together to discuss their differences. When Travis asked why he always had to play host, Tess cried: "Maybe if you came over to play with your nephews once in a while, you'd know my house is a disaster! I have four kids; I'm thrilled if I can see the floor half the time. I'd love to have company sometimes, if I could get the time to clean the house." So they compromised: Tess would host alternate family gatherings, and Travis would take the boys for a day or two beforehand to give Tess and her husband time to get the house in order. When Travis told his mother about their arrangement, Leila said: "You worked it out much better than I could have. I could never have offered up Tess's house or volunteered you to baby-sit, without your permission anyway." By staying out of it, Leila enabled her children to act like adults toward one another. She didn't have to worry about taking sides.

Sometimes in the parent and siblings triangle, it is the parent who feels favored by one child and neglected by another. Stephen had two children, Matt and Freda. Matt, thirty-two, had settled down in his hometown, just a few blocks away from his dad, and the two of them played basketball several times a week and spoke often on the phone. Freda, twenty-seven, had moved to the city with her husband, forty miles away. Stephen often complained to

Matt of how little he saw of Freda. Matt said, "Dad was always grumbling about how Freda made no time for him, that he barely knew her husband, and that she didn't care that her father was lonely. He was always trying to get me to 'talk some sense into her.' But I told him, 'Dad, it's not my job to nag Freda on your behalf. If you don't like your relationship, talk to her yourself. I'm not my sister's keeper.'" Because Matt refused to relay his father's messages to Freda for him, Stephen was forced to confront his daughter. Freda had no idea that she was hurting her father's feelings—she had thought her biweekly phone calls were enough. "After all, dad," she told him, "It's not like you ever call me, or offer to visit me here. How was I supposed to know?" The father now understood that his daughter was disappointed that he had not made overtures to her. They could now craft a new way of interacting. We cannot change relationships to which we don't belong. Matt wisely did not try to change his sister's relationship with their father. He left that for his father and sister to do themselves.

Parents-Children-Children's Kids or Friends

In addition, we as well as our adult children belong to triangles that do not include each other. These other triangles can involve in-laws, siblings, significant others, and friends and, as in the previous triangles, can easily foster a sense of insecurity or exclusion. Here again, two can team up against one. Parents often react like spurned lovers when they see their children make time for friends but not for family. As adults, your children need the support network of friends. Such relationships offer goods and services, such as swapping babysitting duties and helping each other with various tasks, for networking and for emotional support, as they are all experiencing a similar stage of life. These peer relationships are important, and you may not always be welcome as a part of them. It may hurt not to be the center of our child's universe, but, at this point in their lives, we are not. We wanted our children to have friends as they grew up; we knew that they needed to bond with others to move on to create new adult lives and new families. If our children are busy with interests and activities in the community, it simply means that we have raised successful, involved people. Inviting your children to bring their friends to dinner or to an interesting outing is one way to mitigate your feelings of being left out. If you are feeling neglected, however, you might want to have a discussion with your children about how you feel and what role you could play. They may have been unaware of your feelings, and may nonetheless have very good reasons for not including you. When you are invited, enjoy. When you aren't, instead of wallowing, find something else to fill your time that brings you pleasure.

Feelings of being spurned or left out can be magnified when the children start their own families. Their parents are no longer the core of the family unit. Our children are now the center of their own children's universe (and vice versa), while we are mere satellites. It is easy to feel neglected when our children are completely involved with their babies, but this is the natural order of things. Now it's their turn. If you haven't discussed your role before the baby is born, after the newborn has settled in, to avoid misunderstanding you and your children need to envision together the role of grandparent in the lives of the baby. If you do not, your children may expect more than you wish to give, or you may try to impose more than is welcome.[2]

Parents-Child-In-Law

Feelings of jealousy or abandonment can come when a child enters into a committed relationship. According to Kerr and Brown (138), unproblematic twosomes are often destabilized by the addition of a third person. For example, the close relationship you had with your son is now shared with his wife or significant other. His loyalties are no longer foremost to you, but to her, her family, and her friends. Even when thrilled with the new in-law child, parents may feel jealous or abandoned. Your child has formed new triangles with his spouse or significant other, his in-laws—and there may be many sets of them—and his new in-law siblings. The triangles that form among us, our children, and their in-laws can become very complex. The in-laws are parents, too, and probably feel all the same desires and hopes for keeping strong bonds with the offspring. This can lead to jealousy and discontent about sharing time with the kids, and conflict around the differences in rules and traditions in the two families. There can be very different relationships formed with each family group, and the parental job is to minimize difficulties.

In the early stages of any romantic relationship or marriage, the couple has little time for others. But over time this can change, as they become more comfortable and confident with their relationship. It takes a while for both parents and the new couple to figure out where they belong in each other's lives. Each member of the young couple will have their own ideas about how frequently they should visit, or the nature of the contact. The family of your in-law child may have had far less frequent or close contact than your child with his or her family. Those adult children may see your desire for involvement as meddling and intrusive.

Conversely, when your child divorces or breaks up with a long-term lover, you may feel a tremendous sense of loss for the significant other. There are no ceremonies for parents who have lost a much-loved actual or potential in-law child to a break-up. Sometimes parents are torn between loyalty to their own child and the affection they feel for the former significant other, and they need to explain the necessity and desire for contact with the divorced spouse. Often the reason for wanting to maintain connection with the ex-spouse is to see the grandchildren. Karen Fingerman of Purdue University interviewed eighty-six grandparents.[3] She looked at quality or relationships with children and grandchildren and concluded that the relationships with children-in-law were more strongly associated with the quality of the ties to the grandchildren than to their own children. Having good relationships with in-law children is important not only to our lives, but also because we want to maintain involvement in our grandchildren's lives.

Other times, you may want to continue the relationship with the ex-spouse because that person is meaningful to you. Joan, who had had a long illness, told her son, without any anger, "I love you and the fact that I still call Lucy weekly is in no way meant to undermine you. Lucy was very good to me when I was ill. She helped me move, and she was a good daughter-in-law. I am truly sorry that she was not a good wife to you, but my relationship with her is mine and I am grateful for what she did for me. I cannot drop her now.' He was angry, but I stood my ground, and after a while, he just left the whole thing alone."

The ever-changing dynamics of your family circumstances are beyond your control. You do not have a final say about whom your children choose to bring into your family circle, nor do you dictate how these additions and losses will affect your various relationships. You and your child may become closer or more distant by the addition or removal of a spouse, a significant other, or a disliked in-law by divorce. You do, however, have control of how you react to these changes.

Children-In-Laws-Other In-Laws

It hurts when your children seem closer to their in-laws than to you. Negotiating the holidays and visits is easier than negotiating the heart. When one set of in-laws are able to help out more than you, either financially, with time, or because they live nearer to the kids, it feels like a loss. It can shatter the concept of oneself as a good parent. However, we can teach ourselves to view this differently. Throughout their lives, we have been grateful to those who have helped our children. Other people do have much that is unique and important to give to our children. Focus on your own goals for the relationship and work to achieve them. Find out what you can do. Also, congratulate yourself that your child is capable of having close relationships with others, including his or her in-laws. You may have felt anger or sadness due to having to "share" your child. Find a way to be meaningful, to be useful, and to reconnect. One father lived thousands of miles from his grandchildren. Every morning, he played with his grandson over an Internet video link. The grandfather would sing songs and dance while the child joined him. In that way, the child's father could go in the kitchen and make coffee, and the grandfather became the grandchild's own personal "Sesame Street."

Tempers can really flare up when parents and in-laws get along better than the child and the in-laws. The children question your loyalty to them. "How could you like my in-laws, who are so unfriendly and unfair to me?" Remember, though, that in any triangle each adult member should make her or his own decisions. You can encourage your child to take up their issues with his or her in-laws, but try not to assume the role of mediator.

Being cognizant of the roles family members play can assist you in negotiating new ways of interacting. Sarita, a widow, was close with her son's in-laws and celebrated the holidays with them annually. One year her son had a major blowout with his father-in-law and decided not to go to the holiday dinner. Sarita, however, decided to accept their invitation as usual. "My son was not happy that I would go to their house. But Fred and Matilda are my friends. I decided to go for dinner." Her son questioned Sarita's loyalty to him. "How could you like my in-laws, who are so unjust to me?" Sarita explained: "Your in-laws have always been kind to me. I like being with them." Again, in any triangle, each adult member should make her or his own decisions. Sarita encouraged her son to resolve the problems with his in-laws, but would not cut off her relationship with them. Nor would she be the intermediary.

It's not easy making judgments about loyalties, nor is it easy negotiating the politics of families. There is a fine line between asking your child to be an ambassador to his or her new family and asking him to be the go-between. Each family unit has its own rules and regulations. It is wise to ask your child about the correct manner of acting or gift-giving or reciprocation to his or her new family to make sure you do not act offensively. However, do not ask your child to act or speak for you. That you must do yourself after you have collected the information from your child. You must choose how to respond.

There are so many conflicting loyalties, so many ambivalent feelings, so many desires for attention and so many people needing reassurance, including ourselves. It can become very complicated! Families who have reached a satisfactory accommodation do so by compromise, sensitivity, and discussion. They agree that one is entitled to choose his or her associates and make decisions for him- or herself. Each adult must choose his or her priorities at any particular moment. Openness and honesty help to ease the tensions of triangles.

Questions:

- Who is the instigator, and who is the peacemaker? Is this always the case?
- Do your children ever accuse you of being unfair? In what situations? What is fair? Why?
- How do you treat the children so that they all feel loved?
- Do you ever intervene and speak for your spouse or for the children's other parent?
- When do you allow negative feelings such as jealousy, competitiveness, or resentment to spill over into your behavior?

11

COMMUNICATION TIPS

When to Talk?

The injunctions to "bite your tongue," "zip your lip," "be quiet," and "don't say anything" frustrate us. We have things to say, opinions to share, and we want to share them in a way that our children can hear or at least in a way that won't lead to a screaming fight or an abruptly ended phone call. After all, we cannot be close to our children if we don't communicate about things meaningful to both of us. Silence doesn't build intimacy. And one shouldn't be deceived by the existence of talk. Silence can take many forms. It can be masked by drivel, by talking, even at great length, about all the things in our lives that don't really matter. It can mean speaking only of safe subjects, such as the traffic on the road or yesterday's weather, a pattern all too common at family gatherings. It can take the form of talking about people who are not present while avoiding conversations about those who are actually in the room. Or it can take the form of one person carrying on a monologue and not allowing a moment's interaction. Peace may reigneth, but not communication.

Many of us fantasize about being best friends with our children. The parent-adult child relationship can include many qualities of friendship: sharing, caring, and reciprocating. But it can never be the same. We choose our friends but not our relatives, especially not our parents or our children. Friendships are voluntary; the parent-child relationship is not. Moreover, while we may have helped friends, we have not sacrificed time and sleep and invested our energies, day after day, year after year, to the extent we have with our children. Thus, we do not believe our friends owe us the same debt of gratitude. When our friends seriously disappoint us we can opt out of the relationship, but our children, like our parents, are ours forever. We can share our friends' failures and achievements, but for most of us those of our offspring reach our core; we are to a greater or lesser extent wrapped up in their successes and failures. We are, as the old saying goes, only as happy as our least happy child.

Relationships with our children can resemble that with a spouse or lover even more than a friendship. They share the same intensity and ability to evoke anger, joy, heartbreak, embarrassment, or pride. With our children as with our spouses, we can have the same arguments in countless forms over the years. And as with our spouses we rarely censor our rage. Both types of relationships involve significant financial entanglements and obligations. And both not only endure, but go through extraordinary transformations. Like the tadpole and the frog, each relationship morphs so completely that the later stages are virtually unrecognizable from the first. And it is different with each child. Thus, what works with one child may not work with another; what works in one situation may not work in another.

Yet unlike our relationships with spouses or friends, our children are literally ours from the very beginning. The memories of their childhood make up our mutual history. Most of us feel that we know as much about being the parent of an adult as we did when we brought that first baby home—precious little. Once again, we feel lost at sea not knowing when to use the power motor, the rudder, the sail, or when to just float along. Again, we are filled with questions with no ready answers. We want to know: Where do I fit into my child's life now that I don't pick out his or her clothes, apartments, or friends? How do I maintain a relationship over thousands of miles? What can I do to make those holiday visits fun or at least pleasant? How do I get to know my new son- or daughter-in-law, or the co-vivant of my child? And, more often: What to say? When to say it? How to say it?

When this feels overwhelming, it is worth remembering that we are actually well-practiced in not knowing the "right" thing to do. Dr. Spock gave us instructions, but they didn't always work. Teachers, doctors, and mentors offered solutions, but they were not always helpful.

While there are no simple answers, we can build a frame of reference. Figuring out how our lives fit together is not only the stuff of deep talks. Those are simply the hurdles and milestones on the long road. Sometimes we get so absorbed in the importance of talking about life's big issues that we forget that the smaller moments lay the groundwork for the bigger ones. Indeed we have probably been constructing that groundwork throughout our children's lives as we have tried to open or keep open the lines of communication. The true substance of any relationship is in the ordinary; the sharing of joys and frustrations, caring and gossip. Small talk is useful in greasing the wheels of communication. It is not, however, the core of important discussions.[1]

One can communicate in many ways, and talking is only one of them. Sometimes we use words. Sometimes a bike ride or a shopping trip serves to cement bonds or to recall happier times.

Martha found that she was having trouble communicating with her daughter. After talking to her friends, Martha creatively made an inventory of what she and her daughter liked to do and used those shared interests to facilitate conversation. They both loved shopping, hiking, and rock music. For one birthday, Martha took her daughter to a rock concert. She had no agenda other than to enjoy the music together. This shared positive experience became the foundation for many future conversations.

You too can create your own inventory and discover where your interests and those of your child intersect. In this way you can build a relationship based on mutual interests, just as you would with a friend. Sharing experiences and bonding over common hobbies is communicating. These intersections make great conversation starters.

The early stages of the relationship with grown children can be difficult. It is easy to feel on uncertain ground: both children and parents are unsure of the boundaries of conversation. We all probably need more flexibility if we are to make sure moments of real communication happen; sometimes we need to adjust our schedules to those of our children, at others vice versa. Finding a good time to talk is part of any conversation. And the notions of time itself can differ. Both parent and child are influenced by the ethos of their own generation and culture. Because of technology our kids are used to making plans with only a moment's notice, whereas many of us were taught that advance notice is a better way to make arrangements. Virtual online conversations are almost as good as the real thing for many younger persons, but can be a real challenge, or just feel less authentic, for the non-computer savvy.

All these factors shape conversation. As the years go on it becomes easier. Children grow less defensive of their adult role and parents develop confidence in their roles in this evolving relationship.

Before Speaking

The first step in any communication is to understand each other. As with anyone else, if our children assume we're going to be wrong or that we couldn't possibly understand, they find no reason even to listen to what we have to say. Only when we've built a firm foundation of trust can we communicate, whether on troublesome issues or on less difficult ones. The basis of trust lies in your shared history, the honesty experienced, the promises kept.

A key element in building trust is respecting one another's boundaries. This often feels like biting one's tongue. Instead of focusing on holding back, that is, the biting, focus on how you might express what you are bursting to say at another time and another place and another way. Ask yourself if whatever it is you think your adult kids are doing is going to harm them. If not, you probably don't need to address it. Next, decide if whatever is happening really matters, and to whom. If you feel your children are running themselves and their children ragged flying from one educational class to another, you don't need to comment. The exhaustion is not yours. Reserve your input for a different time, a different issue.

Another key element in communicating is knowing and understanding your own intentions. Are you really just sharing an opinion? Are you offering another perspective? Or do you hope to convert your child to your way of doing things? If you are trying to change your child, think again. Investigate first what she or he thinks, whether change is something she or he is even interested in considering. And think about your reasons and motives for wanting your child to change; make sure to put yourself in your child's shoes and try to see the issue from his or her point of view.

When to Say It?

Timing is everything. If the issue is important enough to raise, choose your moment carefully and thoughtfully. As much as we may wish it were different, it is impossible to have a productive conversation with someone who doesn't want to talk. There are many reasons our adult children might wish to opt out of a discussion. Our job is to understand why. Perhaps they are busy. Perhaps they want to solve their problem themselves. For whatever reason, if the moment isn't right, step back.

Billy came home after a year of traveling in Europe. He was gracious and talked about his trip in terms of what he had done and what he had seen. His parents were anxious to talk about his plans for a job or the next stage of education, but he avoided the topic. They heard, took note of his silence, and waited. After a few days, he said, "I'm not going to tell you my plans because I don't want any advice." His message couldn't have been clearer. They promised not to offer any advice, if he shared his plans. When your children make it clear that they don't want your input on a given topic, then respect that, and save your breath for an area where your input is sought. Your children will be more likely to listen if they feel you listen to them. You can, however, let them know that you are anxious to talk with them when they are ready to hear your point of view, always reiterating that your point of view is only one opinion, not meant as a command.

As we know, timing has always been a part of parent-child communication. We may fantasize about the good old days when we could say anything, anytime, to our kids. The truth is, even when they were toddlers, we thought before we spoke. If we told them too far in advance that we were going for ice cream, hours of nagging would ensue. "When are we going?" "Can't we go now?" And bedtime was not the time to break exciting news if we ever wanted them to sleep. It is the same in all of our interpersonal communications. We are capable of being exquisitely sensitive to the appropriate time to ask the boss for a raise. We don't ask when she or he is upset, when we have just missed a deadline, or when she or he is rushing to a meeting. We know about timing!

Too often, though, our timing is bad, in spite of our best efforts. Either we or the children are always running out the door. There never seems to be a "good" time for the serious talk we need to have. How do we find the right time when it seems there is no time?

Maybe our grown children's lack of time has less to do with us and more to do with the crowded lives they lead as they try to combine work and family. It's best not to take their abruptness and lack of communication personally. Remember when they were toddlers? It was impossible to finish a sentence, let alone have a heart-to-heart talk with a friend or a partner. If finding the perfect time to talk is not possible, think about other creative ways to be a part of their lives.

Bob, a sixty-six-year-old former technology worker, was frustrated. He had just retired and wanted to spend time with his children and grandchildren, but there never seemed to be a good time to call, visit, or talk. Finally it occurred to him, "I need to fit into their lives. They seem happy to see me when I attend a kid's soccer game or play. Their lives really are busy with jobs and raising a family. I just have to fit into their schedules. If I can help them cheer on their child, they'll be happy to socialize with me while they themselves are cheering."

Often the geographic distance is so great that we need to settle for the virtual sharing of our lives. New technologies make it possible to receive online pictures so that we can share the growth of the grandchildren, the purchase of a new sofa, or the refurbishing of the bachelor pad. It is even possible to set up a system that allows you and your children to use your computers to see each other and communicate in real time.

Seven-year-old Jack got to see his grandparents only once every other year. Not wanting their son's grandparents to be strangers just because of distance, Jack's parents used a picture of the grandparents as the screen saver on their computer. Jack was around the computer all the time, so he was able to recognize them when he saw them and wasn't shy or uncomfortable with them. Another parent created an album of pictures of all the grandparents, aunts, and uncles who lived far away and made going through this simple album part of the bedtime ritual.

Problems of emotional distance may be harder to overcome than those of physical distance. Demands from spouses, grandchildren, loud music, and work pressures may contribute to the inability to communicate. Try to identify what is getting in the way of your ability to listen. Only when both participants understand the distractions, the disturbances in the field, can you both figure out a better time and place for real conversation. This change of venue can sometimes relieve emotional distance or help bridge the gap.

Sometimes we revert to our caretaker role and are frustrated that a child has not listened when, in fact, they may have listened and chosen not to follow our advice. Even though we have reiterated to our children and to ourselves that they do not need to follow our advice, we may keep repeating it. Sometimes we cannot stop ourselves. If you are tackling a recurrent issue, at least acknowledge that this has been much discussed and that what you are adding is new. This is better than just hoping that repetition will eventually convert your kids to your opinion.

How to Say It?

How should you say what you want to say? There are no right answers. The ways to communicate are unlimited. Obviously your children are the first ones you should ask about their preferred methods of communication. If you are lucky, they can tell you when they want to hear from you; when they want you to say something and when they'll be able to listen. Sometimes they will tell you verbally and other times through their actions. Sometimes they will be close-mouthed. We need to listen with our eyes, ears, and hearts. Here, however, are some guidelines:

Listen to yourself. If you are always inclined to suggest how to do things differently and criticize, then your child will probably hear only the implication, "I am the parent and I know; you don't." Try listening to yourself with an outsider's ear. Hear your own words, as though you were a third party. Rather than offer helpful hints, see if through raising questions you can enable your child to come up with ideas or coping mechanisms on his or her own. In other words stop, look, and listen: stop criticizing, look at your adult child's reactions to your comments, and listen to yourself and to your child.

Be honest. Let's face it, though: we have never been completely and absolutely honest with our kids. When they loved that ratty old blanket, bunny, or bear, we did not lecture them for hours on its filth and lack of aesthetic appeal. We overlooked its obvious flaws and when it disappeared we searched for it, because we knew it comforted our child. It was in our own interest. That security object was a soporific, a crutch. We let them have it, while gently encouraging them to leave it behind. We knew they'd grow out of it when they were ready. There is a lesson here for how to deal with the adults our children have become. Even in speaking honestly, we need to be sensitive to what is meaningful in their lives.

Be positive. Focus on what you love about your child and his or her life. No one likes to be criticized. We all dread going places where we will be looked over, taken apart, and told our failings. We avoid those places, and so will our kids. Understanding that there are many definitions of success, both in terms of your relationship and in viewing your adult child's life, helps us to be positive. Remember, positive reinforcement works. While criticism used constructively and judiciously and around specific issues can be useful when requested, honest praise sets a better tone for the relationship. It's always nicer to be where you are greeted warmly and praised, and it is easier to hear alternative suggestions when they are given with a dose of love.

Betty had two great aunts in their late eighties who lived alone in a different state. Trying to be a good niece, she called them three or four times a year just to keep in touch. One aunt would always begin the conversation with, "Betty, I haven't heard from you in so long." The other always opened with, "Betty, aren't you nice to remember an old aunt like me. How are you and the kids?" Betty dreaded the guilt she would feel when she called the first aunt and reveled in the pleasure she was able to give the second aunt and herself. After her conversation with her first aunt she felt inadequate. After a conversation with her second aunt she felt like a nice person. The way we talk with each other can influence the frequency of those conversations.

As a corollary, it's important to thank your children. Simple, but so often forgotten. None of us likes to be taken for granted. When we thank our children we model the behavior we want, and we have the pleasure of letting our children know we are grateful to them.

Invite communication. Think of conversations as explorations. If our children believe that we are offering perspectives, not answers or instructions, all of us will take more away from the discussion. By aiming to discover what your child is thinking and by what route he or she arrived there, you're more likely to gain mutual understanding.

Ask questions. We can only begin to understand what their issues or concerns are by asking. We need to be sensitive to phrasing and tone if we want to get a response. Otherwise our questions are seen as criticisms. We might describe what we think we have observed, what it's led us to think or worry about. Ask whether there's any basis for our concerns. Ask about the facts so you are both considering the same information. When we ask questions or bring up new perspectives, doing so with a real desire to understand increases the likelihood of being heard. We really don't know their context or all the various pieces of their lives, and we should acknowledge this. Thankfully we don't need to solve all their problems, because we can't anyway. None of us knows enough or is powerful enough to take on that task. More important, they generally are capable of solving their own problems, and doing so will help them grow.

Acknowledge that you could be wrong. Our children have grown up in a society in which they have learned to question authority, and they will question us, so we'd best question ourselves first. And, when we are wrong, apologize. We all are wrong sometimes. Admitting our mistakes or lack of insight emphasizes that it is OK to make mistakes and that apologizing for them is just ordinary politeness.

Don't look for perfection or allow perfection to be the enemy of the good. Sometimes we feel inadequate in a discussion, either because we've never been in that situation, or because our relevant experiences have been poor. We don't have to possess all the answers; just sharing what experience we do have can be enough. For example, if your marriage failed you could say, "You saw the pain and suffering dad and I went through. I understand your terror of marrying and I know you are not me, but maybe some of what I learned applies to you."

Allow your children to demonstrate their expertise. As adults they too have experience, information and insights to share. They have wisdom learned from their lives, their jobs, and their hobbies. Among the great joys of parenting adult children is learning from our children.

If you give advice: Because our children hear our words in high definition, louder, and with more insistence than we probably mean them, it is important to remind them that our advice is just one piece of information. Remind them they don't need to follow it! They can and should talk to others, and you might suggest whom. Express the limits of your knowledge: "when I faced this I had no money or no kids" or "I never faced this decision" and share other views you might have been given on the subject.

When talk is urgent: Sometimes, however, it is absolutely necessary that we speak. Destructive behaviors—drug or alcohol abuse, domestic violence, gambling, or even child abuse—need to be confronted, however challenging they might be. So are family medical histories. When your children's behavior or context is or can be dangerous or life-changing, you simply must intervene. Your child has to know not only the facts, but also how you feel about what is going on.

But it is also critical to step delicately. Nobody likes to be told they have a problem. Statements like, "You need to stop doing this," or "You have a problem" are almost certain to evoke a defensive, tight-lipped response.

And when the timing is key and "together" time is rare, then you must make the opportunity. You might make a date, an allotted time for talking together. Perhaps try to lay the groundwork for the conversation by assuring your child of your love and caring, and then introduce your concerns. You might want to start by talking about yourself: "I am worried," or "I would feel guilty if I didn't tell you. . . ." You might allow that your concerns might not be warranted, and be sure your child knows that you are keeping an open mind. But be honest about your concerns and the grounds for them. Ask questions, and wait for responses before drawing conclusions. Keeping limited goals for such conversations is necessary and realistic. Probably the best you can do is to begin to talk about the problem. It is unlikely to go away with this or many discussions. Just because behaviors don't change doesn't mean you haven't been heard. Don't expect your words to have a sudden, dramatic effect. Let your child know your concern, your willingness to listen, and your availability for whatever they think they need.

But be prepared. Broaching difficult subjects can lead to angry words. Tempers may rise, but we have all heard angry words before, and most of us have maintained relationships with our children despite the difficult moments.

Sometimes it is our children who approach us with concerns, either about our lives or their own. If they do, be prepared to listen with an open mind, just as we would expect from them, and be honest about your reactions. Being open and honest, while uncomfortable and often against precedent, is often the only way to achieve any real understanding. This may not be a time to keep family secrets.

Max, a forty-six-year-old engineer, called his father, Philip, to express his concerns about his own inexplicable feelings of panic. He'd felt constantly on edge for some time. It was starting to affect his work and family life. His father confided in Max that there is a family history of mental illness, and Max seemed to be displaying symptoms that sound similar. Max was upset, he had been suffering for over two years, and his father had kept this crucial fact about his gene pool a secret. Philip tried to explain that he was only trying to protect his son. To Philip, even talking about mental illness was difficult because of the attached stigma. The whole family would be seen as damaged goods. Max couldn't understand. To him, as he told his father, "People talk to therapists all the time. It's not taboo to talk about mental illness anymore." Max felt betrayed, and confused; he was used to talking openly with his peers about problems and considered doing so natural and healthy, although he had not talked with his own parents about his difficulties.

Openness with parents is often limited; that in itself can make communication awkward at best. That's why asking questions is so important: it's too easy to fall into assumptions, and if no one volunteers any information the truth may never come forward. Assumptions can be dangerous. We all too often make them without testing them and therein lies more potential for miscommunication. Only by exploring together can we find out what we and our adult children assume.

Educate yourself. Learning as much as we can about the attitudes of our children's generation by reading books, by talking with people in their age group or from their community can help us understand their context. Being a parent of an adult child requires us to educate ourselves, to keep up with current trends so that we can discuss and understand the differences in our social environments and theirs. Ultimately we need to talk with our own children and ask them what we want to know. When, for one reason or another, communicating with our children is difficult, it is important to let them know that we are willing to cooperate in figuring out what might work. It helps to lay foundation for communication: ask your children what they hope for in the new adult-adult relationship and let them know you are willing to compromise in figuring out when and how to keep in touch.

Molly, a sixty-seven-year-old mother from Boston, wanted to talk more with her son Patrick, a stockbroker in New York. Patrick was busy building his career and enjoying city life. He didn't want to spend the time and money to come home very often, and seemed fairly indifferent about how often he spoke to his parents. So Molly asked, "Can we find a time to talk? I really enjoy hearing what's doing!" When they would talk, Patrick would chat for a moment or two and rush off the phone. Molly realized the phone was not his preferred method of communication. So Molly sent a no-pressure e-mail on the subject of "checking in" and filled it with chatty news from home. She kept the e-mail short and ended it with "What's up in NYC?" A couple of days later Patrick answered with a short update. Molly realized that at this stage of his life, short notes would probably have to suffice unless she had a particular item to discuss.

While we can ask our children their best method to stay in touch, they may not know the answer. And at times, little communication may serve them better than it serves us. They may need distance or want to feel independent. We can explain our feelings, but our explanation might fall on deaf ears. Asking is the best way to find out if you and your child can work out a solution.

Not all conversations go well, whether with children, spouses, or friends. Patrick might make it clear he really doesn't want to talk, at least for now. Friends, other parents, and colleagues can give us pointers about how they communicate with their adult children. And we might try some methods out on our kids, as Molly did. Don't be discouraged by the fact that children do not want to talk. Words, gifts, favors, and small details of life are all communication channels. You can begin with any one of them. If you choose to begin with words, next decide if you want to talk face-to-face, over the phone through voicemail or text-messaging, by e-mail, or with picture postcards. Both the situation and the personalities involved will determine the answer.

But remember, there are many ways to communicate without words. When a death or an illness strikes, friends and neighbors bring food, flowers, chocolates, a favorite CD, a book, or they might run an errand or send a news clipping. Often, as in the cliché, such actions speak louder than words. There's no need to wait for a tragedy to do something for or with our kids.

Cheryl, a fifty-four-year old librarian, had little in common with her daughter-in-law, Patty, a freelance carpenter. Try as Cheryl might, she seemed unable to get past pleasantries. When her daughter-in-law became pregnant, Cheryl decided to take her shopping for maternity clothes. Patty was from a very poor family.

Because no one had ever done anything like this for her, she was honored and touched. Cheryl said, "I doubt Patty ever wore the clothes, but they helped us begin to talk and were worth every penny! Somehow shopping together demonstrated to Patty that I wanted to build a relationship and that I cared about her."

Here are a few suggestions to assist you in building communication:

Spend leisure time with your child. It matters little what you do as long as you both enjoy the activity. You can eat, play sports, climb rocks, go shopping, walk the dog, go to a concert. Or try doing something decadent, like going for a manicure (yes, even some men like manicures, so invite your sons, too), or going to a palm-reader. You can enter your child's life by volunteering together at a local soup kitchen, or for the local sports league, or at your grandchildren's school. You can help each other clean closets, bake bread, or build a bookshelf. Organize old pictures into an album. Spend time reminiscing, laughing, and remembering the "old times." Again, these sorts of things build your relationship only if *both* of you enjoy these tasks or if one of you really needs the project done. Then they can yield real pleasure. Having a common project to focus on is a great way to build rapport through conversation and inside jokes.

The activity list is endless. Even watching TV together can lead to conversation. The point is to enjoy the pleasures of life together without waiting for special occasions.

These methods are particularly useful when first establishing a relationship with a new daughter- or son-in-law or your child's partner. You can let the new "family" member know you care without worrying about getting the specific words just right. Because so many parents fantasize about spending extended time with their children, they cannot enjoy the brief moments. As with most things in life, we need to enjoy the reality of each moment, rather than wishing for an ideal and failing to appreciate what is available.

Greta, a sixty-one-year-old mother of four married sons, wanted to be close to her daughters-in-law, but each one lived at least 1,000 miles away. The annual visit was fun, but all too short. So she suggested that she and her daughters-in-law exchange chicken recipes. They all agreed to make a specific one the same night. They then did an e-mail exchange of their husbands' reactions. They roared with laughter at the different reactions of the four brothers. Greta enjoyed sharing this experience rather than wasting time on wishing she could spend more time with her family.

Nonverbal communication can also be useful when you want your children to know that you are trying to be supportive even though they seem reluctant to talk at any particular moment. Sometimes a certain topic is too hot to handle by talking through it. Either you or your child is just too upset to talk. At such times, a quiet presence may be enough.

It is painful to watch when your child is really in trouble, or suffering from rejection, a broken heart, or any kind of failure. Nonverbal actions are a great way to let your child know you care, by being supportive without prying, smothering, or ignoring.

Elaine, a lawyer, was distraught when her thirty-five-year-old, single daughter was diagnosed with breast cancer. She phoned daily, but after a while her daughter let her know that the phone calls undermined her confidence in both taking care of herself and in the eventual outcome. Her mother's worries magnified her own. Elaine heard and instead sent postcards every few days. The cards varied and had different messages, such as "Thinking of you" or "Went shopping today." Her daughter felt supported instead of disquieted.

Distance and physical infirmity, too, can be overcome with creativity. Lucy, eighty-six, and her daughter Suzanne, fifty-eight, loved to do crossword puzzles, so they would each work on the Sunday *New York Times* puzzle by themselves until Thursday. Then they would talk on the phone, completing it together. It gave them each a chance to praise the other and to enjoy the mental gymnastics of puzzling together.

Sometimes a gesture or a good, old-fashioned hug may be enough to communicate your love and affection for your child. Other times, these actions can serve to begin a conversation. You are not bound by mere words. There are many ways to let your children know that you want to talk, you love them, and you want to be a part of their lives. Remember, a good relationship is not synonymous with a smooth one. The biggest step is to accept each other, by focusing on the strengths and by respecting each other's point of view.

It takes courage to communicate. Ten years into my marriage, I had two children, ages four and six, and had developed a cordial relationship with my mother-in-law. I guess she wanted more, because she called me out to the porch one day. However, first she arranged to send our husbands on an excursion with the kids. She sat me down and said, "I sense some tension between us and wonder what I can do to change things." I gasped and decided that if she had the courage to ask, I should find the courage to answer. I respected her directness and her willingness to confront our perfectly pleasant but not especially warm relationship. I explained, "I feel criticized for my lack of domestic interest. I have many other talents. Focusing on my weaknesses just makes me uncomfortable and less than thrilled to visit with you." She responded by listening and then, over the next days, weeks, months, and years focused on my talents. When I began graduate school, although neither she nor my own parents thought it a wise choice, she stepped in to cook and babysit. Our relationship became more mutually fulfilling over time, as we came to understand each other better.

We all have more than one opportunity to improve our relationships. The great Babe Ruth had a batting average well under .400. That means he successfully connected only a little more than a third of the time. We probably won't have a meeting of the minds with our kids every time, but the hope is that, like Babe Ruth we will hit a few home runs. The home runs, the good, solid connections, may sustain us through the challenging times.

We can find many positive opportunities to connect. There will always be moments of aggravation and of anger, but our aim is to balance those with more and more loving, caring, and joyful interactions.

It's easier to keep trying when we are not keeping score. Set aside that temptation to keep a ledger. The goal is an exchange in which both parties feel nurtured and respected. Thinking in terms of "global reciprocity" can help. Your children give to you in very different ways at different times, just as you do with them.

Parenting adult children is a work in progress. In the end if something isn't working, we can do things differently. We, too, are growing adults.

Questions:

- In relationships where you have felt tension, have there been times that you remained silent and it felt good?
- With what people and in what situations do you avoid talking about emotions and matters that are meaningful to you?
- When and with whom do you talk about things that matter?
- What aspects make that conversation possible?
- How can you translate that into such conversations with your children? How might it differ for each child?
- List all the ways people have communicated to you without words.
- What are some of your favorite nonverbal ways of communicating? Which of these work with each of your children, and when?
- What secrets are you keeping from your children? Upon reflection, are there some it would be better to share?
- When have you had an altercation and later been able to improve the relationship?

12

CONCLUSION

Then and Now

Three years ago, when my mother-in-law died, I had the extraordinary experience of finding every letter I had ever received from age eighteen to age twenty-three in her attic. I had stashed them there in 1965 when my husband and I went to work in India and had forgotten about them. Piled in with missives from old boyfriends and other friends were letters from my mother and father written between 1958 and 1962, my college years. The letters were filled with instructions on what to wear, how to behave, and orders to visit my aunt each week. While the specific instructions, "to wear skirts to class . . . [and] going to breakfast in bathrobes sets a poor tone," were products of their period, the disapproval of the younger generation's norms by the older generation was familiar. How annoying these instructions were when I was young. As an adult I can still hear the messages of support amid the instructions, and I miss them. What I now read as gentle reminders—"write often, call so and so, and keep us informed"—I read at the time as scoldings. What I then perceived as a "guilt trip," I now see as instructions for polite living or reminders not to take my parents for granted. I now know how lucky I was to have parents who cared about all aspects of my life including the minutiae.

Revisiting these letters, I see their support and belief in me, and as an adult I realize the importance of that gift. Mixed with the directives about dress and behavior were messages of support, love, and faith that, whatever I was worrying about, I would make a good decision and execute it well. After chastising me for not sharing my post-college plans (I had none), we had lengthy exchanges about whether I should work in New York and live the big city life, which I wanted to do, or come home to Massachusetts so I could save money for graduate school. They discussed alternatives, but then reminded me that the final decision was mine, as I would be the one living with the consequences. "Yours is the choice, ours is but to advise," they often said, followed by questions to ask myself before I made a decision. Though at the time I wanted to stay in New York and live the big city life, their insistence that a master's degree was important, and that I would need to earn money to pay for graduate school, turned out to be wise advice. It gives me pleasure and reassurance to know that the past looks quite different in the present, and to see that the disagreements of those past moments have morphed into fond memories of caring and support. Perhaps some day my children will look back on my advice with the same affection.

The content of other letters in that collection made clear that I did not share every facet of my life with my parents. Letters from friends were filled with more details about the drama of my life. Here, too, lies a lesson: we need not be all-involved in our children's adult lives. A window can suffice.

But after my adventures in India and once I had children, mine and my parents' lives became closely intertwined once again. I needed their help. As my oldest daughter says, "Behind every great woman is a great set of grandparents who help out in the crisis." I have not achieved greatness, but whatever I have achieved was made possible by the support of my children's grandparents. The help my parents and in-laws gave me in my child-bearing and child-rearing years set examples for me about tending to others' needs, models I could follow as they aged. Finally, as my parents became frail, I again became more involved in their lives. It was, I admit, far easier to be attentive to them once my children were more independent; I no longer felt sandwiched between the needs of the two generations. Parents and children exchange and receive aid as well as love and emotional support from one another. Grandparents who extend themselves when their children are stretched are hopefully planting seeds for future reciprocation. As in many families, my parents and I blended back into each other's lives as our needs required. We all need each other at the beginning and the end of life, and for all the large and small crises in between. This global reciprocation or exchange of services over a lifetime is typical of families.[1]

Why We Need Each Other

Rereading my letters with hindsight and through the lens of sociology and psychology, I realize that the thoughts and behaviors depicted in them—while not universal—are quite common. The distancing that occurs when children emerge into adulthood often is not permanent. Families grow and change throughout the years. It also demonstrated what I have read so many times; good intergenerational relationships are important for both parents and children. In times of crises, parents and children can help each other, and often do, when poor health strikes either generation, finances dry up, or support systems unravel.

Many studies have shown that an exchange of communication, care, and gifts across the lifetime increases the quality of life for both parents and adult children. Aging parents who have maintained connections with their children are less likely to become depressed and more likely to receive adequate elder care; and adults who have had a longstanding healthy relationship with their parents are more willing to be actively involved in their aging parents' care.[2] Widows and widowers, especially, benefit from close ties to their children. One study of widows in America showed that the stronger their social network, the lower their mortality rate.[3] Our relationships with our children are indeed vital.

Gender differences are another factor that influences the form reciprocity takes. Women spend more hours caregiving for their elders than men, even though men now make up 39 percent of family caregivers (up from 25 percent only a few years ago).[4] Divorce is another component influencing reciprocity, especially for fathers. According to a 2003 study in the *Journal of Family Issues*, noncustodial fathers tend to live farther away from their adult children and enjoy less contact and exchange of aid.[5] About 44 percent of Americans between the ages of 45 and 55 have aging parents or in-laws as well as children under age twenty-one. This sandwich generation tries to balance their time and resources between caring for their children, advancing their careers, and providing care for their aging parents.[6]

The stress and financial burdens that are present during the latter stage of life can be overwhelming, including feeling guilty about burdening our stressed children. In many ways, for many of us, the better the relationship we build over the years with our children, the easier our aging years are likely to be. As we near the end, often our children are our main lifeline. It is never too late to start the building process. I have encountered families estranged for years who have reconciled sometimes because of a crisis and other times because one generation has grown internally. Children provide all kinds of assistance—physical, emotional, or financial—to parents, and aging parents continue to provide support to their adult children for as long as they can. When there is no exchange, parents become despondent.[7] Not being allowed to help our children can be detrimental to us. And, not having children who help may damage us in the long run. As we near the end, our children are often our main lifeline. Those who have maintained this lifeline will reap benefits. Our relationships with our adult children might determine the quality of the care we receive in our elder years.

Social Policy

Parenting is a mix of successes and failures, exhilaration and disappointment, harmony and discord. Each of us has our own unique blend of these ingredients. Some of the difficulties of intergenerational support are magnified or mitigated by social policies. Our intergenerational relationships are important to us on an emotional level, but they are also an important factor in America's cultural and economic fabric. In our society the generations are interdependent: so much depends on continuing family relationships because there are few institutional systems in place to pick up the slack when families fail to support one another. Most employers offer only limited maternity, paternity, and sick leave; many offer none at all. Many employers offer no affordable childcare, and many parents are uncomfortable leaving young children in institutional daycare centers of indeterminate quality; they may not be able to afford high-quality, dependable nannies or daycare. Thus working parents often rely on the grandparents to fill the care gap: when maternity leave has run out, when a child has a prolonged illness, or when a parent's job does not allow for adequate time off for any of the myriad complications that come with having a family, grandparents are asked to step in. At the same time, no laws require adult children to care for their aging parents, nor does the tax system provide incentive to do so, though some long-term care insurance policies pay for the services provided by family members. Moreover, the United States' Social Security system has not kept up with inflation and many elderly people find it difficult to survive on that pension alone. Thus parents must rely on their children and even on their grandchildren for assistance when they can no longer support themselves, financially or physically. When parents and adult children feel so alienated that they are unwilling to help each other, the whole economy suffers.

Use Your Wisdom

The glue that holds us together is affection. We need time and support for building and maintaining relationships. If you feel excited by the idea of crafting government policies to support families, then become politically active. You can do it by going to your local city hall and finding out about the political parties or interest groups in your town. If you are computer literate, finding groups on the Internet is easy. Expanding your own life is one of the important factors in continuing to develop your relationship with your children, and political activity is one way to do it. Public policy can affect both independence and connection. You not only help yourself, but also the greater society. Politics gives you a chance to influence others, to share your wisdom, and to leave a legacy. Our nation needs good people to run for school boards, attend town meetings, and participate in state legislatures. We need volunteers for town or city boards and commissions.

We cannot depend on the world to change itself; we have to make change happen. Look around: are there things you'd like to change to make your life as a parent or grandparent easier? Parents across the political spectrum have many issues in common, and if we join together to make our concerns and ideas known—across generations, geography, and party lines—we may become a force to be reckoned with. If we all remain isolated, we cannot work for policies that facilitate building good relationships such as paid family leave.

There are many ways we can use the hard-won wisdom we have earned as parents even if we are frustrated with our own families. Not all of us will be able to resolve our differences with our adult children. We or they may not have the time, the inclination, or the geographic proximity to do so. Whether you have peace in your own family or not, now that our first stage of parenting has ended many of us have time and energy to use our skills to benefit the greater "family," our society. We can mentor our friends' children, or help our children connect with others who can mentor them; we can tutor in schools or community centers or become a mentor to a new moms' support group. There is no dearth of need. Whatever our experience, it is useful to someone. If you have not been lucky in the lottery of life, you can share how you managed. Charlotte Bloomberg, the ninety-eight-year-old mother of New York City's mayor, told the *Boston Globe* why she volunteers: "I'm perfectly able to, and I like to do it, and they need people, so there is no need not to."[8] Many older parents are in a position to be on the giving end. We have emotional capital and wisdom to impart. We have much to give and potentially many years to give it. We all can keep giving and growing and learning.

The future looks good for parents and their adult children.[9] The boomers' children are reaching adulthood; as parents of adult children, they form a large and vocal cohort likely to press for policies to meet their needs. As immigration continues in

America and the numbers of intermarriages continue to expand, many of us will be exposed to new models of interacting with family members. This will increase our own repertoire of interpersonal skills. The popular press is already chronicling the changing ways families spend time together. We already see manifestations of these changes. Children and parents are going on trips, cooking, singing, and exercising together, and generally enjoying each other. Psychologists are reexamining long-held theories that the paragon of adulthood is the independent human being, and are instead emphasizing remaining connected rather than letting go.[10] Advice books for teenagers are emphasizing intergenerational conversation.[11] Even advertisements focus on the importance of parental discussion, as in "Parents: the antidote to drugs?" At the same time, though, we see the demonizing of "helicopter parents" who seek close and ongoing involvement with their college-age children.

We can also redefine and clarify our roles by joining together in small groups to identify our needs and wants more specifically. I encourage you to use this book to form groups to grapple with all the ambiguities of this phase of our lives. We can all learn from the ways others have handled situations. We can exchange ideas on both what to do and what to avoid. Appendix I provides guidelines for organizing and conducting those groups. Select a topic for each meeting, give each participant a chance to talk about his or her feelings about the topic, and over time, as more and more groups tease out what attitudes and laws inhibit close interactions, social change can result.

The power of small groups sharing their experiences is proven. It led to dramatic social change in the 1960s and 1970s after women and men gathered to talk about their lives. As more and more people begin to analyze the forces that encourage or discourage close connections, as they share their insights, maybe even write articles, soon the whole society is reexamining itself, its attitudes, and its laws and remolding them in light of new understandings. Maybe your group will figure out how to subsidize grandparents who give respite care or how to assist the sandwich generation, or how to mentor parents of emerging adults. Minimally, you will be able to share with others some of the things that work with your adult children. Who knows, your group might invent a new term to replace the oxymoron "adult child."

Some of you may be more comfortable talking about relationships "in the third person," for example by discussing books or movies. You can join or create a book or video club in which you talk about the main characters and their relationships. Appendix II lists a number of relevant readings. Appendix III suggests movies that should provoke thoughtful explorations. Or you can create a book club with the readings suggested in Appendix IV.

Our time is now. Though some of us will have many more years, many of us will have a much shorter time. Our days are numbered. They always were, but now we know it. This is the time to make amends, to focus on what really matters to us, to make peace with old demons, to forgive ourselves and our children. This is the time to make the world a bit better while we are here and the time to leave a legacy of goodwill with our families. It takes work to do this. Reframe when we see only the downside of ourselves and our relationships, focus on the positives. Nothing is perfect. Using our time to help others can make us feel better and might help others respect us. We cannot undo the past, but we can create a better future for ourselves and others by sharing the talents we have.

Whether you decide to become politically active, or you decide to join a formal group, I urge all of you to be proactive in your relationships. Think about them; modify them so that they bring both joy and sustenance to both you and your children. You have worked too hard not to enjoy the fruits of your labors. You can share what you have learned from years of work and from being part of a family and a community. You can motivate and mentor young people. You can listen, care, and praise good work. You can challenge, and teach and give feedback to young persons starting on their paths. As you do this you give purpose and meaning to your lives.

I end with a quote I found among the letters in my mother-in-law's attic. It was written by my soul sister from college, Barbara Friedman Chambers, who died in her early forties. Despite an Internet search, I do not know the source of the quote, but because of the person who gave it to me, it reminds me of the fragility of life, and because of its content, it helps when my relationships become strained:

"All human relations are ambivalent. The only complete relations are those in which hostility can be expressed and the relationship maintained."

13

YOURS TO WRITE

I leave this page blank to encourage you to write your story of how you forged new and enduring bonds with your adult children.

APPENDIX I:
HOW TO START
A SUPPORT GROUP

To form a group, gather eight to twelve people; they can be friends or strangers, they can be from one or many generations. Begin by introducing yourselves and describing your families. Then proceed by following the guidelines below. Pick a topic each week and make sure each person has a chance to express his or her point of view before others talk a second time.

Group Guidelines:

1. No one speaks twice until everyone speaks once or has had a chance to speak.
2. Make no comments on or criticisms of what another member has said during her or his turn.
3. What you say here in this group is confidential, not to be repeated outside of the group.
4. Your feelings are welcome here; talk in the first person about what you feel since there are no rights or wrongs with feelings.
5. You are not here to solve problems but to expand your knowledge.

This model changed the roles in American families as women and men all over the United States joined to discuss how they felt about their roles in the family during the sixties. It might just work as we forge new roles in this century.

APPENDIX II: FURTHER READINGS

This list is by no means comprehensive, but these are a few of my favorites, and those I found most helpful.

Adams, Jane. *I'm Still Your Mother: How to Get Along with Your Grown-up Children for the Rest of Your Life* (New York: Delacorte Press, 1994). You raised your kids to be independent, strong, and to think for themselves. Jane Adams interviewed over a hundred mothers and fathers of young adults to learn how they've created closer, more authentic relationships with their kids than they had with their own parents. She offers practical wisdom about how to keep families together even when distance tugs at the ties that bind, and gives sensible tips on how to get children out of your house as well as good advice about helping them to start their careers. She gives advice on getting along with children's mates, giving or lending money, offering or asking advice, and being a grandparent.

Adams, Jane. *When Our Grown Kids Disappoint Us* (New York: Free Press, 2003). This book is *very* worthwhile and discusses many issues. However, it states in the introduction and throughout the book that it is meant for parents of adult children who have problems (i.e., dependency issues, alcoholism, drug issues, etc.). The book goes on to discuss coping methods, beginning with admitting a problem, to "limits of love," and how to be a good parent to an adult child during rough times.

Campbell, Ross and Chapman, Gary. *Parenting Your Adult Child: How You Can Help Them Achieve Their Full Potential* (Chicago: Northfield Publishers, 1999). This book has a Christian focus. The authors provide superb insights and practical hints for relating to one's adult children. They discuss everyday issues that parents and adult children face—such as communication and dealing with life choices—rather than focusing on more difficult or unusual issues.

Coleman, Joshua. *When Parents Hurt: Compassionate Strategies When You and Your Grown Child Don't Get Along* (New York: Harper Collins, 2007). This book focuses on problems and troubled relationships, and offers very sound advice for negotiating difficult territory. The book also explores ways for parents to deal with their own emotions and reactions to their children's problems, suggesting ways to alleviate stress, worry, and guilt. This book has a very positive and realistic message about parenting in difficult times.

Davitz, Lois and Davitz, Joel. *Getting Along (Almost) With your Adult Kids: A Decade by Decade Guide* (Notre Dame: Sorin Books, 2003). While this book gives insight into adult developmental stages, it frequently suggests parental silence rather than more creative solutions. The book is worth reading, however, for its depiction of the tasks of each adult decade.

De Vaus, David, *Letting Go.* (New York: Oxford University Press, 1994). This is a very readable study of adult children and their relationships with both their mothers and their fathers. Although the interviews are of their children, the insights will benefit both children and parents. The author suggests that parent-child relationships fall into three broad categories: parent-centered, children-centered, and mutually attached. The author and subjects are Australian, but the issues discussed are universal. This book is useful in helping to diagnose the problems with one's child and for outlining what a good relationship might look like.

DiGeronimo, Theresa Foy. *How to Talk to Your Adult Children About Really Important Things* (San Francisco: Josey-Bass, 2002). This book tends to focus on problems, crises, or issues rather than healthy relationships. The chapters are broken down into life issues: alternative lifestyles, homosexuality, marriage, sibling relationships, divorce, etc. There is a great deal of advice especially for parents of adult children, including advice in their children's relationships, living together, and grandparenting.

Friedman, Edwin H. *Generation to Generation* (New York: Guildford Press, 1985). This book is intended for church and synagogue groups. However, it has a superb chapter with insights into family triangles. The author is comprehensive in his descriptions of how these triangles work and how to handle them. Also worth noting are its chapters on life cycle ceremonies, which can be useful for those with interfaith marriages in their families.

Gross, Zenith. *And You Thought It Was All Over!* (New York: St. Martin's/Marek, 1985). This book provides an examination of new parenting roles after the child is grown. Despite being more than twenty years old, the questions the book raises are still pertinent, demonstrating that parental concerns and the felt need for a good relationship with adult children is not new. Situations may change, but the desire for parents to reach out to their children does not. It is a thorough and accessible reference.

Isay, Jane. *Walking on Eggshells: Navigating the Delicate Relationship Between Adult Children and Parents* (New York: Doubleday Flying Dolphin Press, 2007). This book deals with healthy, normal relationships. Isay offers practical advice on a variety of topics as well as lengthy, thorough anecdotes. Using interviews and vignettes, she gives good practical advice. My own disagreement with her is that she suggests that parents should never, ever give advice. I suggest that it is acceptable to give advice, just don't expect it to always be followed.

Jacobs, Ruth Harriet. "Mothers, Daughters, Grandmothers, Granddaughters: Personal Reflections on Relationships." Wellesley College Center for Research on Women, 1982. This paper discusses the dilemmas that mothers, daughters, grandmothers, and granddaughters face in their relationships. Generations clash in views on behavior, sexual norms, and whether to start a family. Jacobs lists her rules for dealing with several generations.

Jonas, Susan and Nissenson, Marilyn. *Friends for Life* (New York: Morrow and Company, Inc., 1997). This book is very sensible reading about the mother-daughter relationship. Both authors have grown daughters, and they drew on their own experience as well as the stories of more than a hundred women across the country to address questions of lifestyle choices, communication, and generational differences.

Kidder, Rushworth M. *Moral Courage* (New York: Harper Collins Publishers, 2005). Kidder clearly delineates the "two rights," rather than right versus wrong, that cause conflict in hard moral situations. The conflicts people face are not between a right and a wrong, but rather deciding between two rights. These include deciding between long-term versus short-term solutions, or between individual growth and familial duty. This concept is especially important for parents to keep in mind as they watch their adult children make choices that are often radically different from the ones they would make.

Miller-Day, Michelle A. *Communication Among Grandmothers, Mothers, and Adult Daughters* (Mahwah, NJ: Lawrence Erlbaum Associates, 2004).This books details a study of three generations in different families, focusing on the structure of these families and how this affected behavior and feeling in each respective family. The families in which there were many problems, such as anorexia, suicide, and depression, tended to be "enmeshed" families, that is, families in which the younger generations are expected to bow to the desires of the older generations. In "embedded" families, each generation was encouraged to develop and stand by their own opinions, allowing for a more open atmosphere. The book focuses on the quality of understanding. The author advises parents to let go of the expectation that adult children should take any and all advice that parents offer.

Tannen, Deborah. *You're Wearing THAT? Understanding Mothers and Daughters in Conversation* (New York: Random House, 2006). This book focuses solely on mothers and daughters and only on conversations, but it is an excellent tool for learning how to communicate effectively. Rather than focusing on solutions or answers, Tannen examines the many layers of meaning in the ways that mothers and daughters communicate. Relying heavily on anecdotes, the author lets the different conversations speak for themselves, allowing the reader to see what works and what doesn't.

APPENDIX III:
FILMS AND VIDEOS

View these films alone or in groups to help explore issues of parenting adult children. The list is by no means comprehensive. Please feel free to add to this list.

Mothers and Daughters

Terms of Endearment: A mother and daughter lead different lifestyles and struggle to maintain their relationship. Stubborn, independent Emma sees her mother as overbearing and intrusive, but Aurora only wants what is best for her daughter. The film spans thirty years, and throughout it we see the different ways that people express love and caring.

Antonia's Line: The story of Antonia and her relationship with her daughter and granddaughter. The film explores the way four different generations relate to and accept one another.

The Joy Luck Club: Four Chinese women in America meet every week to play mah-jongg. The story explores their lives in America and in China, and focuses especially on the contrasts between themselves and their Westernized, Chinese American daughters.

Autumn Sonata: Charlotte, a world-famous pianist, visits her daughters after years of neglecting them in favor of her career. One is mentally impaired, and the other has taken her out of the institution where Charlotte placed her. Tension builds until daughter and mother finally confront each other with all the things they've never said.

Gas, Food and Lodging: A single mother working as a waitress in New Mexico struggles to raise two teenage girls who dream of leaving their small town. One dreams of having a father and a "normal" family, while another sleeps around and defies their mother.

Mildred Pierce: A devoted and doting mother spoils her ungrateful and manipulative daughter. A reconciliation only leads to more tears when mother concedes to her daughter's every demand. A good warning on the dangers of overindulgence and trying to give our children everything we never had.

One True Thing: A career-driven New Yorker is brought home to upstate New York when her mother is diagnosed with terminal illness. She resents having to quit her job and leave her boyfriend to care of her dying mother, but she begins to learn more about her mother and father and the lives they've led, and this brings her to reflect on her own life.

Secrets and Lies: A lonely, world-weary mother who struggles with her sullen daughter and a difficult relationship with her brother is contacted by the child she gave away. The two quickly develop a close bond, but this new relationship brings into sharp relief all the problems in both of their lives. This film explores the different ways people react when confronted by hard truths.

'Night Mother: An intensely honest film that follows a mother as she tries to talk her daughter out of suicide. The film deals with emotionally difficult issues, such as a mother's powerlessness over her daughter's epilepsy, and the blame and shame they both feel.

Steel Magnolias: A story of female friendship and of the tensions and love between mother and daughter. A diverse group of women meet in the local beauty shop to gossip, grouse, and celebrate their lives with one another. The film focuses on the strength women find to help each other through hard times.

Fathers and Sons

My Son, the Fanatic: The son of a Pakistani cab driver living in England becomes an Islamic fundamentalist and begins to reject his family's Westernized ideals. The film explores the effect of his behavior on his mother and father, and the ways that families cope with divergent views and the way parents cope with disappointment.

Big Fish: A charming, charismatic father upstages his son at his wedding; as a result the son doesn't talk to his father until he is on his deathbed. There the son finally confesses to his father how much he resents him, but realizes how much he is like his father. This film explores how we must accept what in ourselves is like our parents.

A River Runs Through It: The story of a Presbyterian minister and his two sons, who have nothing in common but a love of fishing. Father and sons drift apart, but retain a lifelong connection. It is the story of a father powerless to help a son who goes astray through drinking, women, and gambling. It deals with difficult truths, such as "when love is not enough."

The Chosen: Set in New York in the 1940s, the story revolves around the friendship between an orthodox Jew and a Chasidic Jew. The son of the Chasidic rabbi chooses not to follow his father into the rabbinate, and his father must learn to accept it. The other father and son have a tender, intimate relationship, and are great role models for sharing and caring. The film artfully depicts a bygone era in which sons were expected to respect their fathers' wishes.

Death of a Salesman: This heartbreaking classic is the story of Willy Lohman, a failing salesman. About to lose his job and confronted with the emptiness in his life, he must also face his sons, who do not respect him and who seem unable to realize their potential.

Bicycle Thief: The classic film about an Italian who has just found a job, only to have the bicycle he needs for work stolen. His adoring son watches him search for it, learning from his father determination and strength in the face of adversity.

Bopha! "Bopha!" means "detain that person!" When a policeman in South Africa finds that his son has joined the anti-apartheid movement, he finds himself torn between his devotion to his family and his sense of duty.

The Sum of Us: The story of two gay young men. One's father disowns him while the other wants only the best for his son, but his open-mindedness and desire to "support" his son in his search for true love border on being annoying and overbearing.

American Chai: An excellent story about the conflicts between generations and cultures. A young Indian American, graduating from college with a music degree, has let his overbearing, traditionalist father believe he is a pre-medical student. This film explores the conflicts when children do not follow the advice of their parents.

Voyage 'Round My Father: A successful lawyer, struck with blindness in middle age, continues his battles in the courtroom with the assistance of his family. His son deals with bitter memories of their relationship, but also seeks his father's respect and love and in the process learns to love in return.

Cat on a Hot Tin Roof: An alcoholic with a troubled marriage is forced to confront a long history of resentment and spite when he discovers that his father is dying of cancer. The film explores what can happen to families and individuals when they are surrounded by secrets and pent-up emotions.

Mothers and Sons

Dancer in the Dark: An idealized depiction of a mother who willingly sacrifices her life for her child. It is against this ideal that mothers are judged.

A Touch of Pink: A Canadian Pakistani lives in England with his male lover. When his mother comes to visit he tries to hide the fact that he is gay. The partner befriends the mother. When his mother discovers the relationship, she goes home very upset. The surprise ending leads us to question the morality of "staying in the closet."

The Namesake: This story of an Indian family's adjustment to America clearly depicts the growth and conflicts within each individual in the family and among all the members. It is a touching story of how both mother and son develop and find strength in each other despite their differences.

Fathers and Daughters

Father of the Bride: A devoted but nervous father is unready to face his daughter's wedding. Funny and often silly, the movie nonetheless takes a good look at the difficulty fathers have with letting their daughters grow up, and suggests ways to make them feel more comfortable with the idea.

Guess Who's Coming to Dinner? A daughter brings home a charming, successful black man who she intends to marry. Her father is upset and eventually comes to respect his future son-in-law. While this movie focuses on race, it brings out many of the feelings surrounding any marriage between members of different social groups. It also is an excellent film about accepting our children's choices, even when they differ from our own.

Both Parents and Children

In the Bedroom: Frank's parents are uncomfortable with his son's girlfriend, an older woman with two young children and an unfriendly, unwelcome ex-husband. When tragedy strikes their son, Matt and Ruth struggle to cope with the turns their lives have taken. A film that calls in to question when it is appropriate to intervene in a child's life, and that emphasizes the importance of honesty and openness.

What's Cooking? It's Thanksgiving, and four families from very different ethnic backgrounds must deal with secrets and lies, cultural clashes and generational disputes. No matter your ethnicity, family foibles will abound, and this film compares and contrasts the troubles and prevailing connections in very different families.

Long Day's Journey: The story of a family of four people—a drug-addicted mother, a failed-actor father, an alcoholic son, and a son with a wasting illness—who are so self-centered and so concerned with their own problems that they cannot help one another.

APPENDIX IV: LITERATURE FOR BOOK CLUBS

This list is just a beginning, but each title explores intergenerational relationships and can lead to marvelous insights and discussions.

Antin, Mary. *The Promised Land*. Cambridge: The Riverside Press, 1925.

Balzac, Honoré de. *Le Pére Goriot*. New York: W.W. Norton & Co, 1998.

Cisneros, Sandra. *The House on Mango Street*. New York: Vintage Books, 1984.

Danticat, Edwidge. *Breath, Eyes, Memory*. New York: Vintage, Inc., 1998.

Eliot, George. *The Mill on the Floss*. London: W. Blackwood, 1907.

Lahiri, Jhumpa. *The Namesake*. New York: Houghton & Mifflin, 2004.

Marshall, Paule. *Daughters*. New York: Plume, 1992.

Miller, Arthur. *Death of a Salesman*. New York: Penguin Classics, 1998.

Morrison, Toni. *Beloved*. New York: Penguin, 1998.

Munro, Alice. *Lives of Girls and Women*. New York: McGraw Hill-Ryerson, 1971.

Norman, Marsha. *'Night Mother*. New York: Hill and Wang, 1983.

Potok, Chaim. *The Chosen*. New York: Simon and Schuster, 1967.

Roth, Philip. *Portnoy's Complaint*. New York Vintage, 1994.

Smith, Betty. *A Tree Grows in Brooklyn*. New York: Harper & Row, 1943.

Tyler, Anne. *Digging to America*. New York: Knopf, 2006.

Sophocles. *Antigone, Oedipus the King.* Oxford: Oxford University Press, 1998.

Sophocles. *Electra.* New York: Penguin Books, 1953.

Tan, Amy. *The Joy Luck Club.* New York: Ballantine Books, 1990.

Williams, Tennessee. *Cat on a Hot Tin Roof.* New York: New Directions Publishing, 1955.

Woolf, Virginia. *Moments of Being: Second Edition.* San Diego: Harvest Books, 1985.

NOTES

Preface

1. Donald Super, *Vocational Development: A Framework for Research* (New York: Teachers College, Columbia University, 1957).
2. Bernice Neugarten, *Middle Age and Aging* (Chicago: University of Chicago Press, 1968).
3. J. James and N. Zarrett, "Ego integrity in the lives of older women: A follow-up of mothers from the Sears, Maccoby, and Levin (1952) Patterns of Child Rearing Study." *Journal of Adult Development* 12 (2005): 155–167.

Introduction

1. I am indebted to Mary Mason and Bonnie Sherr Klein for pointing out the complexity and ambiguity of the terms "health," "illness," and "disability." They also emphasize that persons with disabilities create their own individual ways of parenting and grandparenting. Mary Mason, Keynote Address, "Taking Care: A Disabled Mother's Dialogue with her Daughter," October 20, 2007, Association for Research on Mothering (ARM) Toronto, Canada. She is also the author of *Life Prints: A Memoir of Healing and Discovery,* (Berkeley, CA: Feminist Press, 2000). Bonnie Sherr Klein, director, *Shameless: the ART of Disability,* National Film Board of Canada (2006) and author of *Slow Dance: A Story of Stroke, Love, and Disability* (Toronto: Vintage Canada, 1997).
2. United Nations World Population Prospects: 2006 revision.

3. U.S. Census Bureau, "Participation in Adult Education: 2004 to 2005," 2007 Statistical Abstract. http://www.census.gov/prod/2006pubs/07statab/educ.pdf.

4. U.S. Census Bureau, "Civilian Labor Force Participation with Projections: 1980 to 2014," 2007 Statistical Abstract. http://www.census.gov/prod/2006pubs/07statab/labor.pdf.

5. U.S. Census Bureau, "Marital Status of the Population by Sex, Race, and Hispanic Origin: 1990–2005," 2007 Statistical Abstract. http://www. census.gov/prod/2006pubs/07statab/pop.pdf.

6. Since the Virginia Tech incident, colleges are reevaluating their strict interpretations of FERPA.

7. David G. Weisstrub, Serge Gauthier Thomasma, and George F. Tomossy, eds., *Aging: Caring for our Elders* (Dordrecht/Boston/London: Kluwer Academic Publishers, 2001).

8. U.S. Census Bureau, "Civilian Labor Force Participation with Projections: 1980 to 2014," 2007 Statistical Abstract.

9. Joan Aldous and David M. Klein, "Sentiments and Services: Models of Intergenerational Relationships in Mid-life," *Journal of Marriage and the Family* 53 (August 1991): 595–608.

10. T. H. Brubaker and E. Brubaker, "Family Caregiving in the U.S.: An Issue of Gender Differences?" in *Family Care of the Elderly: Social and Cultural*, ed. J. L. Kosberg, 210–231. (Newbury Park, CA: Sage, 1992).

11. Umberson, 1992.

12. Chris Knoester, "Transitions in Young Adulthood and the Relationship between Parent and Offspring Well-being," *Social Forces* 81 no. 4 (2003): 1433–1444, provides a review of previous studies showing the interrelatedness of parents and adult children over the life course. A family "offers individuals a feeling of connectedness to society." The parent-child bond is especially important because "the relationship is permanent and involuntary," "parents and children remain connected through their shared histories," "parents and their children are encouraged by societal norms to identify themselves with one another throughout the life course," "parents and their children share many beliefs and values," and "because of increased longevity, the life spans of parents and their children overlap more now than ever." See also: Debra Umberson, "Relationships between Adult Children and Their Parents: Psychological Consequences for Both Generations," *Journal of Marriage and the Family*, 54, no. 3 (August 1992): 664–674.

13. Albert Ellis developed the concept of Rational Emotive Behavior Therapy in the 1950s. The method requires people to focus on their current lives and then take steps to change their behaviors. He and I both believe people can change themselves. His methods and those of Dr. Aaron Beck provide the basis for cognitive behavior therapy. While this book is *not* therapy, the notion that one can modify one's behavior is based in their theories.

1 Don't Let Go, Don't Bite Your Tongue

1. Caryl Rivers, *Selling Anxiety: How the News Media Scare Women* (Lebanon, NH: University Press of New England, 2007).
2. Dave Marcus, "A Generation of Parents Learns to Let Go," *Newsday. com*, June 17, 2007. http://www.newsday.com/news/local/education/ ny-libye0617,0,4334678.story.
3. Progressive Business Audio Conferences held a "webnar," a conference on the web entitled "Difficult Parents on Campus: Tips to Handle 'Helicopter Behavior,'" which addressed this emerging issue.
4. Luann Brizendine, in *The Female Brain* (New York: Broadway Books, 2006), suggests that we are just learning about how hormones and other chemicals affect men and women's brains.
5. Barbara Crooker, "In October, Everything Starts to Come Apart," *Whetstone*, (Barrington, IL: 2001).
6. Chaim Ginott, a school teacher turned psychologist, talked about "congruent communication." He advocated for consistency in communicating with children because he thought poor communication could "damage progeny" and hinder the formation of healthy relationships. (www.hodu.com).
7. Judith Warner, *Perfect Madness: Mothering in the Age of Anxiety* (New York: Riverhead Trade, 2006). This book talks about the extreme perfectionism that drives motherhood in the current era and analyzes its impact on today's mothers and children.
8. Joyce Antler, in *You Never Call! You Never Write! A History of the Jewish Mother* (New York: Oxford University Press, 2007), elucidates the interaction between culture and popular images. She says: "Although novels about Jewish mothers in the 1970s also blamed mothers for being weak and submissive, or malevolent, it was through film and television that the 'whining' and 'nagging,' overbearing Jewish mother

reigned over the public imagination" (p. 170). She credits Janet Burstein's *Writing Mothers, Writing Daughters: Tracing the Maternal in Stories by Jewish Women* (Urbana, IL: University of Illinois Press, 1996) for illuminating mothers and daughters in 1970s fiction (especially chapter four) for this insight.

9. The issue of grandparental rights in divorces varies by state. Visitation rights can be denied or granted as mandated by court order. For more information, visit http://www.divorcehq.com/grandparent.html.

10. Carl J. Boyd, "Mothers and Daughters: A Discussion of Theory and Research," *Journal of Marriage and the Family* 51 no. 2 (May 1989): 291–301.

2   Know Yourself

1. Barry Kosmin, "1990 National Jewish Population Survey," *Council of Jewish Federations* (1991). Fifty-two percent of Jews who have married have done so outside the faith.

2. U.S. Census Bureau, *"Immigration 1901–2005,"* 2007 Statistical Abstract, http://www.census.gov/prod/2006pubs/07statab/pop.pdf.

3. Beverly Birns and Dale F. Hay, *The Different Faces of Motherhood* (New York: Springer, 1988) and Paula J. Caplan, *Don't Blame Mother: Mending the Mother-Daughter Relationship* (New York: Harper and Row, 1989) both address the "mother-blaming" phenomenon.

4. U.S. Census Bureau, "Income of Families and Primary Individuals by Selected Characteristics—Occupied Units," American Housing Survey (2005). http://www.census.gov/hhes/www/housing/ahs/ahs05/tab220.html.

3   Say Goodbye to Fantasy and Hello to Reality

1. U.S. Census Bureau, "Married Couples by Labor Force Status of the Spouse: 1986 to 2005," 2007 Statistical Abstract, http://www.census.gov/prod/2006pubs/07statab/labor.pdf.

2. U.S. Census Bureau, "United States: Selected Social Characteristics," American Community Survey (2002), http://www.census.gov/acs/www/Products/Profiles/Single/2002/ACS/Tabular/010/01000US2.htm.

3. U.S. Census Bureau, "Marital Status of the Population by Sex and Age: 2005," 2007 Statistical Abstract. http://www.census.gov/prod/2006pubs/07statab/pop.pdf.

4   Emerging Adulthood

1. Elizabeth Bernstein, "A Mother Takes on MIT," *Wall Street Journal*, September 10, 2007: 1.
2. Samuel G. Freedman, "Calling the Folks about Campus Drinking," *New York Times*, September 12, 2007. The University of Wisconsin has started a parent notification program and is asking parents to become partners with them in reducing binge drinking. They alert parents if the child is found to have a high blood alcohol level.
3. Michelle Miller-Day, *Communication Among Grandmothers, Mothers, and Adult Daughters* (Mahwah, NJ: Lawrence Erlbaum Associates, 2004).
4. Rushworth M. Kidder, *Moral Courage* (New York: Harper Collins, 2005). Kidder posits that most people know right from wrong, but that adults differ on various continua in decision making.
5. According to www.socialsecurity.gov, the "normal" age of retirement depends on your birth year. For example, for those born before 1938, the age of retirement is sixty-five. For those born between 1938 and 1955, the age increased by two months with every year until the age leveled out at sixty years old. Now, the age of retirement reaches its maximum at age seventy.
6. Miranda Hitti, "Older Moms Among Latest Birth Trends in U.S.," *WebMD Medical News*, March 7, 2005. http://women.webmd.com/news/20050307/older-moms-among-latest-birth-trends-in-us. Although many women still have babies in their twenties, the window of opportunity is expanding into the mid-thirties. Those women aged thirty to forty-four are experiencing the highest birth rate in thirty years.
7. U.S. Bureau of Labor Statistics, "Number of Jobs Held, Labor Market Activity, and Earnings Growth Among Younger Baby Boomers: Recent Results from a Longitudinal Survey," August 25, 2004, http://www.bls.gov/nls/nlsy79r20.pdf.
8. Daniel Altman, "Managing Globalization: Has it Hurt the U.S. Worker?" *The Herald Tribune*, April 18, 2007, http://yaleglobal.yale.edu/display.article?id=9075.

5 Refilling the Nest

1. Pulte Homes, Inc., "Empty Nester Syndrome: When the Kids Go Away Will the Baby Boomers Play?" *Del Webb Baby Boomer Survey* (2004), http://www.pulte.com/PressRoom/2004BabyBoomer/BabyBoomerDet ailReport.pdf.

2. Department of Health and Human Services, Centers for Disease Control and Prevention, National Center for Health Statistics, "Cohabitation, Marriage, Divorce, and Remarriage in the United States," July 2002. http://www.cdc.gov/nchs/data/series/sr_23/sr23_022.pdf.

3. "National Jewish Population Survey 2000–01," United Jewish Communities, 2004. http://www.ujc.org/local_includes/downloads/5086.pdf.

4. U.S. Census Bureau, "Fertility of American Women: June 2004," December 2005, http://www.census.gov/prod/2006pubs/07statab/ vitstat.pdf.

5. U.S. Census Bureau, "Children's Living Arrangements and their Characteristics: March 2002," Annual Demographic Supplement to the March 2002 Current Population Survey. http://www.census.gov/ population/socdemo/hh-fam/tabAD-1.pdf.

6. I am indebted to Sherry Israel, retired associate professor, Hornstein Program, Brandeis University, for clarifying the concept of public and private space within the home.

7. Mireya Navarro, "My Child's Divorce is My Pain," *New York Times*, September 2, 2007.

8. U.S. Census Bureau, "Married Couples by Labor Force Status of Spouse: 1986 to 2005," 2007 Statistical Abstract, http://www.census.gov/prod/ 2006pubs/07statab/labor.pdf.

6 Relationships

1. In his *Boston Globe* article, "Downside of Diversity," Michael Jones quotes Robert Putnam author of *Bowling Alone:* "Growing up in the 1950s in a small Midwestern town Putnam knew the religion of virtually every member of his high school graduation class because, he says, 'such information was crucial to the question of "who was a possible mate or date."' The importance of marrying within one's faith has largely faded. . . ."

2. comScore Networks, "Online Paid Content: U.S. Market Spending Report," Online Publishers Association, 2005.
3. Bruce Tulgan and Carolyn A. Martin, *Managing Generation Y: Global Citizens Born in the Late Seventies and Early Eighties* (Amherst, MA: HRD Press, 2001).
4. Diane Swanbrow, "Intimate Relationships between Races More Common Than Thought," University of Michigan News Service, March 23, 2000, http://www.umich.edu/news/index.html?Releases/2000/Mar00/r032300a.
5. U.S. Census Bureau, "Married Couples by Race and Hispanic Origin of Spouses: 1980 to 2005," 2007 Statistical Abstract. http://www.census.gov/prod/2006pubs/07statab/pop.pdf.
6. U.S. Census Bureau, "Resident Population by Race, Hispanic Origin, and Age: 2000–2005," 2007 Statistical Abstract, http://www.census.gov/prod/2006pubs/07statab/pop.pdf.
7. U.S. Census Bureau, "Current Population Survey, March and Annual Social and Economic Supplements, 2005 and Earlier," http://www.census.gov/population/socdemo/hh-fam/ms2.pdf.
8. U.S. Census Bureau, "Unmarried-Partner Households by Sex of Partners: 2004," 2007 Statistical Abstract, http://www.census.gov/prod/2006pubs/07statab/pop.pdf.
9. Books such as *The Sexual Spectrum: Why We Are All Different* by neuropsychologist Olive Skene Johnson can help parents understand a parents' role in homosexuality.
10. U.S. Census Bureau, "Married Couples and Unmarried Partner Households," Census 2000 Special Report, February 2003. http://www.census.gov/prod/2003pubs/censr-5.pdf.
11. For more information, visit http://www.sec.state.vt.us/otherprg/civilunions/civilunions.html or http://www.glad.org/marriage/howtogetmarried.html.

7 Weddings

1. This knowledge derives from the personal experience and travels of both my family members and myself.
2. Judith Martin, *Miss Manners on Weddings* (New York: Crown, 1999).

3. Edgar Schein, *Organizational Culture and Leadership* (San Francisco: Jossey-Bass, 1992), 30. "A culture exists in an organization when a group has enough shared history to form a set of shared assumptions." By this definition every family is a culture. Schein writes about businesses, but the concept is equally relevant to families.

8 Grandparenting

1. Nell Porter Brown, "Grand Adventures: Finding Family Time Away from Home," *Harvard Magazine Online*, July–August 2006, http://www.harvardmagazine.com/on-line/070641.html.

2. CDC, *Assisted Reproductive Technology Report: 2005 Preliminary Accessible National Summary*, http://www.apps.nccd.cdc.gov/AR2005/nation05acc.asp.

3. Victor Flango and Carol Flango, *The Flow of Adoption Information from the States* (Williamsburg, VA: National Center for State Courts, 1994).

4. P. L. Maza, *Adoption Trends: 1944–1975*. Child Welfare Research Notes #9 (Washington, DC: Administration for Children, Youth, and Families, 1984).

5. K. S. Stolley, "Statistics on Adoption," *The Future of Children: Adoption* 3, no. 1 (Spring 1993), http://www.futureofchildren.org/usr_doc/vol3no1entire_journal.PDF.

6. U.S. Department of State, *Immigrant Visas Issued to Orphans Coming to the U.S.*, http://travel.state.gov/family/adoption/stats/stats_451.html.

7. U.S. Census Bureau, "Births to Teens, Unmarried Mothers, and Prenatal Care: 1990 to 2004," 2007 Statistical Abstract, http://www.census.gov/prod/2006pubs/07statab/vitstat.pdf.

8. Anne Holden, "Who Needs a Grandpa?" *Inkling Magazine*, August 2, 2007, http://www.inklingmagazine.com/articles/comments/who-needs-a-grandpa/.

9. Natalie Angier, "Weighing the Grandma Factor: In Some Societies, It's a Matter of Life and Death," *New York Times*, November 5, 2002.

10. Jennifer Lee, "The Incredible Flying Granny Nanny," *New York Times*, May 10, 2007.

11. Peter Flemming, "Where Should Babies Sleep at Night? A Review of the Evidence from the CESDI SUDI Study," *Mothering Magazine*, September/October 2002, http://www.mothering.ocm/articles/new_baby/sleep/fleming.html.

12. Nicholas Wade, "Is Do Unto Others Written into our Genes?" *New York Times*, September 18, 2007.

9 Money

1. Baldwin Haspel, LLC website, "Louisiana is the only State that provides for forced heirship, that is, a percentage of one's estate that must be left to one's children. At various times in the State's history, forced heirship consisted of one-third of an individual's estate (if he or she had one child), one-half of an estate for individuals who had two children and two-thirds of an estate for individuals having three or more children." But now they have reduced the shares and made it applicable only until the child is twenty-four years old with an exception for handicapped children.
2. Daniel C. Vocek, "States Let Adult Kids Keep Insurance Longer," *Stateline.org*, August 15, 2007, http://www.stateline.org/live/details/story?contentId=232292.
3. Neale Godfrey, *Money Still Doesn't Grow on Trees: A Parent's Guide to Raising Financially Responsible Teenagers and Young Adults* (Emmaus, PA: Rodale Books, 2004).
4. Lydia I. Marek and Jay A. Mancini, *Mother-Child Relationship Quality and Support Patterns in Adulthood*, Department of Family and Child Development, Virginia Polytechnic Institute and State University, Blacksburg, VA. Presented at the annual meeting of the National Council on Family Relations, Seattle, Washington, November 1990.
5. Sandra Block, "Students Suffocate Under Tens of Thousands in Loans," *USA Today*, February 23, 2006, http://www.usatoday.com/money/perfi/general/2006-02-22-studentloans-usat_x.htm.
6. M. Thakor and S. Kedar, *On My Own Two Feet* (Avon, MA: Adams Media , 2007), and Beth Kobliner, *Get a Financial Life: Personal Finance in Your Twenties and Thirties* (New York: Fireside Press, 2000).
7. Anna Bahney, "The Bank of Mom and Dad," *New York Times*, April 20, 2006.
8. Anya Kamenetz, *Generation Debt* (New York: Riverhead, 2006) and Tamara Drair Eclore, *Strapped: Why 20 and 30 Somethings Can't Get Ahead* (New York: Doubleday, 2006).

9. Christopher Shea, "Are Parents Getting Short-Changed?" *Boston Globe*, April 11, 2004.
10. Andrea O'Reilly and Sharon Abbey, eds. *Mothers and Daughters: Connection, Empowerment, and Transformation* (Lanahm, MD: Rowman and Littlefield, 2000).
11. Tamara D. Golish, "Changes in Closeness between Adult Children and Their Parents: A Turning Point Analysis," *Communication Reports*, Summer 2000.
12. Thakor and Kedar, *On My Own Two Feet* (Avon, MA: Adams Media) 2007.
13. Ninette Sosa, Bob Franken, Rich Phillips, and Susan Candiotti, "Terry Schiavo has Died," Cnn.com, March 31, 2005, http://www.cnn.com/2005/LAW/03/31/schiavo/index.html.
14. I am indebted to Elinor Yudin Sachse, Ph.D. for coauthoring this chapter.

10 Eternal Triangles

1. Michael E. Kerr and Murray Bowen, MD, *Family Evaluation: An Approach Based on Bowen Theory* (New York: W.W. Norton & Company, 1988). Edwin H. Friedman, *Generation to Generation: Family Process in Church and Synagogue* (New York: Guilford Press, 1985). Kerr, Bowen, and Friedman talk about how basic the triangle is to all human dynamics, in families and institutions. Many of the ideas in this chapter are based on their work.
2. Karen Hube, "Baby-sit? Maybe Next Time," *Wall Street Journal Online*, September 22, 2007.
3. Karen Fingerman, "The Role of Offspring and In-Laws in Grandparents' Ties to Grandchildren," *Journal of Family Issues* 25 no. 8 (November 2004): 1026–1049.

11 Communication Tips

1. Charles Lemert and Ann Branaman, ed., *The Goffman Reader* (Oxford: Blackwell Publishing Limited, 1997): 27.

12   Conclusion

1. John Ermisch, "Fairness in the Family: Implications for Parent-Adult Child Interactions." *Lecture at the Policy Studies Institute*, November 21, 2004.
2. Mayur M. Desai, Harold R. Lentzner, and Julie Dawson Weeks, "Unmet Need for Personal Assistance with Activities of Daily Living Among Older Adults," *The Gerontologist* 41 (2001): 82–88.
3. Merrill Silverstein. "Do Close Parent-Child Relations Reduce the Mortality Risk of Older Parents?" *Journal of Health and Social Behavior* 32 no. 4 (Dec. 1991): 382–395.
4. *National Alliance for Caregiving*, 2004.
5. Adam Shapiro, "Later Life Divorce and Parent-Adult Child Contact," *Journal of Family Issues* 24 no. 2 (March 2003): 264–285.
6. www.sandwichgeneration.com. This term, sandwich generation, has become an increasingly prevalent concept in pop culture and numerous websites offer advice.
7. Ermisch, 2004.
8. Rich Barlow, "A Bloomberg's Love Affair with Faith," *Boston Globe*. September 1, 2007.
9. Pew Research Center, "Adult Children and Parents Talking More Often," February 23, 2006.
10. Jean Baker, *Toward a Psychology of Women* (Boston: Beacon Press, 1976). Researchers at the Stone Center at Wellesley College have posited that the mature adult needs interdependence.
11. Anne Fishel, *Treating the Adolescent in Family Therapy: A Narrative and Developmental Approach* (Lanham, MD: Jason Aronson, 1999).

BIBLIOGRAPHY

Aldous, Joan and M. David Klein. "Sentiments and Services: Models of Intergenerational Relationships in Mid-life." *Journal of Marriage and the Family* (August 1991): 595–608.

Altman, Daniel. "Managing Globalization: Has it Hurt the U.S. Worker?" *International Herald Tribune.* April 18, 2007. http://yaleglobal.yale.edu/display.article?id=9075.

Angier, Natalie. "Weighing the Grandma Factor: In Some Societies, It's a Matter of Life and Death." *New York Times,* November 5, 2002.

Antler, Joyce. *You Never Call! You Never Write! A History of the Jewish Mother.* Oxford University Press, 2007.

Bahney, Anna. "The Bank of Mom and Dad." *New York Times,* April 20, 2006.

Banks, Amy, and Judith Jordan. "The Human Brain: Hardwired for Connections." *Research and Action Report* (Wellesly Centers for Women), Spring/Summer 2007.

Barlow, Rich. "A Bloomberg's Love Affair with Faith." *Boston Globe,* September 1, 2007.

Bernstein, Elizabeth. "A Mother Takes on MIT." *Wall Street Journal,* September 10, 2007: 1.

Birns, Beverly, and Dale F. Hay. *The Different Faces of Motherhood.* New York: Springer, 1998.

Block, Sandra. "Students Suffocate Under Tens of Thousands in Loans." *USA Today.* Feburary 23, 2006. http://www.usatoday.com/money/perfi/general/2006–02–22-studentloans-usat_x.htm.

Boyd, Carl J. "Mothers and Daughers: A Discussion of Theory and Research." *Journal of Marriage and the Family* 51, no. 2 (May 1989): 291–301.

Brizendine, Luann. *The Female Brain.* New York: Broadway Books, 2006.

Brubaker, T. H, and E. Brubaker. "Family Caregiving in the U.S.: An Issue of Gender Differences?" in *Family Care of the Elderly: Social and Cultural*, edited by J. L. Kosberg, 210–231. Newbury Park, CA: Sage, 1992.

Burstein, Janet. *Writing Mothers, Writing Daughters: Tracing the Maternal in Stories by Jewish Women*. Urbana, IL: University of Illinois Press, 1996.

Caplan, Paula J. *Don't Blame Mother: Mending the Mother-Daughter Relationship*. New York: Harper and Row, 1989.

Centers for Disease Control and Prevention. *Assisted Reproductive Technology Report: 2005 Preliminary Accessible National Summary*. http://www.apps.nccd.cdc.gov/AR2005/nation05acc.asp.

Crooker, Barbara. "In October, Everything Starts to Come Apart." *Whetstone* (Barrington, IL: 2001).

Department of Health and Human Services. "Cohabitation, Marriage, Divorce, and Remarriage in the United States." Centers for Disease Control and Prevention: National Center for Health Statistics. July 2002. http://www.cdc.gov/nchs/data/series/sr_23/sr23_022.pdf.

Eclore, Tamara Drair. *Strapped: Why 20 and 30 Somethings Can't Get Ahead*. New York: Doubleday, 2006.

Ermisch, John. "Fairness in the Family: Implications for Parent-Adult Child Interactions." *Lecture at the Policy Studies Institute*. November 21, 2004.

Fingerman, Karen. "The Role of Offspring and Children-in-law in Grandparents' Relationships with Grandchildren." *Journal of Family Issues* 25, no. 8 (November 2006): 1026–1049.

Fishel, Anne. *Treating the Adolescent in Family Therapy: A Narrative and Developmental Approach*. Lanham, MD: Jason Aronson, 1999.

Flango, Victor, and Carol Flango. *The Flow of Adoption Information from the States*. Williamsburg, VA: National Center for State Courts, 1994.

Flemming, Peter. "Where Should Babies Sleep at Night? A Review of the Evidence from the CESDI SUDI Study." *Mothering Magazine*. September/October 2002. http://www.mothering.ocm/articles/new_baby/sleep/fleming.html.

Freedman, Samuel G. "Calling the Folks about Campus Drinking." *New York Times*, September 12, 2007.

Friedman, Edwin H. *Generation to Generation: Family Process in Church and Synagogue*. New York: Guilford Press, 1985.

Godfrey, Neale. *Money Still Doesn't Grow on Trees: A Parent's Guide to Raising Financially Responsible Teenagers and Young Adults*. Emmaus, PA: Rodale Books, 2004.

Hitti, Miranda. "Older Moms Among Latest Birth Trends in the U.S." *WebMD Medical News.* March 7, 2005. http://women.webmd.com/news/20050307/older-moms-among-latest-birth-trends-in-us.

Holden, Anne. "Who Needs a Grandpa Anyway?" *Inkling Magazine.* August 2007. http://www.inklingmagazine.com/articles/comments/who-needs-a-grandpa/.

Hube, Karen. "Baby-sit? Maybe Next Time." *Wall Street Journal Online,* September 27, 2007.

Johnson, Olive Skene. *The Sexual Spectrum: Why We are All Different.* Vancouver: Raincoast Books, 2004.

Jonas, Michael. "Downside of Diversity." *Boston Globe,* April 5, 2007. http://www.boston.com/news/globe/ideas/articles/2007/08/04/the_downside_of_diversity.

Kamenetz, Anya. *Generation Debt.* New York: Riverhead, 2006.

Kerr, Michael E., and Murray Bowen. *Family Evaluation: An Approach Based on Bowen Theory.* New York: W.W. Norton & Company, 1988.

Kidder, Rushworth M. *Moral Courage.* New York: Harper Collins Publishers, 2005.

Klein, Bonnie Sherr. *Out of the Blue: One Woman's Story of Stroke, Love, and Survival.* Berkeley, CA: Page Mill Press, 1998.

Shameless: The ART of Disability. Directed by Bonnie Sher Klein. Performed by Film Board of Canada. 2006.

Knoester, Chris. "Transitions in Young Adulthood and the Relationships Between Parent and Offspring Well-being." *Social Forces* 81, no. 4 (2003).

Kobliner, Beth. *Get a Financial Life: Personal Finance in your Twenties and Thirties.* New York: Fireside Press, 2000.

Kosmin, Barry Alexander. *Highlights of the CJF 1990 National Jewish Population Survey.* New York: Council of Jewish Federations, 1991.

Lee, Jennifer. "The Incredible Flying Granny Nanny." *New York Times,* May 10, 2007.

Marcus, Dave. "A Generation of Parents Learn to Let Go." *Newsday.com,* June 17, 2007. http://www.newsday.com/news/local/education/ny-libye0617,0,4334678.story.

Marek, Lydia I., and Jay A. Mancini. "Mother-Child Relationship Quality and Support Patterns in Adulthood." Seattle: National Council on Family Relationships Annual Meeting, 1990.

Martin, Judith. *Miss Manners on Weddings.* New York: Crown, 1999.

Keynote Address. Performed by Mary Mason. Association for Research on Mothering (ARM), Toronto. October 20, 2007.

———. *Life Prints: A Memoir of Healing and Discovery.* Feminist Press, 2000.

Mayur M, Desai, PhD., MPH, PhD., Harold Lentzner, PhD., Julie Dawson Weeks. "Unmet Need for Personal Assistance with Activities of Daily Living Among Older Adults." *The Gerontologist* 41 (2001): 82–88.

Maza, P. L. *Adoption Trends: 1944–1975.* Child Welfare Research Notes #9, Washington, DC: Administration for Children, Youth, and Families, 1984.

Michael E. Kerr, and Murray Bowen. *Family Evaluation: An Approach Based on Bowen Theory.* New York: W.W. Norton & Company, 1988.

Miller, Jean Baker. *Toward a Psychology of Women.* Boston: Beacon Press, 1976.

Miller-Day, Michelle. *Communication Among Grandmothers, Mothers, and Adult Daughters.* Mahwah, NJ: Lawrence Erlbaum Associates, 2004.

Navarro, Mireya. "My Child's Divorce is My Pain." *New York Times.* September 2, 2007.

Neugarten, Bernice. *Middle Age and Aging.* Chicago: University of Chicago Press, 1968.

O'Reilly, Andrea and Sharon Abbey. *Mothers and Daughters: Connection, Empowerment, and Transformation.* Lanaham, MD: Rowman and Littlefield, 2000.

Pew Research Center. "Adult Children and Parents Talking More Often." February 23, 2006.

Pulte Homes, Inc. "Empty Nester Syndrome: When the Kids Go Away Will the Baby Boomers Play?" *Del Web Baby Boomer Survey.* 2004. http://www.pulte.com/PressRoom/2004BabyBoomer/BabyBoomerDet ailReport.pdf.

Putnam, Robert. *Bowling Alone.* New York: Simon & Schuster, 2000.

Rivers, Carol. *Selling Anxiety: How the News Media Scare Women.* Lebanon, NH: University Press of New England, 2007.

Schein, Edgar H. *Organizational Culture and Leadership.* San Francisco: Jossey-Bass, 1996.

Shapiro, Adam. "Later Life Divorce and Parent-Child Contact." *Journal of Family Issues* 24, no. 2 (2003): 264–285.

Shea, Christopher. "Are Parents Getting Short-Changed?" *Boston Globe,* April 11, 2004.

Silverstein, Merrill. "Do Close Parent-Child Relations Reduce the Mortality Risk of Older Parents?" *Journal of Health and Social Behavior* 34, no. 4 (December 1991): 382–395.

Sosa, Ninette, Bob Franken, Rich Phillips, and Susan Candiotti. "Terry Schiavo has Died." *Cnn.com.* March 31, 2005. http://www.cnn.com/2005/LAW/03/31/schiavo/index.html.

Stolley, K. S. "Statistics on Adoption." *The Future of Children: Adoption* 3, no. 1 (Spring 1993): http://www.futureofchildren.org/usr_doc/vol3no1entire_journal.PDF.

Super, Donald. *Vocational Development: A Framework for Research.* New York: Teachers College, Columbia University, 1957.

Swanbrow, Diane. "Intimate Relationships Between Races More Common than Thought." *University of Michigan Institute for Social Research.* 2000. http://www.umich.edu/~newsinfo/Releases/2000/Mar00/r032300a.html.

Tallant, Jeannette. "Niche Dating Sites Allow Special Interest Singles to Find Each Other." *Easty Valley Tribune,* April 5, 2005. http://www.eastvalleytribune.com/story/39078.

Thakor, M., and S. Kedar. *On My Own Two Feet.* Avon, MA: Adams Media, 2007.

Trahan, Erin. "Connection as the Center of Girls' Mental Health." *Girl Matters.*

Tulgan, Bruce and Carolyn A. Martin. *Managing Generation Y: Global Citizens Born in the Late Seventies and Early Eighties.* Amherst, MA: HRD Press, 2001.

U.S. Bureau of Labor Statistics. "Number of Jobs Held, Labor Market Activity, and Earnings Growth Among Younger Baby Boomers: Recent Results from a Longitudinal Study." August 25, 2004. http://www.bls.gov/nls/nlsy79r20.pdf.

U.S. Census Bureau. "Births to Teens, Unmarried Mothers, and Prenatal Care: 1990 to 2004." *2007 Statistical Abstract.* http://www.census.gov/prod/2006pubs/07statab/vitstat.pdf.

———. "Children's Living Arrangements and Their Characteristics: March 2007." *Annual Demographic Supplement to the March 2002 Current Population Survey.* http://www.census.gov/population/socdemo/hh-fam/tabAD-1.pdf.

———. "Civilian Labor Force Participation with Projections: 1980 to 2014." *2007 Statistical Abstract.* http://www.census.gov/prod/2006pubs/07statab/labor.pdf.

U.S. Census Bureau. "Fertility of American Women: June 2004." December 2005. http://www.census.gov/prod/2006pubs/07statab/vitstat.pdf.

———. "March and Annual Social and Economic Supplements." *Current Population Survey*. 2005. http://www.census.gov/population/socdemo/hh-fam/ms2.pdf.

———. "Marital Status of the Population by Sex and Age: 2005." *2007 Statistical Abstract*. http://www.census.gov/prod/2006pubs/07statab/pop.pdf.

———. "Married Couple and Unmarried-Partner Households." *Census 2000 Special Report*. February 2003. http://www.census.gov/prod/2003pubs/censr-5.pdf.

———. "Married Couples by Labor Force Status of Spouse: 1986 to 2005." *2007 Statistical Abstract*. http://www.census.gov/prod/2006pubs/07statab/labor.pdf.

———. "Married Couples by Race and Hispanic Origin of Spouses: 1980 to 2005." *2007 Statistical Abstract*. http://www.census.gov/prod/2006pubs/07statab/pop.pdf.

———. "United States Social Characteristics." *2002 American Community Survey*. http://www.census.gov/acs/www/Products/Profiles/Single/2002/ACS/Tabular/010/01000US2.htm.

———. "Unmarried-Partner Households by Sex of Partners: 2004." *2007 Statistical Abstract*. http://www.census.gov/prod/2006pubs/07statab/pop.pdf.

———. "Income of Families and Primary Individuals by Selected Characteristics—Occupied Units." *American Housing Survey for the United States: 2005*. http://www.census.gov/hhes/www/housing/ahs/ahs05/tab220.html.

———. "Marital Status of the Population by Sex and Age: 2005." *2007 Statistical Abstract*. http://www.census.gov/prod/2006pubs/07statab/pop.pdf.

———. "Marital Status of the Population by Sex, Race, and Hispanic Origin: 1990 to 2005." *2007 Statistical Abstract*. http://www.census.gov/prod/2006pubs/07statab/pop.pdf.

———. "Married Couples by Labor Force Status of Spouse: 1986 to 2005." *2007 Statistical Abstract*. http://www.census.gov/prod/2006pubs/07statab/labor.pdf.

———. "Participation in Adult Education: 2004 to 2005." *2007 Statistical Abstract*. http://www.census.gov/prod/2006pubs/07statab/educ.pdf.

———. "Resident Population by Race, Hispanic Origin, and Age: 2000–2005." *2007 Statistical Abstract.* http://www.census.gov/prod/2006pubs/07statab/pop.pdf.

U.S. Department of State. *Immigrant Visas Issued to Orphans Coming to the U.S.* http://travel.state.gov/family/adoption/stats/stats_451.html.

Umberson, Debra. "Relationships Between Adult Children and Their Parents: Psychological Consequences for Both Generations." *Journal of Marriage and the Family* 54, no. 3 (August 1992): 664–674.

United Jewish Communities. "National Jewish Population Survey 2000–01." 2004. http://www.ujc.org/local_includes/downloads/5086.pdf.

United Nations. "World Populations Prospects." *2006 Revision.* http://esa.un.org/unpp/.

Vocek, Daniel C. "States Let Adult Kids Keep Insurance Longer." *Stateline.org.* August 15, 2007. http://www.stateline.org/live/details/story?contentId=232292.

Wade, Nicholas. "Is Do Unto Others Written into Our Genes?" *New York Times.* September 18, 2007.

Warner, Judith. *Perfect Madness: Mothering in the Age of Anxiety.* New York: Riverhead Books, 2005.

Weisstrub, David N., David G. Thomasma, Serge Gaunthier, and George F. Tomossy. *Aging: Caring for our Elders.* Dordrecht/Boston/London: Kluwer Academic Publishers, 2001.

Wellesley Centers for Women. "The Human Brain: Hardwired for Connections." *Research and Action Report*, Spring/Summer 2007.

Wenger, Clare C. "Across the Generations" in *Aging: Caring for our Elders*, by David N. Weistubb, David G. Thomasma, Serge Gauthier, and George F. Tomossy. Dordrecht: Kluwer Academic Publishers, 2001.